Look, a White!

Look, a White!

Philosophical Essays on Whiteness

George Yancy

TEMPLE UNIVERSITY PRESS   PHILADELPHIA

TEMPLE UNIVERSITY PRESS
Philadelphia, Pennsylvania 19122
www.temple.edu/tempress

Copyright © 2012 by Temple University
All rights reserved
Published 2012

Library of Congress Cataloging-in-Publication Data

Yancy, George.
  Look, a white! : philosophical essays on whiteness / George Yancy.
    p. cm.
  Includes bibliographical references and index.
  ISBN 978-1-4399-0853-2 (cloth : alk. paper) — ISBN 978-1-4399-0854-9
(pbk. : alk. paper) — ISBN 978-1-4399-0855-6 (e-book) 1. Race. 2. Racism.
3. Race awareness. 4. Whites—Race identity. 5. Blacks—Race identity.
I. Title.
  HT1521.Y36 2012
  305.8—dc23

                                                            2011047600

Printed in the United States of America

110712P

That we may all *see with greater clarity*

Contents

Foreword
Racist Onions and Etchings

NAOMI ZACK

I taught two classes on race at the University of Oregon during the 2011 spring term, an upper-level undergraduate course and a graduate seminar. The usual coursework was supplemented by video conferences with authors of course readings, including George Yancy speaking about *Black Bodies, White Gazes: The Continuing Significance of Race* (2008).

The video conference room had two large screens. George wore a bright red-orange sports cap that glowed almost phosphorescently, and he was so upbeat and energetic that it took a while for my mostly white male undergrads to process what he was telling them. (The more worldly grad students seemed to get Yancy's message right away and take it in stride—or, in some cases, dismiss it.) Yancy told the undergrads that despite their best intentions about not being racist, their whiteness, and its attendant racism, was not like an onion layer that could be peeled off so that the good nonracist would remain. Rather, he said, a person's racism infested his or her entire being.[1]

After Yancy's video visit, I thought it was my pedagogical responsibility to leave the white male students feeling less doomed about ever becoming nonracist—which could be an excuse to not even try. I gave them a Sartrean perspective on the subconscious, self-reflection, action, and so forth. My idea was to keep alive the choice to be implicitly racist or not. Yet we know that even if we are able and obligated to recognize radical Sartrean freedom, most people will make choices about what they are told they *can* do. And many undergrads have already been told that they cannot escape from their "conditioning."

Yancy has now given us *Look, a White! Philosophical Essays on Whiteness.* The Introduction sets the tone and scope of the project in two very important ways. First, Yancy explains to whites that they are more dangerous and frightening to blacks than some (many? all?) whites take blacks to be. Second, he invites whites to develop a white double consciousness to mirror the black double consciousness that W.E.B. Du Bois claimed blacks could not avoid having. As a result, *Look, a White!* is much more optimistic than *Black Bodies, White Gazes.* This time, Yancy directly addresses whites, in their better selves of double consciousness, to get them to see themselves as blacks see them. (This would not be possible without a history leading to the formal equalities on which we all now stand, so Yancy is implicitly recognizing that.) Moreover, Yancy exhibits an existential trust in the goodwill of his white readers. Why else would he invite them to consider themselves *with* him?

The beginning of Chapter 1 lucidly captures Yancy's methodology:

While the focus on demonstrating the nonreferential status of race is important work within the context of liberation praxis vis-à-vis racism—indeed, indispensable work—my sense is that it is at the level of the *lived* density of race that so much more work needs to be done. The former, while necessary, I judge to be conceptually thin; the latter, also necessary, I judge to be existentially thick.

I think that the nonreferential status of race is conceptually *thick*, but I agree with Yancy that the lived density project is still in progress.

Yancy is right to point out in these pages that there can be and often is a split between proclaimed antiracist ideals held by some whites and their unexamined racial narcissism and conformity to racial exclusion. He is correct to raise the issue—which is about Western history as much as it is about academic life—that some white antiracist progressives have done very well for themselves while at the same time leaving unexamined their own racist assumptions, behavior, and covetous investment in white dominance. They need to hear a more traditional version of Audre Lorde's famous dictum "You cannot have your cake and eat it too!"

Whites ought to give up their racial dominance, but they won't unless there is something in it for them. And there is. If whites relinquish whiteness-as-antiblack-racism, they will be able to disgorge indigestible "etchings," a term that Yancy traces etymologically to mean "eatings," of the sort suffered by the person who wrote him this e-mail message after hearing him speak on public radio:

My dear Yancy: Do you know what you remind me of? You remind
me of somebody like that stupid Henry Gates who got a Ph.D. and
ivy league tenure at Harvard by being an expert on himself. Maybe
you ought to go to the White House and have a beer with yourself
and wait for Obama at his door to show up like his dog, "Bo."

Yancy's *etchings* = *eatings* metaphor invites whites to consider how white
antiblack racism is lodged in the lived body of the white person who ingests
it. Getting rid of these etchings is a more positive ongoing project than peeling onions, because excretion is sustainable, whereas endless excoriation has
the limit of "nothing left" at some point.

After following Yancy through this new exploration of how white dominance plays out in the classroom (not his), nursery school, hiring, conferences, the media, and much more of our shared world, I think we all—
blacks, whites, mixed, and others who think about race—should, once again,
thank Yancy for using philosophy where psychology and basic ethics have
not yet effectively ventured.

Acknowledgments

I thank Micah B. Kleit, executive editor at Temple University Press, for his enthusiasm for this project from the start. I truly appreciate his respect for my body of work. I am also grateful to Micah for the important work that he does to expand our collective critical imaginations through books. I thank all those at Temple University Press and Newgen–Austin for their professionalism in this book's publication process. I am greatly indebted to Naomi Zack—who has made a tremendous impact on philosophical discussions of race and mixed race and whose work is intellectually expansive, fruitfully interdisciplinary, and philosophically rigorous—for writing the Foreword. I continue to admire her prolific philosophical output. I extend a huge thank-you to the two anonymous readers for Temple University Press who read the proposal and a sample chapter. Their feedback was both encouraging and insightful. I also thank Steve Martinot for his excellent scholarship and his encouragement.

I am grateful to those who generously agreed to read parts of the book and offer their feedback: Barbara Applebaum, Kathy Glass, Linda Furgerson Selzer, Clevis Headley, Bill Bywater, Floyd W. Hayes III, and Maria del Guadalupe Davidson (Lupe). I thank Bill Bywater and Floyd W. Hayes III for creating important critical dialogical spaces at their respective academic institutions where I could share and test my ideas. I thank Barbara Applebaum for giving so freely of her time and energy. In response to my request that she read through a few chapters (even as school was beginning), she agreed without hesitation. I greatly appreciate her time, effort, and giving spirit. I also thank Joe R. Feagin, who remains as prolific as ever and who continues to fight the good fight. I am most grateful to Joe for being in my corner.

I thank my late colleague and friend John Warren for his important body of work dealing with questions of whiteness, performativity, and pedagogy. We never got a chance to fulfill our plan to meet. I am willing to wait for that opportunity! I also thank those colleagues and scholars who continue to support the work that I do, including James Swindal, Fred Evans, Manomano M. M. Mukungurutse, James Spady, Victor Anderson, Janine Jones, and E. Lale Demirturk. I owe a special debt of gratitude to the prominent literary figure and philosopher Charles Johnson, who has continuously shown tremendous generosity and friendship toward me. Thanks, Chuck.

Chapters 2, 3, and 4 are revised versions of previously published essays. I thank Routledge for permission to reprint a revised version of George Yancy, "Engaging Whiteness and the Practice of Freedom: The Creation of Subversive Academic Spaces," originally published in Maria del Guadalupe Davidson and George Yancy, eds., *Critical Perspectives on bell hooks* (New York: Routledge, 2009); the *CLR James Journal: A Review of Caribbean Ideas* for permission to reprint a revised version of George Yancy, "Political and Magical Realist Semiotics in Kamau Brathwaite's Reading of *The Tempest*," *CLR James Journal* 12, no. 1 (2006): 85–108; and the *African American Review* for permission to reprint a revised version of George Yancy and Tracey Ann Ryser, "Whiting Up and Blacking Out: White Privilege, Race, and *White Chicks*," *African American Review* 42, nos. 3–4 (Fall/Winter 2008): 1–16.

As none of us works in a vacuum, we must not forget those who help to create the conditions that support our creativity. Toward that end, I thank Michelle Bonaventura for making it possible for Susan, my amiable consort, and me to have free time to work on projects that we love. I am most grateful to Michelle for her love for our boys. I also thank the Yancy boys for their patience this past summer (2011), especially as I consumed so much of it. And to Susan, who has read almost everything I have written and who has long been a critic and supporter of my ideas, I offer my eternal gratitude.

Look, a White!

Introduction

Flipping the Script

High in the tower, where I sit above the loud complaining of
the human sea, I know many souls that toss and whirl and pass,
but none there are that intrigue me more than the Souls of
White Folk. —W.E.B. Du Bois, "The Souls of White Folk"

To look directly was an assertion of subjectivity.
—bell hooks, *Black Looks: Race and Representation*

"I Give You Your Problem Back. You're the 'Nigger,' Baby; It Isn't Me"

"Look, a Negro!" The utterance grabs one's attention. It announces something to be seen, to be looked at, to be noticed, to be watched, and, in the end, to be controlled. "Look" catches our attention, forcing us to turn our heads in anticipation, to twist our bodies, to redirect our embodied consciousness. The entire scene is corporeal. "Negro!" functions as a signifier that gives additional *urgency* to the command to "Look." So the imperative "Look" becomes intensified vis-à-vis the appearance of a "Negro." "Look, a shooting star!" elicits a response of excitement, of hoping to catch sight of the phenomenon and perhaps even to make a wish. "Look, a Negro!" elicits white fear and trembling, perhaps a prayer that one will not be accosted. In short, "Look" has built in it—when followed by "a Negro!"—a gestured warning against a possible threat, cautioning those whites within earshot to be on guard, to lock their car doors, to hold their wallets and purses for dear life, to gather their children together, to prepare to move house, and (in some cases) to protect the "purity" of white women and to protect white men from the manipulating dark temptress.

Frantz Fanon writes about his experiences when a little white boy "sees" him:

> "Look, a Negro!" It was an external stimulus that flicked over me as I passed by. I made a tight smile.
>   "Look, a Negro!" It was true. It amused me.
>   "Look, a Negro!" The circle was drawing a bit tighter. I made no secret of my amusement.
>   "Mama, see the Negro! I'm frightened!" Frightened! Frightened! Now they were beginning to be afraid of me. I made up my mind to laugh myself to tears, but laughter had become impossible.[1]

Note the iterative "Look, a Negro!" It is repetitive and effectively communicates something of a spectacle to behold. Yes. It's a Negro! Be careful! Negroes steal, they cheat, they are hypersexual, mesmerizingly so, and the quintessence of evil and danger. The tight smile on Fanon's face is a forced smile, uncomfortable, tolerant. Fanon feels the impact of the collective white gaze. He is, as it were, "strangled" by the attention. He has become a peculiar *thing*. He becomes a dreaded object, a thing of fear, a frightening and ominous presence. The turned heads and twisted bodies that move suddenly to catch a glimpse of the object of the white boy's alarm function as confirmation that something has gone awry. Their abruptly turned white bodies help to "materialize" the threat through white collusion. The white boy has triggered something of an optical frenzy. Everyone is now looking, bracing for something to happen, something that the Negro will do. And given his "cannibal" nature, perhaps the Negro is hungry. Fanon writes, "The little white boy throws himself into his mother's arms: Mama, the nigger's going to eat me up."[2]

Fanon has done nothing save be a Negro. Yet this is sufficient. The Negro has always already done something by virtue of being a Negro. It is an anterior guilt that always haunts the Negro and his or her present and future actions. After all, this is what it means to be a Negro—to have done something wrong. The little white boy's utterance is felicitous against a backdrop of white lies and myths about the black body. As Robert Gooding-Williams writes, "The [white] boy's expression of fear posits a typified image of the Negro as behaving in threatening ways. This image has a narrative significance, Fanon implies, as it portrays the Negro as acting precisely as historically received legends and stories about Negros generally portray them as acting."[3] One can imagine the "innocent" white index finger pointing to the black body. "Here the 'pointing' is not only an indicative, but the schematic foreshadowing of an accusation, one which carries the performative force to constitute that danger which it fears and defends against."[4] The act of pointing is by no means benign; it takes its phenomenological or *lived* toll on the black body. As Fanon writes, "My body was given back to me sprawled out, distorted, recolored, clad in mourning in that white winter day. The Negro is an animal, the Negro is bad, the Negro is mean, the Negro is ugly; look, a nigger."[5] Fanon is clear that the white boy, while not fully realizing the complex historical, psychological, and phenomenological implications, has actually distorted his (Fanon's) body. "Look, a Negro!" is rendered intelligible vis-à-vis an entire play of white racist signifiers that ontologically truncate the black body; it is an expression that calls forth an entire white racist worldview. The white boy, though, is not a mere innocent proxy for whiteness. Rather, he is learning, at that very moment, the power of racial speech, the power of racial gesturing. He is learning how to think about and feel toward the so-called dark Other. He is undergoing white subject formation, a formation that is fundamentally linked to the object that he fears and dreads.

To invoke Fanon, "the [white] collective unconscious is not dependent on cerebral heredity; it is the result of what I shall call the unreflected imposition of a culture."[6] Or, as I would argue, the white boy's racial practices are learned effortlessly, practices that are always already in process. In short, the white boy's performance of whiteness is *not* simply the successful result of a *superimposed* superstructural grid of racist ideology. Rather, the white boy's performance points to fundamental ways in which many white children are oriented, at the level of everyday practices, within the world, where their bodily orientations are unreflected expressions of the background *lived* orientations of whiteness, white ways of being, white modes of racial and racist practice.[7] It is a process, though, where the white embodied subject is intimately linked to the black embodied subject. "Therefore," as Mike Hill argues in reference to Toni Morrison's insightful concept of American Africanism, "the distance implicit in presumptive white purity is false, and covers an occluded racial proximity."[8]

"Look, a Negro!" draws its force from collective fear and *misrecognition*. Although Fanon does grant that, within the field of culturally available racial descriptors, it is true that he is a "Negro," he recognizes how the term is fundamentally linked to various racist myths. This is why Fanon also writes, "'Dirty nigger!' Or simply, 'Look, a Negro!'"[9] There is no distinction here within the context of the white gaze. To "see" a Negro is to "see" a nigger; it is to "see" a problem—a problem that is deemed, from the perspectives of whites, ontological. In the face of so many white gazes, one desires to "slip into corners."[10] Yet as Fanon makes clear, it is not easy to hide. Metaphorically, he describes how his "long antennae pick up the catch-phrases strewn over the surface of things—nigger underwear smells of nigger—nigger teeth are white—nigger feet are big—the nigger's barrel chest."[11] He cannot live a life of anonymity, etymologically, "without a name" or "nameless." Apparently, only whites have that wonderful capacity to live anonymously, thoughtlessly, to be ordinary qua human, to go unmarked and unnamed—in essence, to be white.[12] They are like Clint Eastwood's white stock characters in his Western shoot-'em-up movies who come into town nameless and mysterious.

Indeed, Eastwood's central character is *the man with no name*. This is the portrayal of white liberalism perhaps at its best. The black lone figure already has a name. Indeed, he has multiple names: "nigger," "rapist," "savage." The white townspeople become fearful as he moves through the street; they know that even as a man of the law, as shown in the comedy *Blazing Saddles* (1974), he is on the verge of "whipping it out." Fanon writes, "The Negro is the incarnation of a genital potency beyond all moralities and prohibitions."[13] To be *the black* or *the Negro*, then, is to be immediately recognized and recognizable. One is in clear view: "Look, a Negro-nigger!" There is no escape; there are no exceptions; it is a Sisyphean mode of existence. Fanon writes, "When [white] people like me, they tell me it is in spite of my color. When they dislike me, they point out that it is not because of my color. Either way, I am locked into the infernal circle."[14]

Yet this infernal circle is not of Fanon's doing. It is the social world of white normativity and white meaning making that creates the conditions under which black people are always already marked as different/deviant/dangerous. "Look, a Negro!" (or perhaps, simply, "Look, the wretched and forlorn nigger!") has the perlocutionary power to incite violence, violence filled with white desire and bloodlust. Call: "Look, a Negro!" Response: "Rape the black bitch!" Call: "Look, a Negro!" Response: "Get a rope!" Call: "Rape!" Response: "Castrate the nigger!" The black body is deemed a threat vis-à-vis the "virgin sanctity of whiteness,"[15] something to be marked, sequestered, and in many cases killed—just for fun. In fact, in 2011 in Jackson, Mississippi, a forty-nine-year-old black man, James Craig Anderson, was targeted primarily by a white eighteen-year-old male, who, according to law enforcement officials, said to his white friends, "Let's go fuck with some niggers." On seeing a black man standing in a parking lot ("Look, a Negro!"), the group first repeatedly beat him. It is alleged that the expression "White Power!" was also yelled out by one of the white youth. As Anderson staggered, he was then brutally run over by a truck driven by the white eighteen-year-old, an event captured on surveillance tape. After driving over and killing Anderson, the white male, who since has been indicted on charges of capital murder and a hate crime, allegedly said to his friends, "I ran that nigger over."[16] While many of the details of this crime are still unknown as of this writing, the racist narrative is certainly consistent with the historical legacy of whiteness in North America as it relates to black people. As I write about this incident, I hear the words of many of my white students: "But our generation has changed when it comes to racism." Call: "Look, a Negro!" Response: "Run the nigger over!"

"Look, a Negro!" is a form of racist interpellation that, when examined closely, reveals whites to themselves. One might say that the "Negro" is that which whites create as the specter/phantom of their own fear.[17] Thus, I would argue that the whites who engage in a surveillance of Fanon's body don't really "see" him; they see themselves. James Baldwin, speaking to white North America with eloquence and incredible psychological insight, says, "But you still think, I gather, that the 'nigger' is necessary. But he's unnecessary to me, so he must be necessary to you. I give you your problem back. You're the 'nigger', baby; it isn't me."[18]

What is so powerful here is the profound act of transposition. One might ask, "Will the real 'nigger' please stand up?" Ah, yes, "Look, a white!" Such naming and marking function to flip the script. Flipping the script, which is a way of changing an outcome by reversing the terms or, in this case, recasting the script[19] of those who reap the benefits of white privilege says, "I see you for what and who you are!" Flipping the script is, one might say, a gift offering: an opportunity, a call to responsibility—perhaps even to greater maturity. "Look, a white!" is disruptive and clears a space for new forms of recognition. Public repetition of this expression and the realities of whiteness that are so identified and marked is one way of installing the legitimacy that there is something even seeable when it comes to whiteness. Moreover, public repetition functions to further an antiracist authority over a visual field[20] historically dominated by whites. It is important to note, though, that the subject of the utterance, "Look, a white!" is not a sovereign, ahistorical, neutral subject that has absolute control over the impact of the utterance. "Look, a Negro!" is already embedded within citationality conditions that involve larger racist assumptions and accusations as they relate to the black body that shape the intelligibility, and the meaningful declaration, of the utterance. "Look, a Negro!" presupposes a white subject who is historically embedded within racist social relations and a racist discursive field that pre-exists the speaker. As a form of repetition, one that would be cited often and by many, "Look, a white!" has the potential to create conditions that work to install an intersubjective intelligibility and social force that effectively counter the direction of the gaze, a site traditionally monopolized by whites, and perhaps create a moment of uptake that induces a form of white identity crisis, a jolt that awakens a sudden and startling sense of having been seen. In response, one might hear, "You talkin' to me?" But unlike the scenario played out in *Taxi Driver* (1976), where Robert De Niro poses this question, in this case the mirror speaks back: "*You're damn right. Indeed, I am!*"

"Look, a white!" returns to white people the problem of whiteness. While I see it as a gift, I know that not all gifts are free of discomfort.[21] Indeed, some are heavy laden with great responsibility. Yet it is a gift that ought to engender a sense of gratitude, a sense of humility, and an opportunity to give thanks—not the sort of attitude that reinscribes white entitlement. As bell hooks writes, "Those white people who want to continue the dominant-subordinate relationship so endemic to racist exploitation by insisting that we 'serve' them—that we do the work of challenging and changing their consciousness—are acting in bad faith."[22]

The gift is not all about *you*. As white, you are used to everything always being about *you*. We have heard, as Du Bois writes, your "mighty cry reverberating through the world, 'I am white!' Well and good, O Prometheus, divine thief."[23] But your cry to the world was followed by exploitation, dehumanization, and death. "I am white!" was egomaniacal and thanatological; it was a process of self-naming that functioned to "justify," through racial myth making, the actions of whites in their quest to dominate those "backward" and "inferior" others. This process of self-naming was *not* a gift but a manifestation of white messianic imperialism. In this case, it was a death-dealing superimposition of white power. As Steve Martinot notes, "As a 'gift,' it must see the world as other, against which it demands of its own citizens (the white members of the white nation) that they stand in allegiance and solidarity, and that the other on whom the 'gift' is bestowed (imposed) be grateful."[24] Flipping the script, within the context of this book, however, is about *us*—collectively.

Sara Ahmed writes, "It has become commonplace for whiteness to be represented as invisible, as the unseen or the unmarked, as non-colour, the absent presence or hidden referent, against which all other colours are measured as forms of deviance."[25] According to George Lipsitz, "Whiteness is everywhere in U.S. culture, but it is very hard to see."[26] He goes on to say, "As the unmarked category against which difference is constructed, whiteness never has to speak its name, never has to acknowledge its rule as an organizing principle in social and cultural relations."[27] Richard Dyer writes, "In fact, for most of the time white people speak about nothing but white people, it's just that we couch it in terms of 'people' in general."[28] Finally, as Terrance MacMullan sees it, "White people remain ignorant of white privilege because of the fact that all aspects of our lives—our institutions, practices, ideals, and laws—were defined and tailored to fit the needs, wants, and concerns of white folk."[29]

But to whom is whiteness invisible? Ahmed is clear that whiteness is invisible to those who inhabit it,[30] to those who have come to see whiteness and what it means to be human as isomorphic. For them, it has become a "mythical norm."[31] This does not mean, however, that whites who choose to give their attention to thinking critically about whiteness are incapable of doing so, though it does mean that there will be white structural blinkers that occlude specific and complex insights by virtue of being white. Therefore, people of color are necessary to the project of critically thinking through whiteness, especially as examining whiteness has the potential of becoming a narcissistic project that elides its dialectical relationship with people of color—that is, those who continue to suffer under the regime of white power and privilege. Pointing to the importance of Audre Lorde's work, which emphasizes the importance of studying whiteness and its significance to antiracism, Ahmed argues that if the examination of whiteness "is to be more than 'about' whiteness, [it must begin] with the Black critique of how whiteness works as a form of racial privilege, as well as the effects of that privilege on the bodies of those who are recognized as black."[32]

The fact of the matter is that, for white people, whiteness is the transcendental norm in terms of which they live their lives as persons, individuals. People of color, however, confront whiteness in their everyday lives, not as an abstract concept but in the form of embodied whites who engage in racist practices that negatively affect their lives. Black people and people of color thus strive to disarticulate the link between whiteness and the assumption of just being human, to create a critical slippage. By marking whiteness, black people can locate whiteness as a specific historical and ideological configuration, revealing it as "an identity created and continued with all-too-real consequences for the distribution of wealth, prestige, and opportunity."[33] The act of marking whiteness, then, is itself an act of historicizing whiteness, an act of situating whiteness within the context of material forces and raced interest-laden values that reinforce whiteness as a site of privilege and hegemony. Marking whiteness is about exposing the ways in which whites have created a form of "humanism" that obfuscates their hegemonic efforts to treat their experiences as universal and representative.

According to bell hooks, "Many [whites] are shocked that black people think critically about whiteness because racist thinking perpetuates the fantasy that the Other who is subjugated, who is subhuman, lacks the ability to comprehend, to understand, to see the working of the powerful."[34] On this score, then, black subjectivity poses a threat to the invisibility of whiteness. Yet this is a specific type of threat. Because of the profound relational reality of whiteness to the nonwhite Other, whites are not the targets of their own whiteness, so the reality of the invisibility of whiteness, its status as normative, does not affect them in the same way. In fact, this is impossible, for as whites continue to strive to make whiteness visible, they do so from their perspective (which is precisely embedded within the context of white power and privilege), not from the perspective of those who constitute the embodied subjectivities that undergo the existential traumas due to whiteness (the terror of whiteness, the colonial desires of whiteness, the possessive investments in whiteness that perpetuate problematic race-based economic orders, residential orders, judicial orders, somatic orders, etc.). Speaking directly to the ramifications of this specific threat, Crispin Sartwell writes, "One of the major strategies for preserving white invisibility to ourselves is the silencing, segregation, or delegitimation of voices that speak about whiteness from a nonwhite location."[35]

While it is true that not all people of color have the same understanding of the operations of whiteness, at all levels of its complex expression, this does not negate the fact that people of color undergo raced experiences vis-à-vis whiteness that lead to specific insights that render whiteness visible. Being "a wise Latina woman,"[36] for example, is one mode of expression of such raced experiences, experiences that have deep socio-ontological and epistemic implications. Yet how can people of color not have this epistemic advantage? After all, black people and people of color, when it comes to white people, are "bone of their thought and flesh of their language."[37] As Du Bois writes, "I see these souls [that is, white souls] undressed and from the back and side. I see the working of their entrails. I know their thoughts and they know that I know. This knowledge makes them now embarrassed, now furious!"[38]

Ahmed, hooks, and Du Bois emphasize the necessity of a black counter-gaze, a gaze that recognizes the ways of whiteness, sees beyond its "invisibility," from the perspective of a form of raced positional knowledge. The black counter-gaze is a species of flipping the script. Indeed, the expression, "Look, a white!" presupposes this counter-gaze. I encourage my white students to mark whiteness everywhere they recognize it. Of course, thinking critically with them about whiteness enables these students to become more cognizant of the obfuscatory ways in which whiteness conceals its own visibility. The critical process creates a more complex epistemic field, as it were, in terms of which whiteness becomes more recognizable in its daily manifestations.

After taking my courses, many white students say, "I can't *stop* seeing the workings of race. It's everywhere." One often gets the impression that they would rather return to a more "innocent" time, before taking my course, before they learned how to see so much more.

The reality is that the "workings of race" are precisely what people of color see/experience most of the time. Important to this learning process, though, is reminding my white students that they are white, that they are part of the very "workings of race" that they are beginning to recognize.[39] For most of my white students, before taking my course their own whiteness is just a benign phenotypic marker. Indeed, for most of them, whiteness has not really been marked as a raced category to begin with. They do not recognize the normative status of whiteness that the marking is designed to expose. For them, "to be white" means "I am not like you guys"—those people of color. Whiteness as normative and their whiteness as unremarkable thus remain in place, uninterrogated, unblemished. Sara Ahmed writes, "There must be white bodies (it must be possible to see such bodies *as* white bodies), and yet the power of whiteness is that we don't see those bodies as white bodies. We just see them as bodies."[40] In short, the process of disentangling the sight of white bodies from the sight of such bodies as just bodies is not easy, but it is necessary.

For many whites, the process of marking the white body ("Look, a white!") is not just difficult but threatening. The process dares to mark whites as racists, as perpetuators and sustainers of racism. Furthermore, the process dares to mark whites as *raced* beings, as inextricably bound to the historical legacy of the "workings of race." Hence, the process encourages a slippage not only at the site of seeing themselves as innocent of racism but also at the site of seeing themselves as unraced.[41] As Zeus Leonardo and Ronald K. Porter write, "Hiding behind the veil of color-blindness means that lifting it would force whites to confront their self-image, with people of color acting as the mirror. This act is not frightening for people of color but for whites."[42] It is frightening because whites must begin to see themselves through gazes that are not *prone* to lie/obfuscate when it comes to the "workings of race" qua whiteness. Indeed, there is no real need to lie about whiteness. People of color have nothing to lose; whites have so much to protect. Yet what do they have to protect? As Richard Wright notes, "Their constant outward-looking, their mania for radios, cars, and a thousand other trinkets, made them dream and fix their eyes upon the trash of life, made it impossible for them to learn a language that could have taught them to speak of what was in theirs or others' hearts. The words of their souls were the syllables of popular songs."[43]

The use of the mirror is effective as a metaphor. White people see themselves through epistemic and axiological orders that reflect back to them their own normative status and importance. Indeed, the script has already been written in *their* favor. It is time for the mirror to speak through a different script, from the perspective of *lived* experiences of those bodies of color that encounter white people on a daily basis as a problem or perhaps even as a site of terror. The mirror will tell the truth: *"No, damn it! Snow White is not the 'fairest' of them all. She is precisely the problem!"*

This returns us to the issue of the gift. Seeing whiteness from the perspective of, in this case, black people functions as an invitation *to see more*, to see things differently. It is a special call that reframes, that results in a form of unveiling, of seeing, and of recognizing a different side. It is a gift that invites an opening, perhaps having a Hubble telescope–like impact: "I had no idea that there was so much more to see, and with such clarity!" I have had this experience while reading works by feminist theorists. I have dared to see the world and my identity through their critical analyses, from their experiences of male dominant culture, from their *mirror*. "Damn, what a sexist! I overlooked that one." Yet I am thankful for *their* gift. And while it is true that I always fail to comprehend the sheer complexity of what it is like to be a woman in a world that is based on male patriarchy, and the multiple forms of male violence toward women, I can use that mirror to make a difference. I can see me differently; I can see the operations of male hegemony differently, in ways that implicate me. And as a gift, I treat it as such. I am humbled by it.

Whites must also be humbled by the gift of seeing more of themselves, more of the complex manifestations of their whiteness, as seen through black experiences of whiteness. As whites use the mirror to see and name whiteness, they do not magically become black. Indeed, accepting the gift ought to involve the recognition of important boundaries. There is no room for white territorialization or white appropriation, features that are symptomatic of whiteness itself. To go it alone implies that whites themselves can solve the problems of whiteness. It would be like men getting together by themselves to solve the historical problem of male hegemony and sexism without the critical voices of women. Within the context of whiteness, after the gift has been given, one still remains white, ensconced within a white social structure that not only continues to confer privileges but also militates against one even knowing "that [whiteness] is there to be shown."[44]

As stated previously, "Look, a white!" presupposes a black counter-gaze. Moreover, it is this black gaze that I encourage my white students to cultivate. "Look, a white!" is a way of engaging the white world, calling it forth from a different perspective, a perspective critically cultivated by black people and others of color. It is a perspective gained through pain and suffering, through critical thought and daring action. Seeing the world from the perspective of a flipped script ("Look, a white!") does not, however, reinscribe a form of race essentialism. In Fanon's case, "Look, a Negro!" was never intended as a gift; it functioned as a penalty. For the "object" so identified, this phrase meant that there was a price to be paid. The public declaration was designed to fix the black body racially, to forewarn those whites within earshot that a "beastly" threat was near. "Look, a white!" is not meant to seal white bodies "into that crushing objecthood"[45] that Fanon speaks of vis-à-vis the white gaze. There is no desire to fix white people "in the sense in which a chemical solution is fixed by a dye."[46] Instead, "Look, a white!" has the goal of complicating white identity. It has the goal of fissuring white identity, not stabilizing it according to racist myths and legends. To say, "Look, a white!" is an act of ostension, a form of *showing*, but it is not limited to phenotype, though this necessarily shows up in the act of ostension. "Look, a white!" points to what has been deemed invisible, unremarkable, normative.

As children, some of us liked counting anything at all, chairs, passing cars, birds on a rooftop. And we counted them partly because we just loved to count. But we also had this ability to notice so many things that adults had relegated to the background. As adults, we count our money, we count the days of the week—the things that apparently "really" matter. "Look, a white!" tells us to be attentive to what has become the background. As a powerful act of pointing, "Look, a white!" brings whiteness to the foreground. Whiteness as a site of privilege and power is named and identified. Whiteness as an embedded set of social practices that render white people complicit in larger social practices of white racism is nominated. It is about turning our bodies (and our attention) in the direction of white discourse and white social performances that attempt to pass themselves off as racially neutral, and it is about finding the courage to say, "Look, a white!" As Christine E. Sleeter writes, "While in an abstract sense white people may not like the ideas of reproducing white racism, and in a personal sense, do not see themselves as racist, in their talk and actions, they are."[47]

"Look, a white!" also points to the historical white regulatory, antimiscegenation norms that produced white bodies. "Look, a white!" points to "the [white racist] discursive rules and regulations that dictated the biological chain that produced these hands, these eyes, and skin tone"[48] that have become privileged as beautiful, normative, *white*. "Look, a white!" assiduously nominates white bodies within the context of a stream of history dominated by white racism. "Look, a white!" unveils the ways in which white bodies are linked to white discursive practices and racist power relations that define those white bodies. "Look, a white!" signifies "compulsory repetitions [that] construct *illusory origins* of [whiteness] that function as regulatory regimes to keep [whites] within a particular grid of intelligibility by governing and punishing nonnormative behavior, interpellating [whites] back into the normative discourse [and back into normative spaces]."[49] "Look, a white!" dares to mark those whites who deem themselves "ethically superior" because they have a "better" grasp of the operations of white racism than those other complacent whites. "Look, a white!" marks those whites who see themselves as radically "progressive" now that they are able to confess their racism publicly or because they publicly demonstrate intellectual savvy in how they engage whiteness with sophistication. As intimated previously, "Look, a white!" militates against its reduction to identifying singular, individual, intentional acts of racism only. Instead, "Look, a white!" also identifies "*what* one is in a social framework or system of social categorizations."[50] In this way, "Look, a white!" does not open the door to facile claims about symmetrically hurtful racial stereotypes, "reverse discrimination," and the rhetoric of a so-called color-blind, perpetrator perspective. "Look, a white!" marks such moves as sites of obfuscation, revealing them as forms of "mystificatory digression from the clearly *a*symmetrical and enduring system of white power itself."[51]

"Look, a white!" flags whiteness in the form of colonialism and imperialism, which function as forms of gluttony and fanaticism that would dare to consume the entire earth. Du Bois asks, "'But what on earth is whiteness that one should so desire it?' Then always, somehow, some way, silently but clearly, I am given to understand that whiteness is the ownership of the earth forever and ever, Amen!"[52]

I want my white students to shout, "Look, a white!" on a daily basis, to call whiteness out, publicly. I encourage them to develop a form of "double consciousness," one that enables them to see the world differently and to see themselves differently through the experiences of black people and people of color. On this score, "Look, a white!" becomes a shared perspective, a shared dynamic naming process, buttressed and informed by the insights regarding whiteness that black people and people of color have acquired. The strategy is to have my white students see the white world through *our* eyes, a perspective that will challenge whiteness, not deteriorate into white guilt or take new forms of white pity to help the so-called helpless. "Look, a white!" is meant to be unsafe, indeed, to be dangerous to whites themselves. By "dangerous" I mean *threatening* to a white self and a white social system predicated on a vicious lie that white is right—morally, epistemologically, and otherwise.

While a powerful iterative practice, "Look, a white!" will not start a revolution. It does, however, unsettle the normative pretensions of whiteness and help to challenge and change whiteness by renaming its social reality. That is why I encourage my white students to engage in risk-taking acts of naming whiteness wherever it appears: while watching TV ("Look, a white!"); while gathering with white friends for holidays ("Look, a white!"); while attending an all-white church ("Look, a white!"); while listening to white politicians, perhaps those who say things like "You lie"[53] ("Look, a white!") or say that America is ready for a black president because he is "a light-skinned African American with no Negro dialect"[54] ("Look, a white!"); while watching Neo (the *white* one) from *The Matrix* save the world ("Look, a white!"); while engaging in white bonding experiences at philosophy conferences ("Look, a white!"); while sitting with other white students in the university cafeteria ("Look, a white!"); while listening to their white friends tell racist jokes ("Look, a white!"); while denying their own racism ("Look, a white!"); while driving in their car and feeling carefree ("Look, a white!"); and while watching themselves in the mirror ("Look, a white!").

There are some, perhaps many, who will say, "Look, a white!" is too general; it lacks analytic specificity; it essentializes all whites. For them, the construction "Look, a white!' is too homogeneous and problematically reifies whiteness as a "thing," obscuring its historicity and plurality. The expression does not allow for exceptions. It does not allow for the fact that whiteness is inflected relative to class, gender, sexuality, and so on. For example, what about those poor whites who are treated as "Others" within the context of whiteness, the ones who are "dirty white"? I will be accused of failing to have been attentive to that other marked site with its own specific identificatory register: "Look, *white trash!*" Yet even poor whites have been able to mobilize whiteness as a piece of property. Consistent with Du Bois's conception of whiteness as wage, Cheryl Harris writes, "Whiteness as the embodiment of white privilege transcended mere belief or preference; it became usable property, the subject of the law's regard and protection. In this respect whiteness, as an active property, has been used and enjoyed."[55] Furthermore, many whites uncomfortable with the "sweeping" indictment of the expression may complain: "But I don't see color"; "But I'm married to a black man"; "But my wife is Latina"; "But I'm Italian and faithful to that culture"; "But my family never owned slaves"; "But I voted for Obama"; "But I occupied Wall Street"; "But I marched with King"; "But I'm gay"; "But I'm a liberal"; "But I like rap music"; "But I attend church every Sunday"; "But we just hired a black person to teach in our department"; "But I attend a black church"; "But I don't use the N-word"; "But I write about whiteness. Hell, I teach courses on whiteness"; "But I hate the Klan"; "But I believe in God"; "But my favorite charity helps people of color"; "But I'm a feminist!"; "But I'm a member of the Black Student Union"; "But I love black people"; "But I so *want* to be black."; "But I have family members who are black"; "But I believe in social justice"; "But I'm a decent human being; *really* I am"; "But we're not like our white parents and white grandparents. Times have changed." What are we to make of these "exceptions" punctuated with "but" throughout? Let's speak frankly: "Look, a white!"

Overview of the Book

I recently gave a lecture on whiteness—its privileged status and power—to an audience predominantly comprising white undergraduate students. I explained to them how whites often refuse to accept the implications of their whiteness in terms of its power and privilege. I also explained how such power and privilege differentially impact the daily lives of whites and blacks and people of color. After the talk, a white female approached me and said something very insightful. She said in effect that, when it comes to whiteness and racism, especially when people of color are discussing their own perspectives on matters of race and racism, white people want to deny the *real* world; it is as if, once confronted by their own whiteness, they begin to create an alternate world, a fantasy world, within which white privilege and power simply do not exist—indeed, never existed. Her point was that whites refuse to face the real world in which whiteness, *their whiteness*, makes a fundamental difference in their lives and the lives of black people and people of color. This was not the sort of possible-world game that philosophers play ("I can imagine a *possible* world in which white racism does not exist"). Her point was that so many whites deny our *actual* world.

   Look, a White! Philosophical Essays on Whiteness consists of six core chapters that refuse whites a fantasy world, a world where their whiteness no longer directly and indirectly implicates them in the maintenance and perpetuation of white racism.

   In Chapter 1, I engage and map whiteness from the perspective of embodied subjectivity—that is, my own embodied identity as a black male. I deploy a narrative style that exemplifies what I like to refer to as the density of race. The *lived space* that is mapped unveils whiteness and its negative impact on the black body. As in each chapter in the text, whites are shown to themselves unflinchingly. Within the context of concrete encounters (while walking across the street in front of cars or watching a movie), I mark whiteness: "Look, a white!" Through a form of discourse that attempts to "mimic" the lived context, I challenge forms of philosophical discourse vis-à-vis race that seem to abandon the real, messy, complex world in terms of which race is fundamentally situated and enacted.

In Chapter 2, I explore whiteness within the context of critical pedagogy, focusing on key dynamics of race that occur in a classroom. Black philosophers have not given sustained attention to this significant area of inquiry. Drawing particularly from the work of bell hooks, I critically rethink ways in which the classroom, particularly classrooms in which white students are in the majority, can function as a radical space for honestly exploring whiteness, working through various forms of white denial, and encouraging white students to render, to the extent that this is possible, whiteness visible, to name it when and where it appears. In line with Chapter 1, the objective is to explore those messy dynamics that happen in a classroom, especially when engaging issues of race, racism, and whiteness.

In Chapter 3, I mark whiteness within the context of its colonial expression through the critical and imaginative work of the literary figure Kamau Brathwaite in his examination of Prospero and Caliban from Shakespeare's *The Tempest*. Through Brathwaite's work, I delineate ways in which Prospero functions as a complex trope of whiteness, white domination, and white normativity, and how Caliban (a subaltern figure) is deemed the racial Other—the colonized. Like Aimé Césaire's Caliban, who is unafraid to mark Prospero's assembly of lies and deceptions, Brathwaite deploys a politically charged form of magical realism that maps and names the historical traces of Prospero's whiteness.

In Chapter 4, I critically engage whiteness from the perspective of film, specifically the film *White Chicks*. It is argued that this movie, while a comedy (some might say a potboiler), engages in an intra-filmic reversed "black gaze," one that teases out various subtle and not so subtle layers of whiteness. I argue that the Wayans brothers reveal whites to themselves through the ways in which black people are depicted by whites. The brothers enact and, indeed, exaggerate, various stereotypical forms of black behavior in order to interrogate the white imaginary; they flip the script with subversive implications and unveil the ways in which whiteness feeds off its own distortions.

In Chapter 5, I provide a critical narrative that demonstrates how the act of directly confronting whiteness can result in great risk. Indeed, this personal narrative confirms that critically engaging whiteness can potentially come at the cost of one's livelihood, especially in a society like ours that prefers, on the whole, to remain cowardly and silent in the face of the problems of race and the existence of racism, a society that would rather avoid challenging the normative structure and status of whiteness. Deploying the figure of Meletus from Plato's *Apology*, I provide an analysis of one white male's attempt to silence the spirit of my pedagogy and my views on whiteness. I theorize how confronting whiteness directly is a function of how I understand the love of wisdom, which I link to a conception of danger and risk. I also link the importance of students raising dangerous and unsettling, but telling, questions in the classroom with the significance of a critical citizenry that is not afraid to critique hegemonic forces that belie the open-ended direction of critical reflection and critical engagement. In this chapter, then, I argue for continuity between certain critical pedagogical practices and norms in the classroom and the cultivation of democratic ideals that contest complacency, dogmatism, and hegemony.

In Chapter 6, I explore what I refer to as the embedded white racist self and the opaque white racist self. I critique the conception of a white autonomous subject, one that is presumed completely free to extricate itself from racist social processes and structural forces. I also explore the assumption that how one determines if one is racist is by engaging in introspection, which functions as a process of retrieval through the inspection of racist mental contents, as it were.

Using the work of Judith Butler, though drawing nuanced implications for whiteness, I argue against the conception of the white racist self as a site of complete transparency—and for its conception as a site of opacity. Indeed, the opaque white racist self and the embedded white racist self are theorized as sites of dispossession that speak to the difficulties and complexities that whites face in their attempt to "undo" racism or to "rehabilitate" whiteness or to become "race traitors." I also theorize the concept of "tarrying" as an important process whereby whites remain open to the experiences of nonwhites and thereby allow for the possibility of being touched. Part of the function of tarrying is to create a space for whites to ask themselves the question: How does it feel to be a problem?

1

Looking at Whiteness

Finding Myself Much like a Mugger at a Boardwalk's End

I feel, I see in those white faces that it is not a new man who
has come in, but a new kind of man, a new genus. Why, it's a
Negro! —**Frantz Fanon**, *Black Skin, White Masks*

I am walking down Broadway in Manhattan, platform shoes
clicking on the pavement, thinking as I stroll of, say, Boolean
expansions. I turn, thirsty, into a bar. The dimly-lit room,
obscured by shadows, is occupied by whites. Goodbye, Boolean
expansions. I am *seen*. —**Charles Johnson**, "A Phenomenology of
the Black Body"

The Lived Density of Race

While the focus on demonstrating the nonreferential status of
race is important work within the context of liberation praxis
vis-à-vis racism—indeed, indispensable work—my sense is
that it is at the level of the *lived* density of race that so much more work
needs to be done. The former, while necessary, I judge to be conceptually
thin;[1] the latter, also necessary, I judge to be existentially thick. So, despite
the thin/thick designations, both are necessary. I have known whites who are
staunchly *against* the claim that race cuts at the joints of reality. Yet how they
live race, how they live their *own racism*, is unmistakable. I was once interviewed by a white male philosopher for a job opening in a department looking for someone whose areas of specialization were the philosophy of race and
African American philosophy. I met with this faculty member for an hour.
My assumption was that we would spend time talking about what I would
teach, what I desired to teach, my curriculum vitae, and so on. However, he
spent the bulk of our time talking about *his* "antiracism." He also narrated a
personal incident that "demonstrated" this. As I recall, there were no questions about my pedagogy or my relatively extensive publication record.

Here was a white philosopher who no doubt, if asked, would have said that the concept of race is scientifically vacuous and has no empirical referent in the natural world, that race is a mere social construction/social category. Yet he felt the need to self-present as "pure," as a "good white," who was above the fray of racism and lived beyond the trappings of race matters. He used my presence, my hour, as a space for white self-confession and self-glorification. There he was—fully visible, "entrails" revealed—desiring that I spend my time bearing witness to his "white purity" so that I could state emphatically and unequivocally that he was one of the "good guys." Yet he doth self-praise too much. It was as if he were preparing me for those white real racist others—you know, the "bad" ones. I was unmoved by the implied dichotomy. He needed my approval and admiration. My black body, my presence, functioned redemptively. I remained steadfast, though: *"Look, a white! What white narcissism! What white hubris!"*

But what did he need from me? What did he need to prove to me or perhaps to himself? I wonder if, had I applied for a position that required specialization in epistemology, he would have wasted my time and his bending over backward to prove to me that he definitely knew the ins and outs of the Gettier problem, the epistemological point of Neurath's boat, and the implications of "Gavagai" for the problem of translation. My suspicion is that his identity would not have been implicated in the same way. Then again, he could have used the entire interview trying to prove, because of my blackness, that I was running a sham and really did not know much at all about epistemology. My point, though, is that a racial dynamic in an interview for a position teaching philosophy of race was asserting itself in an otherwise pretty mundane social encounter. Indeed, it is at the level of the socially interstitial that race/racism is existentially robust. No matter how scientifically empty the concept of race, its lived reality permeated his office, shaped his disclosures and silences, and shaped his perception of me and how he thought of himself (or needed to think of himself) in my presence.

In our contemporary moment, the *lived* experience of race is anterior to the question of its empirical referential status. Black people are always already raced in relation to the history of the term as a marker of black inferiority. White people are always already raced in relation to the history of the term as a marker of white superiority. The point here is that the conceptual analysis of the scientific or empirical status of race is a second-order process that must not overlook the quotidian reality of race as experienced, as constitutive of interstitial socially lived dynamics. Indeed, before race becomes a self-consciously *philosophical* problem, we are already raced; we are already hurt by race, injured by it, celebrate it, fight because of it, lose our freedoms over it, maintain our privilege because of it, differentiate ourselves from others based on it, enslave others because of it, decimate others because of it—our perceptions are already shaped by it, our fears are already formed by it, who we choose to love is already mediated by it.

Race is similar to our prereflective knowledge about the sun. For example, before we think about the sun as a massive star, a stellar body, among trillions of other stars, as 93 million miles from the earth and warping the vicinity of space around it, we delight in its warmth, we plan family events around that warmth, we enjoy picnics on sunny days, sunny days are days for falling in love and playing outside. We also eagerly anticipate watching sunsets, gathering in social groups to do so. In short, we move and have our being within the warmth of the sun, not as an object of scientific knowledge but as something experienced in the everyday world of our meaningful social activities—activities that are as regular and unnoticed as breathing or blinking. As Clevis Headley writes, "In Heideggerian language, an existential phenomenological approach exposes race as a ready-to-hand-concept, a concept that immediately structures various practical activities."[2]

My point is twofold. First, to restrict the problem of race to conceptual analysis full stop is too limiting. Second, an exploration of race as lived takes one beyond what is thought about in the abstract to the level of how race is meaningfully lived as an embodied and messy phenomenon. I realize that part of the aim of conceptual analysis is precisely to unpack the messiness of race. Yet this messiness reveals its complexity, a complexity that often transcends and outstrips abstract conceptual analysis.

In their epigraphs at the beginning of the chapter, both Fanon and Johnson capture moments in the lived experience of blacks in an already constituted, *messy* world, a world of values, of stereotypes, of being rendered invisible or hyper-visible, of racist assumptions, racist narratives, and embodied others. In short, then, Fanon and Johnson point to a world of sociality. As Maurice Natanson writes, "The experience of the self with other selves is the meaning of 'sociality.'"[3] In a form of sociality that is fundamentally structured by race and racism, black people, for example, undergo ontologically truncating traumatic experiences in the face of white others who refuse to recognize their humanity. In short, blacks are reduced to their epidermis, and so the experience of black people vis-à-vis race/racism presupposes the existence of white others. I take this to be socially axiomatic when it comes to black people in an antiblack world.

Fanon writes, "It will be seen that the black man's alienation is not an individual question."[4] When, *as a black man*, Fanon shouts a salutation to the world and the world cuts away his joy and exuberance, this presupposes a white world—indeed, an antiblack white world—that refuses him the sense of being at home in it. His experience of alienation is one that raises the discussion to the level of a *social* origin; it is *not* a question about his lack of constitution or about *individual* psychological maladies. "The focus on the personality of the individual," according to Cynthia Willett, "does not come to terms with the fact that sociality is not only a dimension of the individual; it is the air that we breathe, the element of our lives."[5]

In Johnson's epigraph, when he writes about thinking of Boolean expansions and being *seen*, he is writing about white gazes and their power to deny the internal complexity of black subjectivity and how such gazes affect the embodied experiences of black people. Johnson's point is that white looks, which presuppose embodied white others, challenge the complexity of his lived subjectivity. This presupposes a social space of intersubjectivity and shared intelligibility. As Ruth Frankenberg writes, "As I, and other colleagues, have argued elsewhere, there are times when whiteness seems to mean only a defiant shout of 'I am not that Other!'"[6] On this score, the "I," as white, in its social ontological constitution, is fundamentally marked through negation. The white "I," then, is constituted within a space of relationality or alterity. At the heart of whiteness is a profound disavowal: *"I am not that!"* In other words, whiteness is secured through marking what it is not. Yet what it (whiteness) is not (blackness in this case) is a false construction that whites themselves have created to sustain their false sense of themselves as ontologically superior. However, it is a form of superiority that involves the subordination of their freedom. As Steve Martinot succinctly states, "White identity loses its freedom through its identity-dependency on the other. But this dependence is then disguised by means of a standard inversion. The ethics of whiteness and white supremacy determines that it is the other (a black person, for instance) who is perceived as the source of one's felt unfreedom."[7]

Theorizing the "dialectics" of white racialization, John Warren writes, "Whiteness does not persist in a vacuum but in relation to nonwhiteness. By uncovering the ways 'white' persons either identify or disavow others, one works to uncover some of the mundane ways [white] people produce race."[8] Or as Barbara Applebaum writes, "A [white] subject's intelligibility . . . is dependent on [ontologically] abject [nonwhite] others who preserve the borders that protect one's ability to be perceived as intelligible. Regulatory norms operate through the subject who repeats and perpetuates the norms that sustain the subject's intelligibility."[9]

Theorizing the issue of negation vis-à-vis the meaning of the human qua white, Sara Ahmed writes, "If to be human is to be white, then to be not white is to inhabit the negative: it is to be 'not.' The pressure of this 'not' is another way of describing the social and existential realities of racism,"[10] particularly in the various ways in which black people face lives of marginalization, exclusion, and ontological and existential erasure. Indeed, I would argue that this "not" functions as a species of the color line. When whites slash away at black joy, then, they install a "color line." When black bodies are objectified by white gazes, reduced to surfaces, and stereotyped, this too is a species of the color line being drawn. The color line, in short, is not just a signifier of *spatial* demarcation, which presupposes a racial economy of spatial management and enforcement that is predicated on the existence, in this case, of white others who have the *sociohistorical* power to delimit space and thus inhibit mobility for, say, black bodies. Rather, the color line also functions as a powerful demarcation that has profound negative *ontological* implications for black people and those of color vis-à-vis whiteness. Indeed, the process of racial spatialization and the process of ontological stigmatization are mutually reinforcing.

Over dinner, after I had given a lecture on racial embodiment at one university, a white colleague argued that children who are racially prejudiced have somehow been "secondarily" taught to be so. My sense is that she wanted to maintain that children, and white children in particular, are blank slates, and only later are they inculcated to be racially prejudicial. I had actually given her an example of a three-year-old white girl, Carla, who, when preparing for rest time in school, said that she did not want to "sleep next to a nigger."[11] Apparently, she "had seen" that there was a "nigger" in the classroom. When asked why, she said, "Niggers are stinky. I can't sleep next to one."[12] After I explained this, the same white colleague insisted that this must have happened in the 1960s. She was shocked when I said that it happened in a study that was conducted in the middle to late 1990s.

While I certainly agreed that children are not born racists, somehow, genetically so, my white colleague missed the subtlety of just how, in Carla's case, racial prejudice is not necessarily an "additional" layer that is forced over an otherwise white innocence—a kind of top-down scenario. Something is far more insidiously operating at the level of simply being bodily in the world as white. In discussing Frantz Fanon's work, Ahmed writes, "We could say that 'the corporeal schema' is already racialized; in other words, race [qua whiteness] does not just interrupt such a schema, but structures its mode of operation."[13]

I want to suggest that something more fundamental or seamless is at work, something that is always already at play, so to speak. Carla's whiteness/racism might be thought of as a fundamental way in which many white children are oriented within the world *ab initio*—a kind of bottom-up scenario, where their bodily orientations have already inherited the background of *lived* orientations of whiteness. This does not mean that every white child of three years old knows the N-word and how to use it. However, it was not simply about prejudices in Carla's case, but about a particular way of being, modes of feeling, perception, and engaging the world from the perspective of whiteness, a form of whiteness unmarked as racist or detrimental to white children. Indeed, it is the quotidian and unmarked ways in which white children simply live their lives within a white family and how various white practices are uneventfully learned that is so crucial here. This point is highlighted in the following example.

After I gave a lecture on whiteness at a university in Perth, Australia, one white woman asked what I thought about whites who adopt aboriginal children. Given Australia's appalling history regarding the "stolen children," Australian Aboriginal and Torres Strait Islander children who were taken from their parents, there were so many obvious dynamics to consider. Yet because there was something less visible at stake, I decided to shift the perspective and talked about how whites, and, by implication, the white woman who asked the question, ought to be focused on how they raise *their own* biological white children. It is within the context of a loving white family structure that the vicious practices of white racism are communicated and learned. This small shift in perspective was to critique the assumption that white parents should take special care to avoid as much as possible their racist practices and sensibilities only when they are the adopters of children of color. And while she raised an important question, my point was to problematize the assumption that white children are not always already the victims of white racism and that white parents are not the primary transmitters of such white racist practices, and that white children's "every gaze and sentence and interaction is inflected, in large or small ways,"[14] by whiteness.

Returning to Carla, I would argue that she is not operating at some abstract level of conceptualization, though she *knows how* to make utterances that are prejudicial or racist. Indeed, she performs the color line effectively, though she is only three years old, has been alive for a little over thirty-six months. For Carla, race is spatial and ontological. Indeed, Carla's sense of herself (how she understands herself, even if only prereflectively) is marked as both spatial and ontological distance. The black child, known as Nicole, inhabited "nigger space." Carla understood her identity through her need to maintain a spatial distance from that "nigger space," a taboo space. One might argue that Carla's identity as white is a process of inheriting proximities that shape how she negotiates space. In short, we are "shaped by what we inherit, which de-limits the [persons] that we might come into contact with."[15] And yet there was also the *ontological* marker of the black body as "nigger," "different," "deviant," "stinky," to be avoided. Carla has become and is becoming white; she is learning how to be in the world—a paradoxical way of being both raced and unraced/marked and unmarked.

Carla is inhabiting, learning, performing, and perpetuating racial spatial logics, racial affective logics, and racial judgmental logics that have begun to feel like "life as usual." These logics are modes of being-in-the-world that are inextricably linked to her whiteness as a site of *here-ness*. And they are formative sites "from which the world unfolds."[16] Moreover, the utterance "little stinky niggers" forms part of the background/orientation of a larger sociolinguistic world that not only is taken for granted but also sanctions (directly or indirectly) such utterances.

Carla is part of an ongoing iterative process, one that is grounded in historicity and social practice. To "see" a "little stinky nigger" and to maintain one's distance, then, does not constitute, from the perspective of the logic of whiteness, a "moral failure" on her part. On the contrary, such a mode of "seeing," which is really a mode of construction, is evidence that Carla has effectively learned *how* to navigate racially saturated social spaces and make racial sense of the world through the lens of a white supremacist society. And while it is Nicole who is the unfortunate target of the racist discourse, it is Carla who, for me, requires unabashed *naming*. Thus, I think it is important and urgent to nominate the scene and call the real problem out—*"Look, a white!"* Through such nomination, the objective is to identify Carla as both the vehicle and the site of the problem.

"Look, a white!" is not simply about Carla. Nomination brings attention to, discloses, renders ethically problematic, a network of iterative power relations, normative assumptions, and calcified modes of being that are created and defined by whiteness. It identifies Carla's racism and also points beyond her, signifying conditions of subject formation that reference thousands of historical acts of repetition, white normative assumptions, ways of being, seeing, comporting, judging, and distancing—that is, infinitesimal ways of drawing and enforcing racial boundaries in the lived social reality, operating within which is a white racist regime of "truth" that "offers a framework for the scene of recognition."[17] In short, Carla's "recognition" of a "little stinky nigger" and her utterance, "Niggers are stinky. I can't sleep next to one," is not an *inaugural* racist moment but an iterative moment that fundamentally speaks to preexisting white racist discursive formations, formations that precede Carla, that render intelligible various racist ontological assumptions and racist utterances.

Carla's racist utterance is indeed racist. Yet it is not Carla who alone endows it with racist meaning as if from the domain of a private language. As Applebaum writes, "The speaker, by uttering the racist speech, makes 'linguistic community with a history of speakers' whose previous citations have invested it with the accumulated force that enables its injurious capacity."[18] In that sense, "Look, a white!" identifies and marks both Carla's individual enactment of whiteness and the dynamic processes of white racist effective history that work through her. And "since one's existence as a [white] subject depends on forced repetition of norms, one's 'being' as a [white] subject is necessarily complicit in the perpetuation of such norms."[19]

That Nicole *comes into view* as a "stinky nigger" is precisely a function of a white orientation that Carla has already taken.[20] For Carla, this orientation is expansive and colonial; it gives her a sense of indefinite spatiality. She is always already given the "right" and the "absolute freedom" to demarcate her white space and to ostracize those who don't "naturally" belong in it. Indeed, she comes to inhabit the world spatially in the mode of an "ability to do" or the "capacity to do." Nicole, from the perspective of whiteness, is the usurped body; a mere object that simply occupies space among other objects. Given the hegemony of whiteness, she may come to experience herself in the mode of an "inability to do" or the "incapacity to do." In short, on the one hand, whiteness expresses a relation to the world in the form of "I can"; on the other hand, blackness expresses a relation to the world in the form of "I cannot."[21] On this score, Barack Obama's mantra-like campaign slogan, "Yes we can!" forces one to question the meaning of the "we" in the expression and to problematize the reality of "can" vis-à-vis differentially raced bodies. As a "nigger," Nicole will learn what it means to undergo social and psychological strangulation within white dominated spaces. She will come to experience what it means to be deemed a problematic body, a suspicious body, a racially profiled body.

Theorizing how black bodies are ontologically truncated and what this means for phenomenology, Sara Ahmad writes, "A phenomenology of 'being stopped' might take us in a different direction than one that begins with motility, with a body that "can do" by flowing into space."[22] Moreover, these different points of phenomenological inquiry, these different ways of describing *lived* experiences that obtain relative to differentially raced bodies, drive home the political and philosophical significance of an identity discourse that assumes *real* identities that have "real-world effects."[23]

Becoming white is like learning a language (say English) as a young child. One learns English in the context of the everyday by hearing it spoken. The "subject" of the language-learning process does not self-consciously incorporate the grammar of English. Yet parents engage in correcting the linguistic performances of their children; this is part of what it means to inhabit a linguistic community. Carla has come to inhabit whiteness. One might say that she has come to *perform or reiterate the grammar of whiteness*. And just as there are ways of speaking that are deemed appropriate/inappropriate, there are also appropriate/inappropriate ways of being white. When mistakes are made in the former, it is not necessary for parents to get the newest edition of Strunk and White's *The Elements of Style* and read it aloud to their children. All that is necessary is a gentle reminder, a linguistic performance (in the stream of everyday language *use*) that shows how it is done. When mistakes are made in the latter case—that is, in the stream of everyday raced contexts—the grimace on the face of a white parent as her white child touches or comes too close to a body of color is enough to communicate that the grammar of whiteness has somehow been performed incorrectly. This is part of what it means to inhabit a community of intelligibility shaped by whiteness.

In other words, my sense is that Carla has *become* white and is repeating/reiterating a fundamental mode of being white-in-the-world. But just as I *become* effective at driving a car on the highway without positioning, as it were, the driving experience as an *object* of my conscious reflection, Carla has already learned (prereflectively) how "to-get-around-in-the-the-world-in-white." By the way, this does not mean that she is completely *thoughtless*. The point is that she *lives* her racism effectively. She has come to inhabit a meaningful world of which certain utterances, movements, gazes, and "acceptable" and "unacceptable" bodies are a part. A meaningful world need not get its meaningfulness from the extent to which it is/becomes an object of conscious reflection. In many ways, meaningfulness is precisely lived/experienced at the prereflective level.

Obviously, I am not saying that white racism does not consist of self-consciously held prejudices, mean-spiritedness, and hatred. My point is that Carla has been thrown into whiteness, has learned to perform whiteness on cue, and that whiteness, for her, has become her structuring orientation. As argued earlier, the self that Carla has become presupposes the reality of sociality. Her performances (whether linguistic or racist) presuppose the not-self in the form of others' existence. Not only are there other whites qua others who make up this social space, but there are also "others" qua nonwhites who are the targets of racial/racist disavowal. The Carla example, it seems to me, illustrates the messiness of race and how race (in this case whiteness) claims, as it were, certain bodies and constitutes bodily repertoires and social practices at the most basic level of coming-to-be-in-the-world.

The white professor who interviewed me, who talked ad nauseam about his antiracism, also illustrates the ways in which racial dynamics play out against the background of "good intentions." Indeed, they often obfuscate the need for greater unflinching self-interrogation and honesty. Gaining conceptual clarity regarding the scientific referential status of race is one thing. Struggling to make sense of how race is performed, how it is lived, is a different matter entirely. One can easily "master" the former with no truly deep and sustained concern for the latter.

I know whites (academic and intellectual types) who are able to engage race and racism critically at the *conceptual* level, but appear to fail at challenging *their* own whiteness at a deeply interpersonal level. In other words, their conceptual sophistication stands side by side with a form of wanton racism that goes unexamined because they refuse to do so. Indeed, they make a fetish, either in writing or at scholarly conferences, of displaying their self-consciousness regarding their whiteness, perhaps even taking the time to offer a personal confession of it. Yet at the end of the day they remain covetous of positions of white power and continue to engage in acts of racism in their daily lives, failing to engage their own racist actions with the same enthusiasm that they bring to theory. After all, there is no necessary connection between (a) the ability to reflect critically on white racism, even on *one's own* white racism, and (b) working hard to mark and challenge one's own racist practices. These white individuals are recognized for their scholarly work on race and racism; they become tenured, acquire book contracts, receive promotions, garner praise for their philosophical acuity and breadth in their academic communities, and become "intellectual leaders." In short, they do well at the level of academic "performance" and academic capital returns. Indeed, as writers, as productive scholars in the areas of race/whiteness, as creators of cultural capital, white philosophers/scholars must not be under the illusion that, because something has implications for their own psychological and material sense of achievement, they transcend their whiteness. There is no liberal, transcendent subject that engages in the cultural production of ideas—an activity linked to larger material conditions of productivity—from the economic outside,[24] as it were.

To write and publish in ways that are not mindful of this fact actually reinscribes the white subject as a site of masterful yet illusory detachment. Furthermore, even as whites perform well academically in terms of exploring white racism, their narcissism and hegemony remain in place, remain unexamined and yet expressed in public and private spaces. This is an important observation as it alerts black people to profound levels of white hypocrisy, ways of *being* and ways of *appearing*. Indeed, it is important not to overlook the real possibility that there are some white scholars, despite the fact that they engage in, and devote their academic careers to, critical studies of race/whiteness, who *self-consciously* engage in acts of white power maintenance, acts of overt racist nastiness, and forms of institutional control that silence and marginalize the voices of black scholars and scholars of color.

It is in such situations that one ought to nominate whiteness unequivocally: "Look, *damn it*, a white!" One has to ask about the "genuine" liberationist ideals of whites. I have watched as many whites pursue issues in the philosophy of race for what seems to be careerist reasons, as a way of diversifying their scholarly profiles. I worry how this might negatively impact the liberationist thrust of critical race discourses.[25] Of course, careerism is not logically incompatible with liberationism. Yet there is something problematic about whites doing this. It reeks of pure opportunism.

Related to this concern of pure opportunism is the fear that white philosophers will approach the problem of race/whiteness as a mere *intellectual* pursuit. As Zeus Leonardo and Ronald K. Porter write, "Whites often conceive of race talks as intellectually stimulating—as in a discovery or another topic in which they can excel—rather than a lived experience that [people] of color in good faith share with their white colleagues."[26] In other words, rather than approaching the problem of race/whiteness as a *lived* experience, as a site of shared vulnerability, as a site of differential cash value,[27] my fear is that white philosophers will treat critical discourses around race/whiteness as sites of *intellectual* mastery, as forms of mastery that do not involve deep personal risk, like being able to rattle off various philosophical movements and thinkers (from, say, Thales to Jacques Derrida) in Western philosophy.

The problem that I delineate here with white theorists regarding race and whiteness reminds me of David J. Kahane's observations that, when he teaches the work of Catherine MacKinnon, many of his students, primarily male, seem to be able to engage her work on eroticized domination without any risk to themselves as gendered beings but "as propositional knowledge only, without taking her views as possibly speaking profoundly to themselves, to privileges and harms in their own lives and the lives of those around them, and to changes the analysis enables or requires."[28]

In this chapter, I expose the lived embodied experiences of black people in an antiblack world. I explore how whites perform the "I am not the Other" dynamic at sites of the everyday. Thus, I explore how white spatial and ontological color line performances *fix* the meaning of the black body as a dangerous outsider or as the hypersexual deviant whose sexual prowess is to be feared and yet desired. In Chapter 4, I argue that the movie *White Chicks* mimics the black imago in the white imaginary as a way of throwing whites back on themselves, as a way of instigating the process of having whites thrown, to the extent that this is possible, into a state of self-recognition. There are many whites and some blacks who will not see themselves in the cases that I examine. To them, I would recommend greater vigilance. There are complex paintings that often appear as incongruent images on initial viewing. By looking longer, staring harder, one will come to see an elephant or an entire city. *I see how you see me, and I damn sure don't like it* constitutes the indictment of whiteness as explored in this chapter. In many ways, this indictment constitutes the entire thrust of this book.

Aimee Sands, Emmy Award–winning filmmaker, has effectively uncovered the density of race with her powerful fifteen-minute 2009 DVD *What Makes Me White?* I have often suggested to my white students that they go back to their dorms and look at themselves naked in the mirror. I ask them to pose the following questions while looking: What is so special about being white? What is so special about *this* white body? The objective of the assignment, once they have explored questions regarding the normative status of whiteness, the ways in which they are privileged in virtue of having phenotypic white bodies, is to have students begin the process of seeing their white bodies as peculiar—that is, not as normative, not as simply the way *human* bodies are. Again, as Sara Ahmed writes, "There must be white bodies (it must be possible to see such bodies *as* white bodies), and yet the power of whiteness is that we don't see those bodies as white bodies. We just see them as bodies."[29]

Sands begins her film with an examination of her own white body by noticing how it is not white like paper or white like clouds but somewhat bone white.[30] She does not interrogate the fact that her own white body is constituted through various racial norms that shaped the behavior of her parents and grandparents; that is, she does not explore how her phenotypic body is an expression of various micro-decisions mediated by race and racism. Yet she poses a very important question immediately after her bodily examination. She asks, "Where do we learn to be white?"[31] The question creates an important slippage between the white body qua white body and the ways in which it engages in various performances in the context of social life. This *does not* mean that racism or whiteness is a state of mind or that antiracism or challenging whiteness is *simply* about the formation of new habits. In fact, we have to be careful that the discourse about habits vis-à-vis whiteness does not obscure just how malignant white racism is.

To think that whiteness as habit formation is akin to picking one's nose is very misleading. I especially emphasize this because we generally think of habits as annoying but fully within our reach to transform with a little effort and self-awareness. Thinking of annoying habits as incidental sidesteps the fundamentally complex and constitutive nature of whiteness.[32] "I'm fine, great in fact, but if only I could rid myself of these damn white *habits*." It is precisely the white self that is "fine" and "great in fact" that is of interest to me. The discourse on habits as they relate to whiteness should not evade the deeper ethical implications of whiteness and how it is inextricably linked to broader issues of injustice, oppression, and suffering when it comes to those who are not white. The importance of whiteness as a *structural evil* should not be reduced to a set of troublesome habits.

"Where do we learn to be white?" Sand's question raises the issue of the messiness of race. She tells the story of how she and her sister would travel from Westchester to New York City with their grandparents. She says that when they reached black neighborhoods the windows of her grandparents' car would close and the doors would lock. She says, "Until dark faces appear on the street. Then the sleek electric windows slide up and suck closed. The automatic locks *click down*. The dark people are sealed out. We are sealed in."[33] It is at this juncture that the camera shifts to antiracist educator and activist Manuel J. Fernandez, who adds to Sands's story. He talks about how whites lock the doors and roll up the windows when approaching black neighborhoods despite the fact that there is no air conditioning in the car. He also adds that, as a man of color, he has experienced whites locking their car doors once he has been seen.[34]

In the film, antiracist activist and whiteness theorist Peggy McIntosh explains to Sands that locking one's doors in the presence of black people is one way that whites are taught to think about blacks as dangerous. She shares her own narrative about how the messiness of race affected her at an early age, describing how, one day before she left her grandmother's house, she kissed the black cook good-bye, someone for whom she felt a great deal of love. McIntosh says that her grandmother protested this show of affection and screamed at her (McIntosh) in a voice that she had never heard before. McIntosh says she was terrified and never touched the black cook again. She explicitly points out the trauma that she felt from such an experience. What we do not hear, however, is the story of the black cook. Think of *her* pain and *her* sense of rejection. Moreover, think of how she may have been made to feel like a diseased body, like shit. However, McIntosh raises an important question that she addresses to Sands: "And what did it do to you to have those windows rolled up?"[35] The camera then pans over to Sands. One can see the contemplative look on her face. Either because of time or because Sands wants those watching the film to explore the question for themselves, she does not answer, though we do hear her voice-over that indicates how seriously she takes McIntosh's question.

Clicks That Install

I have experienced the *clicking* sounds of car doors as white people in their cars catch a glimpse of my black body. I know what Sands is talking about, though from the other side, as it were, of the clicking sounds. I will build on a discursive strategy that I used in *Black Bodies, White Gazes: The Continuing Significance of Race* (2008), where the words on the page create a "syncopated cadence,"[36] and deploy it here, though in greater detail, as a way of addressing McIntosh's question to Sands. The use of such a strategy is *to do* philosophy differently, to write philosophy differently.

To communicate an experience that is difficult to express, the very medium itself may need to change. On this score, perhaps philosophers need to write poetry or make films. When it comes to a deeper, thicker philosophical engagement with issues of race, the medium has to change to something dynamically expressive, something that forces the reader/listener *to feel* what is being communicated, to empathize with greater ability, to imagine with greater fullness and power. Dry and nearly incomprehensible prose needn't mark the "importance" or "brilliance" of philosophical speech or writing. When it comes to race, we need forms of expressive discourse that unsettle us, that make us uncomfortable with its daring frankness that pulls us in even as it unnerves. If philosophy is to become relevant to life as *lived* in its messiness, then we need forms of philosophical discourse that do not lie about and obfuscate life. Instead of avoiding the funk of life, we need to communicate that funk with greater richness. The process of writing with such frankness of style, then, a style that is graphically abrasive, is an attempt on my part to mimic the world of *lived* pain and suffering, and to challenge styles of writing typical of so many academic philosophers, styles that I find fail to capture the nitty-gritty, vivaciousness of the everyday. This raises larger issues of philosophical authority as instantiated through a particular preferred style of writing, questions of philosophical voice, and the marginalization of certain voices in favor of others.

So what did it do to Sands as those windows were rolled up, as the sounds of clicks were heard? My sense is that the clicks signified her identity in the form "I am not that Other." Not only are the white bodies that initiate the clicks performing their white identities through them; the clicks themselves install white identities, hail white identities, and solidify white identities. Sands and her sister were having their identities *as white* constructed and solidified. Though there were no words that accompanied the clicks, the performance of locking the doors marked the space inside the car (and those in it) as normative, as a site of safe and sound distance from those *different* and *deviant* black Others outside. The clicks functioned as constitutive of what it means to be white vis-à-vis nonwhite Others, especially blacks in this case.

It does not require *coercion* to install and fix white identity as a spatial relationship of distance from nonwhites. Through a process of repetition, and subtle policing, a continuously enacted performance of locking car doors and rolling the windows up in the presence of black bodies, the reality of white identity as spatial distance and ontological difference from blacks, takes on the appearance of something natural and inevitable as opposed to something that has been socially constructed, the product of racist regulatory norms. Furthermore, the clicks are not isolated, pure auditory data but markers of social meaning, signifiers of regulated space, forms of disciplining bodies, and part of a racial and racist web of significance that bespeaks the sedimentation of racist history and racist iteration. Through an uneventful,[37] mundane act of white index fingers locking a car door or a white hand rolling up a car window, the color line is drawn, a boundary is created.

But what if those clicking sounds could speak? What would they say to whites? My sense is that the clicks would reinforce multiple ways in which *they* (whites) understand their identity. The clicks would reinforce, over and over again, the stability of white identity qua normative as a noun as opposed to a verb or a succession of acts—that is, a "doing."[38] *Click* (white). *Click, click* (white, white). *Click, click, click* (white, white, white). *Click, click, click, click, click* (white, white, white, white, white). *Click, click, click, click, click, click* (white, white, white, white, white, white). *Click* (pure). *Click* (innocent). *Click* (vulnerable). *Click* (decent). *Click* (threatened). *Click* (true American). *Click* (better than those dark Others). *Click* (epistemologically credible). *Click* (superior). *Click* (clean and unsullied). *Click* (whites only). *Click* (reliable). *Click* (*our* white space). *Click* (sexually responsible). *Click* (well educated). *Click* (godly). *Click* (civilized). *Click* (law abiding).

Within the context of the clicks, however, the car's occupants' (white) safety is a fabrication. They have created a false dichotomy: an outside (the blacks) as opposed to an inside (the whites). But if that inside, that feeling of safety, that fabricated space, is a construction that is parasitic on the false construction of the black body as dangerous, then the occupants' sense of themselves as "safe" (and white) is purchased at the expense of denigrating the black body as unsafe. The clicks control the ways in which blacks become visible (or invisible) to whites. The clicks occlude the possibility of the social world unfolding in a way that might challenge white modes of being. The clicks install white insularity, reinforcing a sense of suspicion and militating against various proximate encounters that might challenge the boundaries of white subject formation.[39] As Robert Bernasconi writes, "Racism wants to make its targets disappear, but it does not want them to disappear into anonymity. It wants to see them without seeing them. It wants to identify its targets unambiguously without having to face them."[40] Yet those clicks occlude the possibility of a greater, more robust sense of human community or *Mitsein*. Whites have cut themselves off from the possibility of fellowship, of expanding their identities, of reaping the rewards of being genuinely touched by black people and thereby shaking the restrictions and fortifications that whites erect to "protect" themselves from those dreaded *racial* Others, those outsiders. Like Odysseus, when he tied himself to the mast of a ship, whites deny the process of *mediation* by black people through the creation of "safe" spaces, spaces that are reflective of a form of self-obsession.

Whites obstruct the possibility of new forms of self-knowledge by creating distances between themselves and nonwhites. It is a "gross attempt to understand the self through the self rather than through the other: narcissism par excellence."[41] The clicks, then, can function to maintain "the self-image and understanding of whiteness and [reveal] a refusal to change through the other."[42] The iterative clicks function as sites of protection against epistemic and affective changes to the white self. Because black people are assigned to be members of the "out-race" or as antithetical to whiteness, whites exclude "the communion that is the condition"[43] for fracturing important aspects of their white identities. The process of shaking the boundaries of the white self is something that McIntosh thinks Sands's work is attempting to accomplish. She says, "I think that you, in making this film, are rolling the windows back down."[44]

Nevertheless, to live a life predicated on a lie often requires more lies to cover it over. Black bodies, then, function to conceal the truth that so many whites lead lives that are constructed around a profound deception—namely, that they need protecting from black people. Hence, the clicks install and shape white sensibilities. The clicks shape white desires. They distort white perception. As suggested, the clicks construct and reinforce "racial" difference and distance. As in the case of Carla, as argued earlier, the clicks demonstrate the inheritance of proximities. They block richer forms of experience, ways of coming to see likenesses.[45] They lay the ground for white fear of black bodies, crush future options, and harden hearts. The clicks are white nation-building micro-events. In short, they imprison the human spirit and cripple the lives of whites.

And yet I have heard whites protest, "But I lock *my* doors because of *strangers*, not because of blacks!" Sands's life experiences, however, pinpoint *white* fears regarding *black* bodies. To argue that one locks one's doors regardless of the "raced" body elevates the white subject to the status of "neutral observer"—that is, the one who sees not race but people. It seems to me that this is just another move toward obfuscation through so-called color-blind discourse. Presumably, when Sands's grandparents drove through Westchester, they encountered *white* strangers. Yet the locks didn't click and the windows didn't roll up until *black* strangers appeared. While it is difficult to do and far more difficult to own, whites need to pay greater attention to how their perception of white strangers eases their discomfort as opposed to how their perception of black strangers actually increases their fear. I certainly acknowledge xenophobia, but for whites there are no strangers qua strangers. There are black strangers, strangers of color—those deemed untrustworthy—and then there are white strangers—those who are coded as simply human persons. Thomas F. Slaughter, Jr., argues that the metaphysical Manichean divide between darkness (evil) and light (good) "became epidermalized, physicalized, by the now fading epoch of African enslavement and world colonization. Thus today, on the one hand, White is exclusive; on the other hand, I am my appearance"[46]—that is, his blackness.

I fear those whites who find themselves in a state of tremulous trepidation once they catch a glimpse of my dark body. I fear them because they have a *need* for me. I make them feel good about themselves; I give them supreme evolutionary status. I am the "proof" that they concocted to confirm their superiority. I am the "nigger" in terms of which the *clicks* signify their white "wholesomeness." Without that "proof," however, where would this leave whites? It would leave them naked, without their illusions. James Baldwin writes, "White people will have to ask themselves precisely why they found it necessary to invent the nigger; for the nigger is a white invention, and white people invented him out of terrible necessities of their own."[47] In many ways, whiteness is a form of make-believe, a game played by children who refuse to grow up, though the existential stakes are high for black people. James Baldwin says that black people "will have to do something very hard . . . which is to allow the white citizen his [or her] first awkward steps toward maturity."[48]

While whites hear the clicking sounds from inside the car (the zone of safety), what of those, in this case, black males who hear the clicking sounds from the outside (the marked zone of "danger")? What do those sounds communicate to those black bodies? *Click* (nigger). *Click* (nigger). *Click* (nigger). *Click* (nigger). *Click, click* (nigger, nigger). *Click* (nigger). *Click, click* (nigger, nigger). *Click, click, click* (nigger, nigger, nigger). *Click, click, click, click* (nigger, nigger, nigger, nigger). *Click, click, click, click, click* (nigger, nigger, nigger, nigger, nigger). The clicking begins to fragment my existence and cut away at my integrity. *Click* (thug), *click* (criminal), *click* (thief). *Click* (dangerous). *Click* (sexually rapacious). *Click* (predator). *Click* (violent). *Click* (wild). *Click* (primitive). *Click* (angry). *Click* (savage). *Click* (rapist). *Click* (irresponsible). *Click* (gang-banger). *Click* (uneducated and uneducable). *Click* (inferior). *Click* (unlawful). *Click* (dirty). *Click* (unreliable). *Click* (evil). *Click* (Satan). *Click* (unpredictable). *Click* (lazy). *Click* (shiftless). *Click* (dreadful). *Click* (stinky). *Click* (malevolent).

The clicks are *doing something*. My body is circumscribed as a site of danger. From the perspective of whiteness, the clicks are necessary for the heinous acts that I will perform by virtue of my blackness. After all, as black, I am always about to do something criminal. Because I am black, I can't bluff; my cards are always already revealed. The clicking sounds might be described as not only an indicative, a form of pointing, but as "the schematic foreshadowing of an accusation, one which carries the performative force to constitute that danger which [whites fear and defend against]."[49] In my case, as a black male, the clicks send me back to myself, enfolded in the form of images I refuse to accept. I deny their terms. Yet after so many clicks, on so many occasions, some blacks may begin to pose a very peculiar question, though one that has significant phenomenological richness: Where *is* my body? The question itself makes sense once the body is theorized not as a brute *res extensa* but as a site of confluent norms, as a function of a complex interpretive and perceptual framework.

In terms of the clicking sounds, my body, through the gazes of white people, manifests a particular modality of volatility (etymologically *volare*, "to fly"). The etymological meaning of volatility captures the sense in which the black body, within the context of white lies and fears, can experience instability, flux, where its meaning appears to fail to remain tethered, as it were, by the power of black self-definitional agency alone. When walking by whites in cars, I might be said to exist ontologically quadrupled. While it is not possible for me to exist in four different places at once, I am after something that arises at the phenomenological or *lived* level of experience. For example, it can be said that I am "here," taking up space outside on the sidewalk or crossing the street before the appearance of any car. However, I am also "ahead of myself." I don't mean this in the way that Heideggerians speak of human beings as always ahead of themselves qua possibility, or in the way that Sartreans speak of human reality as being for itself and as always *future* oriented, as always more. Rather, "being ahead of myself" suggests the sense in which I am always already *fixed, complete, given*.

From the perspective of white looks, my being—the dynamic possibility and openness of being other than I am—can never transcend the fixity of my presumed *racial essence*. After all, a "nigger" will always be a "nigger." In other words, before I walk by a car filled with whites, and before they catch a glimpse of me and lock their doors, I exist in the form of a static racial template. My being is "known" by whites before my arrival. I reside in a fixed place, always already waiting for me. In short, then, I exist ahead of myself.

In Charles Johnson's brilliant phrase, and from which the title of this chapter is derived, I encounter myself "much like a mugger at a boardwalk's end."[50] My destiny has already been determined; the meaning of my life is forever foreclosed by my blackness. As Frantz Fanon writes, "And so it is not I who make a meaning for myself, but it is the meaning that was already there, pre-existing, waiting for me."[51] Whiteness has created a world in which *necessity* is the foundation of being black-in-the-world. As black, I am possessed by an essence that always precedes me. I am always "known" in advance. Please welcome the "person" who needs no introduction: *the black*.

Once next to the car (or once whites "see" my black body approaching), though physically separated from it, I find myself "over there" floating like a phantasm in their imaginary—much like a thought bubble. Yet I am also "alongside" myself as I catch a glimpse of me through their gaze—I have become a predator, *their* predator. It is as if I carry myself in the form of an extraneous appendage, a superfluous meaning. Brent Staples offers a fascinating phenomenological description of what it means when the black body, *his* black body, experiences a sense of ontological disjointedness and multiplicity vis-à-vis white looks:

> I'd been a fool. I'd been walking the street grinning good evening to people who were frightened to death of me. I did violence to them by just being. How had I missed this? I kept walking at night, but from then on I paid attention. I became an expert in the language of fear. Couples locked arms or reached for each other's hands when they saw me. Some crossed to the other side of the street. People who were carrying on conversations went mute and stared straight ahead, as though avoiding my eyes would save them. . . . I tried to be innocuous, but didn't know how. *The more I thought about how I moved, the less my body belonged to me. I became a false character riding along side it.*[52]

Staples's point is that he felt removed from his body, disembodied. Under the white gaze, his body undergoes a process of volatility, a form of ontological destabilization. In my case, then, to exist ontologically quadrupled is to experience myself as "here-ahead-over-there-alongside." In this way, I have become, under the white gaze, "immaterial" and "vaporous." I am spatially "here." Yet I am "over there," ahead of myself, fixed as a dangerous predator even before I am "seen" by white gazes. Then again, once "seen," I am also "there," residing in the minds of whites as a fixed stereotype. Further still, I am "there," alongside myself—a fourth place. As Robert Gooding-Williams says, the clicking "performances which [produce] this sense of being enslaved to an image . . . leave one feeling literally and utterly dislocated in physical space."[53]

The metaphor of finding oneself much like a mugger at a boardwalk's end is a profound way of depicting the black body's meaning as always already ahead of itself. Think about it. One is typically unaware of the presence of a mugger. The mugger is secretly hiding, waiting to attack. The mugger, if successful, robs you of something precious, valuable. You feel violated. To be black, in the context of antiblack racism, is to have one's meaning determined—already in place. As Johnson argues, "All that I am, can be to them [whites], is as nakedly presented as the genitals of a plant since they cannot see my other profiles. Epidermalization [or reduction to the black epidermis] spreads throughout the body like an odor, like an echoing sound."[54]

So, then, the meaning of my blackness is no mystery. There is no deeper meaning waiting to express itself. All is surface; there is no depth; I am known already. In this way, too, the meaning of my being awaits me. Indeed, just when *I* thought that *I* was an *individual*, someone with inner complexity and layers of psychological sophistication and subtlety, I am laid bare, the "secret" of my being is out: "I am your worst nightmare." In fact, when in the presence of many whites, I discover that I am a *universal*, one who is plagued by an inner racial teleology that is indelibly fixed. And like a mugger at a boardwalk's end, I am robbed of ontological upsurge. I feel as if the capacity to transform the meaning of my life, to define the terms of my existence, has been stolen from me.

It is important to note that I do not wish to conflate black female bodies vis-à-vis racism with black male bodies, because white racist responses to female bodies have their own specific valence. As Marcia Y. Riggs has argued, "Thus, while it is true that Black women and men experienced a common oppression deriving from life in a racist society, women experienced racism in a qualitatively different manner because of the additional constraints of gender oppression upon their lives."[55] In that sense, black women have come to experience themselves as fixed racial universals as well, but more often as prostitutes, as Jezebels, or as whorish. Black males are read as predatory; black females as always sexually available, as if waiting just to fulfill their roles as sexual objects, and treated as gaping black holes to be penetrated. These gendered differences are important and add complexity to the ways in which black women's bodies undergo multiple interwoven forms of oppression and how their bodies are specifically defined as problematic.

When a black woman experiences herself under the white gaze as "ahead of herself" or when she finds herself much like a mugger at a boardwalk's end, she may experience the poisonous version of double consciousness wherein she "sees" herself through the eyes of the white other as a wild, irresponsible, libido-driven black bitch. In Frantz Fanon's discourse, we need a fuller picture of how black women suffer from corporeal malediction. We need to be more attentive to the thousand details, anecdotes, and narratives that have been provided to black women by white America that have led them to sketch a historio-racial schema below the corporeal schema.[56]

Sold from auction blocks, black women were commodified, defined, and sold as chattel. In this economy of selling black bodies, "advertisements announcing the sale of black females used the terms "breeding slaves," "child-bearing woman," "breeding period," "too old to breed," to describe individual women."[57] Standing naked on the auction block, witnessed by both white men and women, the black woman became a blood and flesh blank slate on which whites could project all their fears, desires, and fantasies. The black female body became the atavistic trope, subject to the white gaze. It was an "open" site of sexual exploitation. As bell hooks notes, "Rape was a common method of torture slavers used to subdue recalcitrant black women. The threat of rape or other physical brutalization inspired terror in the psyches of displaced African females."[58] White women were of very little help in situations involving the rape of a black woman. Hooks observes, "Often in desperation, slave women attempted to enlist the aid of white mistresses, but these attempts usually failed. Some mistresses responded to the distress of female slaves by persecuting and tormenting them. Others encouraged the use of black women as sex objects because it allowed them respite from unwanted sexual advances."[59]

Hooks also notes that "in most slaveholding homes, white women played as active a role in physical assaults of black women as did white men. While white women rarely physically assaulted black male slaves, they tortured and persecuted black females."[60] Hooks suggests that white men and women formed an alliance against black women on the grounds of shared racism (whiteness). Black women's experiences were shaped not only by shared physical threats of rape and death but also by a semiotic field of whiteness that led to a form of internal "epistemic violence." In other words, black women came to internalize the destructive images created in white procrustean imaginative spaces.

Even as black women came to acquire more "respectable" jobs as domestic workers, they were constantly in fear of being raped, sexually harassed, and treated as inferiors. Patricia Hill Collins notes that "The treatment afforded Black women domestic workers exemplifies the many forms that objectification can take. Making Black women work as if they were animals or 'mules uh de world' represents one form of objectification. Deference rituals such as calling Black domestic workers 'girls' and by first names enables employers to treat their employees like children, as less capable human beings."[61]

Within such a sociohistorical context, it is no wonder that many black women came to see their homes not as sites of oppression but as spaces of safety away from the racist outside world, a world that constructed them as Jezebels. In some cases, black women had to fight against misogynist black boyfriends and husbands and endure micro-social acts of racism on a daily basis within the larger white social sphere; as well, they had to work for wages that barely allowed for their survival.

Within our contemporary context, black women continue to be represented as "welfare queens." This is simply another way of controlling the semiotic medium in terms of which black women are constructed. "She is portrayed," according to Collins, "as being content to sit around and collect welfare, shunning work and passing on her bad values to her offspring."[62]

Yet even as we must recognize and theorize differences between black men and black women in their experiences of white racism, there are points of shared trauma. For example, critical race theorist Taunya Lovell Banks provides a narrative in which she and four other black women law professors were on an elevator and on two separate occasions of the elevator stopping a white woman, upon seeing the black women, decided not to get on. Keep in mind that the elevator is described as large and spacious. Banks writes, "I used to think that whites were afraid only of black men, and I felt safe from that form of racism due to my gender; now I realize that any black person is threatening. Groups of black women are very threatening even to their white 'sisters.'"[63]

Granting the fact that women, because of the history of patriarchal violence against them, frequently fear being sexually objectified, attacked, and harassed, Banks realizes that gender and class did not occlude the white racist response to her and her colleagues. She writes, "In this instance, by virtue of color alone, we too were feared. Thus, being feared is not simply a black male experience, it is part of the black experience."[64] In a similar phenomenological discourse that describes what it means to be "ahead of myself" vis-à-vis the clicking of car locks, Banks writes, "We were instantly categorized, stripped of our individuality, well before those [white] women waiting for the elevator had a chance to know us."[65] As racially premarked dangerous black women, they were ahead of themselves—already anticipated and prefigured by their white "allies."

While I have theorized black agency elsewhere,[66] I bracket that concern here. It is my way of uncovering what it means to suffer in black bodies in white America; it is my effort to delve into the specific configured *meaning* of black existence in relationship to whiteness. The objective is to lay bare the invidious ways of whiteness vis-à-vis the black body. It is my way of saying that to be black in white America means that the experience of oneself as metastable is often complicated by a white world that perceives black bodies in terms of distortions that it (the white world) has itself created. It is my way of saying that when constantly up against stereotypes and treated like an "essence" to be feared, policed, and imprisoned, black people can begin to experience themselves ontologically and existentially as beings who are *not* robustly trans-phenomenal.

While not a totalizing experience, the sense of finding oneself much like a mugger at a boardwalk's end is the reality of what Johnson insightfully refers to as the reduction of black people to the "Black-as-body," where the interiority of black embodiment is constantly challenged. And despite the fact that black resistance to white racism is inextricably tied to the history of black people in America, it is important to *tarry with* the complex and overly burdensome *experience of* racism, to describe the existential and ontological *weight* of being-black-in-the-world in our contemporary moment lest we make the mistake of believing that such experiences have become empty or even superseded under the assumption of a "postracial" America.

Encountering Myself at the Movies

I have "seen me" in movies. And while I have "seen me" on many such occasions, it remains a peculiar and dreadful experience to find oneself ahead of oneself as already fixed and negated. Try as I might to outrun the possibility of being fixed, I fail. Temporally, it is as if I always arrive much too late, as if history, *white* history, has defined my role well in advance. Then again, it is absurd to outrun my "racial destiny." Yet as I argued previously, this experience is not unusual when it comes to the conceptualization of the black body as ontologically fixed. For example, as black, I am often reminded of my purpose, my inner *racial* teleology, writ large in filmic display. I sit in movie theaters waiting for "me" to appear on screen, waiting to see "my body" appear before me.

I saw myself recently in the movie *The Heartbreak Kid* (2007), where a white woman, the wife of the character played by Ben Stiller, pleads with him while having sex, "Fuck me like a black guy!"[67] Stiller's character really tries, with pronounced gyrations, "to fuck her like a black guy." There is something violent in her racist demand. She wants something "bigger," "wild," perhaps "savage." Yet she wants him to be "me." She wants a white man to perform sexually like the mythical sexually insatiable black man. In short, she wants the "white-body-in-black." She is married to whiteness but craves and desires "raw" blackness. Her demand calls *to me*. She wants me to be the fiction that she has helped to create and sustain through her iterative demand. I, in short, feel the tug and pull on my body's so-called intrinsic racial meaning; I feel the historical weight of the call of the white Other. The call violates my complexity, but I slip into the black-as-genital much as I put on a well-worn overcoat. I watch and listen against the backdrop of the racist Manichean divide played out right there on film, in the bedroom. I begin to feel the sensation of being a fiction, a plaything in the world of white fantasy. As Ralph Ellison insightfully writes, "In our society it is not unusual for a Negro to experience a sensation that he does not exist in the real world at all. He seems rather to exist in the nightmarish fantasy of the white American mind as a phantom that the white mind seeks unceasingly, by means both crude and subtle, to slay."[68]

Given the insidious nature of racism, its dramaturgical presentation in films is taken as axiomatic. Everyone in the audience seems to get the intended meaning. After all, as the myth would have it, he is not black and thus cannot possibly do what she demands. I, on the other hand, feel fixed at the level of the genital, pure and simple. The meaning of my body has already been configured, before my arrival, in the (dominant) filmic narrative of the black as the quintessence of sexuality. I was somehow already there. Malcolm X understood this sense of being face to face with his caricatured raced body and the sense of shame and reduction that results. He discusses this experience in a story of going to the theater to see *Gone with the Wind*. He writes, "When it played in Mason, I was the only Negro in the theater, and when Butterfly McQueen went into her act, I felt like crawling under the rug."[69]

Juxtaposed to the white Scarlett O'Hara (played by Vivien Leigh), Butterfly McQueen (who played Prissy, the black stereotyped maid) functioned as one of those filmic controlling images of black women that Collins critically theorizes: "Analyzing the specific, externally defined, controlling images applied to African American women both reveals the specific contours of Black women's objectification and offers a clearer view of how systems of race, gender, and class oppression actually interlock."[70] Hence, unlike Malcolm X, black women would have felt negated, marginalized, in multiple ways, and erased as they watched the controlling image of Butterfly McQueen qua black racially caricatured maid.

In another movie, *Deuce Bigalow: Male Gigolo* (1999), I was the black man (played by Eddie Griffin) who entered a closet with a white woman (played by Dina Platias) who was blind. After having sex with him in the closet, the woman not only miraculously gains sight but also exclaims, "You're black? I knew it!"[71] The white woman didn't need sight. The black body, with its unmistakable hyper-protrusion, functioned like an indubitable sense datum. In the closet, the black body functioned as an epistemological given. The black body is, one might argue, the *foundation* of the distorted white epistemic architectonic of racist North America. In both movies, I have been made into stone, stiff, forever erect. It is as if Viagra runs through my veins. I have become a phantasm. So fictive has the black body become that one might argue that its very material presence (to create the needed response) has become superfluous. All that is needed is the imago—the racial phantasm. As Fanon observed, "A [white] prostitute told me that in her early days the mere thought of going to bed with a Negro brought on an orgasm."[72]

The movie *Big Stan* (2007), staring Rob Schneider as the title character, opens with a scene that depicts the power of the black imago in the white imaginary that is in stream with Fanon's analysis. *Big Stan* is about a feeble white guy who goes to prison as a result of conning people. He eventually becomes a skilled martial artist after being trained by a martial artist sage-like figure played by the late David Carradine. At the very beginning of the film, I am again reduced to my genitalia, the oversized, dangerous, and yet desired black penis. In the opening scene, we see Big Stan attempting to persuade a white woman, who appears to be in her eighties, to buy a timeshare condo, which we find out later is a scam. Because the white woman has discovered that the condo is located in a "bad neighborhood" (a trope for a poor black neighborhood), Stan has to convince her to forgo her feelings of being unsafe for something far more desirable and taboo, something for which it is worth facing "danger."

In this case, the elderly white woman, who is in a wheelchair, can't possibly resist being surrounded by sexually aggressive and physically endowed black men. After admitting that she would not feel safe in such a neighborhood, Stan exploits the black imago in the white imaginary; he deploys white racist lies and fantasies to his advantage. He explains to the white woman that black men *love* white women. He says that black men want *your* white flesh. He even calls this a scientific fact. He also adds that age doesn't matter just as long as you are a *white* woman. He says that black men, "these big black bucks, don't care whether you're young or old, skinny or fat, walking or with two wrinkled stumps right below the knees."[73] As he continues to embellish what she can expect, the viewer sees her changed expression. Her mouth opens slightly while her breathing becomes noticeably deeper. There is a look on her face of having been insulted, and yet the viewer discerns deep interest and excitement. It is at this point that Big Stan says, "I can just imagine you there, all alone in that big condo awash in a sea of Negro cock."[74] It is at this point, with a slight stutter of excitement and with tremendous enthusiasm, that she says, "I'll—I'll take it."[75] As federal agents come into the room to take Big Stan away, the camera pans over to her face. She has a large smile on it as she turns around and signs the contract.

While humorous, it was because of this same white imaginary, particularly when it came to white women believed to be sexually "innocent," that black men were lynched and castrated for their sexually "large" appetites for white women. Think of the panic, the madness, and the bloodlust on the part of white men that would ensue from the knowledge (or even the fantasy) that white women, *their* white women, sexually desired black men. Imagine the white terrorism visited upon black people (let's say in the South in the early nineteenth century) if a white woman, in the act of coitus, let slip, "Fuck me like a black guy!" Imagine what would happen as white men fantasized about *their* white women fantasizing about themselves "awash in a sea of Negro cock." The white writer and social theorist of southern culture Lillian Smith explores this sexually twisted white saga:

> Guilt, shame, fear, lust spiralled each other. Then a time came, though it was decades later, when [the white] man's suspicion of white woman began to pull the spiral higher and higher. It was of course inevitable for him to suspect her of the sins he had committed so pleasantly and often. *What if,* he whispered, and the words were never finished. *What if. . . .* Too often white woman could only smile bleakly in reply to the unasked question. But white man mistook this empty smile for one of cryptic satisfaction and in jealous panic began to project his own sins on to the Negro male. And when he did that, a madness seized our people.[76]

As a result of being bombarded with so many problematic images and representations that depict the black body as a solid type, one often feels the stress of always being on the lookout. Like a sentinel, one forever watches for the next distorted projection, the next racial profile, the next caricature. This takes effort. One's body becomes geared up, ready for battle. As bell hooks warns, "All black people in the United States, irrespective of their class status or politics, live with the possibility that they will be terrorized by whiteness."[77]

So I sit in movie theaters waiting for the confrontation, waiting to engage in semiotic warfare. "Nope, that isn't me. You've got me wrong again, damn it!" When I hear that *click*, I shake my head in disgust. "I had no intentions of stealing your car. In fact, I don't even like the make." Given enough time, and enough white representational distortions, one walks the street with trepidation that one will be gotten wrong, misunderstood, falsely accused, profiled and arrested, perhaps even shot in the back (as in the case of Oscar Grant in 2009),[78] or arrested for indignation as a result of being questioned about the ownership of one's own home (as happened to Henry Louis Gates in 2009).[79]

"Let's Go, Nigger!"

Frantz Fanon profoundly understood the sense of being the object of white representational distortions, the feeling of being gotten wrong. He writes that he "wanted to come lithe and young into the world that was ours and to help to build it together."[80] To come *lithe* into the world signifies a sense of effortless openness toward the future; it is to undergo moments of existential vertigo in the face of the possibilities of one's being toward the future. To come lithe into the world implies a certain freedom of movement/motility; it suggests a certain spontaneity and eagerness that has *spatial* implications in terms of being "unrestricted." Yet, for Fanon, there were white racist myths and narratives that came with their own expectations of and restrictions on the black body. While some men—white men—were simply expected to behave like men, Fanon writes, "I was expected to behave like a black man—or at least like a nigger."[81] At the age of ninety-one, W.E.B. Du Bois assessed his relationship to North America, writing, "Even while in my own country for near a century I have been nothing but a 'nigger.'"[82]

In his short story, "Big Black Good Man," which was originally published in France in 1958, Richard Wright explores the theme of black *Erlebnis* through Jim, the protagonist, and how he is ontologically truncated through the white gaze of Olaf Jenson, the white man who owns a hotel (in Denmark) where Jim is temporarily staying. Olaf has internalized white racist myths and narratives that relegate Jim's black body to sheer physicality; Jim *is* his body, a body that is described as a "black looming mountain," as having a "clawlike hand," as having "gorillalike arms," as "buffalolike," as a "hunk of blackness," as a "huge black *thing*," and as "black mass." He is also depicted as the "devil of blackness," a "black beast," a "nameless terror," and something that "didn't seem human." As we know, Jim is none of these things. In fact, Jim is a gentle figure, agential, dignified, and comfortable in his body.

I think that Wright explores with tremendous psychological acuity the ways in which the white gaze exaggerates and distorts the black body's appearance, leading to two almost incommensurable perspectives—Jim's and Olaf's. Depicted in animalistic terms as dangerous and racially reified as the essence of evil, Jim has become the expulsion, the by-product, of a racist-infused sickness that "originated" with Olaf. Jim is stereotyped as a black beast, primitive, and the very essence of danger. The moment that Jim walks into the hotel, Olaf fears him, not because he is a stranger but because he is black. And even as Olaf attempts to deny his white racist prejudices, the reader knows that, "try as he might, [Olaf] could not shake off a primitive hate for that black mountain of energy."[83] As suggested, Jim is Olaf's creation, a freak of nature of Olaf's white imaginary.

Wright prefigures the contemporary dynamic of racial profiling. Through "Big Black Good Man," we encounter the power of white racist stereotypes in distorting perception, creating an alternate racist reality. In the real world, a black man (Amadou Diallo, in 1999)[84] reaches for his wallet. In the alternate racist reality, the wallet magically becomes a gun. In the real world, a white man (Charles Stuart, in 1989)[85] murders his pregnant wife in cold blood and wounds himself. In the alternate racist reality, a black man magically becomes the shooter and killer, an "urban savage." In "Big Black Good Man," at the very beginning, Olaf has developed white racist perceptual practices/surveilling practices shaped by a racist dualism where whiteness functions as the transcendental norm within the overall context of the novella. Furthermore, as the title implies, there is something oxymoronic when it comes to the black body *and* its moral standing as *good*.

Contemporary black people are constantly under the surveillance of the white gaze, are fixed by white looks that see only "niggers," haunted by white racist naming processes, and subjected to white America's microtomes. To be expected to behave like a black man or at least like a "nigger" precisely invokes Ahmed's contention (cited earlier in this chapter) that a phenomenology of being stopped can take us in another direction than one that begins with a sense of *white* motility. Cornel West provides two personal examples of what it is like to have one's *lived* body spatiality truncated, fixed, or typified as suspicious, known as "driving while black" ("DWB"). He notes, however, that the incidents he experienced "are dwarfed by those like Rodney King's beating or the abuse of black targets of the FBI's COINTELPRO efforts in the 1960s and 1970s."[86] West recalls that he was stopped three times in his "first ten days in Princeton for driving too slowly on a residential street with a speed limit of twenty-five miles per hour."[87] As Ahmed writes, "To be black in 'the white world' is to turn back towards itself, to become an object, which means not only not being extended by the contours of the world, but being diminished as an effect of the bodily extensions of others."[88] In West's case, to be stopped implied that there was something to be *seen*, a spectacle, something to be found, perhaps something dangerous and hidden. On this score, to be stopped implies a site of suspicion and therefore interrogation. Ahmed writes, "Who are you? Why are you here? What are you doing? Each question, when asked, is a kind of stopping device: you are stopped by being asked the question, just as asking the question requires that you be stopped."[89]

To be white in a white world, however, is to be extended by that world's contours. The world opens up, reveals itself as a place called home, a place of privileges and immunities, a space for achievement, success, freedom of movement. Joe R. Feagin captures this sense of expansive motility through his interpretation of whiteness as a site of symbolic capital: "Living in a society where the dominant framing constantly maintains the prized white identity, and denigrates the identities of racialized 'others,' a white person is typically taken as having positive symbolic capital and thus worthy of racial privileges. This symbolic capital makes it much easier for whites to interact in most societal arenas, and it often shapes how decisions are made and what their outcomes will be."[90]

As one example of her forty-six ways that whites experience white privilege, Peggy McIntosh says, "If a traffic cop pulls me over . . . I can be sure I haven't been singled out because of my race."[91] In her case, because she is white, the operative dimension of race as a trigger for being profiled and stopped is inapplicable. After all, to be white is to be human, to be a person unencumbered and unburdened by the messiness of race matters.

Tim Wise demonstrates what it is to be stopped by white police and how his whiteness signifies good moral standing a priori. Indeed, in Wise's case, whiteness reinforces a sense of expansive motility and moral credibility such that when he is "stopped" there is no sense of social stress, just inconvenience. While in New Orleans in 1993, Wise was pulled over by two white police officers. He mentions the fact that he had not committed any moving violations, was wearing his seatbelt, and had not made any lane changes without properly signaling. In fact, Wise says, he knew why he was stopped and it was for the same reason that he had been stopped three other times during that year, stops that did not result in tickets or any proven violations, just warnings. Wise writes, "I was driving a beat-up car (though fully functioning) with tinted windows (though not illegally tinted) and an anti–David Duke sticker on the back bumper, and as such the cops thought I was black."[92] How did Wise know this? As the white officers approached his car and he rolled down his tinted window, one, seeing his face, said, "Oh."

Here, "Oh" functions as an interjection indicating surprise, perhaps shock, that Wise was white, not a person of color. Indeed, "Oh" suggests that a grave error had been made, a case of mistaken identity. Notice also how the expression "Oh" functions as a site of disorientation, a moment of hesitancy, followed by silence. Wise notes that the police officer stumbled around for a few minutes, talked with his partner, and then returned to tell Wise that his license tags said 1993. The problem here is that it was 1993—the tags were still valid. However, the white police officers needed to justify the stop after being mistaken about the *raced body* that was driving the car. As it turns out, Wise's insurance had lapsed two weeks earlier. Wise describes the police officer as being relieved once he discovered something for which he could write a ticket. Yet at the end of the day, whiteness prevailed; it provided affordances. In fact, Wise and the police officer engaged in white bonding. Wise writes, "But because he was apparently still thrown off by my lack of melanin, he did proceed to tell me how to beat the ticket at the courthouse, by pleading a section something-or-other, which for first-time offenders would result in the ticket being thrown out."[93] To be white in America is to traverse social space with presumptive innocence and assurances. In this instance, Wise's white embodied engagement with the world signified a reciprocal relationship, a mutual "we can."

Cornel West, however, had the "wrong" body (read: black body). He describes driving from New York to teach at Williams College in Massachusetts and being stopped on concocted charges of trafficking cocaine. In this case, there was no "Oh," but he tried to explain to the police officer that he was a professor of religion. The police officer replied, "Yeh, and I'm the flying Nun. Let's go, nigger!"[94] In stream with Ralph Ellison's observations in *Invisible Man*, West is rendered invisible because the white police officer refuses to see him.[95] The white officer's white gaze militated against West's self-description as a professor of religion or a philosopher. Fanon notes, "No exception was made for my refined manners, or my knowledge of literature, or my understanding of the quantum theory."[96] Within the context of America's white microtomes, West asks, "Can genuine human relationships flourish for black people in a society that assaults black intelligence, black moral character, and black possibility?"[97] This sense of "black possibility" has overtones of becoming, the sense of existential and ontological reach. Under America's white microtomes, however, black bodies inhabit a social universe that is constantly blueshifting or contracting. However, whites vis-à-vis blacks might be said to inhabit a social universe that is constantly red-shifting or expanding.

The white police officer's actions are part and parcel of a larger white racist regime that is designed to control/stop black bodies. West notes, "White supremacist ideology is based first and foremost on the degradation of black bodies in order to control them."[98] It is the act of naming, which involves the reiteration of racist norms,[99] that militates against the bodily integrity of West and other black bodies. As a "nigger," it is impossible for West to be a professor of religion. After all, to be called a "nigger" presumes a white normative and epistemic framework that constructs one as ontologically stagnant, worthless, stupid, and inferior.

In his encounter with the white police officer, West's voice possesses little or no power. He is stripped, so to speak, of the ability to render actionable his interior knowledge of his own identity. His self-knowledge, in this case, does not make a difference in a white world predicated on the premise "*Stop the niggers!*" West's knowledge is inconsequential against the white officer's so-called epistemic authority to recognize a "nigger" when he sees one. As a professor of religion, West is effectively rendered invisible. Yet he is rendered hyper-visible as a drug dealer, which "is a case of seeing without seeing."[100] Seeing and stereotypification are congealed in a single act of misperception and distortion.

As white, the police officer, like those whites locking their doors (*click*), is the norm. He knows a "nigger" when *he* "sees" one. He also thinks of himself as good, as a protector of the (white) body politic. There is something inherently threatening about West's black body, and especially threatening about West's description of himself as a professor of religion. When West asserts that he is a professor of religion, he discloses an identity that conflicts with the white police officer's stereotypes of black bodies. Indeed, West's self-knowledge challenges and renders false the white police officer's perception, but the former does not render the latter inconsequential. West, for all intents and purposes, is laying claim to his own gaze, his own subjectivity. Perhaps experiencing a slippage between the racist stereotype that presumes West (and other black bodies) to be always already guilty of something, and the possibility that what West says about himself is true, the police officer retreats to sarcasm: "Yeh, and I'm the Flying Nun." He subverts West's gaze by hiding behind the truth that since *he* cannot be the Flying Nun, West cannot be a professor of religion.

The subtext of the officer's caustic "wit" is designed to portray West as an *irony* (etymologically, a dissembler, one who simulates, puts on the appearance of). The racist presumption is that there is no way that a black man can be a professor of religion. History books "confirm" this. The media "confirms" this. Perhaps as this white police officer sat on his mother's lap, he was taught—even if unconsciously—to associate blackness with evil and malevolence and whiteness with goodness and beauty. Of course, white America has a long history of attempting to convince black people "that their bodies are ugly, their intellect is inherently undeveloped, their culture is less civilized, and their future warrants less concern than that of other peoples."[101] This is part of what Feagin importantly refers to as an enduring racial frame. He writes, "From the beginning of this country, this white frame has been deeply held and strongly resistant to displacement, and it includes many important 'bits'—that is, frame elements such as the stereotyped racial knowledge, racial images and emotions, and racial interpretations."[102]

In the police officer's view, West's description of himself as a professor of religion is only a fantasy, just as the 1960s sitcom *The Flying Nun* was a fantasy. For him, West is engaging in wishful thinking, perhaps a stratagem to fool the police officer who has caught him in an act of selling drugs. In fact, the police officer "sees" West as crazy, delusional. It is during times like these that one's other identities (professor of religion or philosophy, for example) are rendered null and void by white America's negative valuation of blackness. It is as if the figure of a black man who is a professor of religion becomes an obscene image, one that registers cognitive dissonance for the white police officer. To be black *and* a professor of religion—even if true—is to synthesize two mutually opposed identities that conjure up something comparable to Frankenstein's monster. Thus, a black professor of religion is *not* simply an exception but a *monstrous* exception, a freak of nature, something grotesque and fit for teratology. West's body has undergone an act of violence. Black bodies are totalized vis-à-vis a white racist epistemology that leaves no ontological surplus for the black body *to be* other than what the white imaginary "dictates." West was not approached by the white police officer as a site of alterity that belies stereotypification; rather, he remained within the space of attempted white mastery of the white police officer. West became the site of the "reduplication of the [white] self."[103] Relevant here is James Baldwin's question "But if I am not the 'nigger,' and if it's true that your invention reveals you, then who is the 'nigger'?"[104] Dare I say, *"Look, a white!"*

The white police officer constructed West as the embodiment of criminality. Yet who is the real criminal? One might argue that West functioned as the site of "an imagined Africanist persona," a fiction according to which the white police officer enacted his racist aggression and nomination through an a priori suspicion of the black body. The black body is stereo-typed as *the* definitive threat. Dialectically, the white police officer is *the* guarantor of (white) safety. Recall that West was in Princeton for only ten days and was stopped three times, a third of the time he was there. He was not speeding but driving "too slowly" on a residential street. Despite the fact that West drove within the speed limit of twenty-five miles per hour, he was still stopped; indeed, as black, always already stoppable. So, even as West obeyed the law, his black body was always already guilty, against the law. West might agree with Fanon, who says, "The movements, the attitudes, the glances of the [white] other fixed me there, in the sense in which a chemical solution is fixed by a dye."[105] Such stereotypical constructions can take their toll on the black body in the form of "psychic scars and personal wounds."[106] Imagine the trauma of being constantly stopped, of having one's identity distorted, "being for the white other" a constant threat. One begins to feel one's body as the site of trouble —it is as if one's body is *ontologically* trouble-some. For Ahmed, "being stopped is not just stressful: it makes the 'body' itself the 'site' of social stress."[107]

The desire to come lithe into the world is belied by the social reality that one's blackness will always be under surveillance, watched, stereotyped, stopped, and controlled. After running some association tests with whites, Fanon relates that when he said "Negro," he observed that the word "brought forth biology, penis, strong, athletic, potent, boxer, Joe Louis, Jesse Owens, Senegalese troops, savage, animal, devil, sin."[108] There are also contemporary studies revealing that when "whites are shown photos of black faces, even for a few milliseconds, key areas of their brains designed to respond to perceived threats light up automatically under medical-type brain scans."[109] Also, con-temporary research gathered through the Implicit Association Test (IAT), which measures racial valences by connecting photos of faces of black and white people to pleasant and unpleasant descriptors, demonstrates that "more than 80% of all those who take this test end up having pro-white [antiblack] associations."[110] However, the black body not only signifies a zone of threat, criminality, danger, and avoidance, and triggers negative attributes; it also signifies perversity—a site of specific *sexual* perversity and promiscuity.

As Joy James notes, "Part of the racialized attraction or aversion for 'the black' in a society obsessed with race, sex, and violence is the appeal of exot-ica tinged with racial savagery and perversity."[111] Because of the presumptive possible eruption of the black body's sexual drives, the black body has to be controlled/stopped, even if not guilty; lines have to be reinforced; borders have to be policed. Pointing to the logic of borders, Robyn Wiegman writes that "lynching figures its victims as the culturally abject—monstrosities of excess whose limp and hanging bodies function as the specular assurance that the racial threat has not simply been averted, but rendered incapable of return."[112]

This brings us back to the issue of the density of race, *race as lived*. It is exhausting to be constantly *against* a white world that suspects you a priori; to be the site of that which must be stopped. Yet black parents must continue to warn their sons and daughters to remain vigilant in a world that continues to demonstrate that their lives are of lesser value. I am reminded of the movie *Higher Learning* (1995) in which the leader of a neo-Nazi group says to a white student, "We're white in America. What more do you need to have a good time?"[113] Many of my white students look with surprise when I attempt to describe for them what it is like for so many blacks in North America. It will take some of them a lifetime (and perhaps not even then) to realize that their sense of America as unconditionally a place called home is directly linked to what it means to be white.[114] Many white students fail to grasp the gravitas of the situation, but those who do, and I have known a few, have shown anger, disappointment, sadness, and deep frustration. Some have even wept.

2

Looking at Whiteness

Subverting White Academic Spaces through the Pedagogical Perspective of bell hooks

To teach in a manner that respects and cares for the souls of our students is essential if we are to provide the necessary conditions where learning can most deeply and intimately begin.
—bell hooks, *Teaching to Transgress*

Critical race pedagogy is inherently risky, uncomfortable, and fundamentally unsafe. This does not *equate* with creating a hostile situation but to acknowledge that pedagogies that tackle racial power will be most uncomfortable for those who benefit from that power. —Zeus Leonardo and Ronald K. Porter, "Pedagogy of Fear"

Through text and dialogue, critical educators need to create an environment of dissonance that brings white students to a point of identity crisis. —Ricky Lee Allen, "Whiteness and Critical Pedagogy"

When I began teaching philosophy at a predominantly white university, I wished that I had been exposed to a critical body of work that explored the unique experiences of what it is like to be a black male philosopher teaching courses in a sea of whiteness, particularly for one teaching courses that explore questions of race, whiteness, and racism. Such narratives would have helped me to negotiate the sheer anger and defensiveness that white students undergo when faced with the question of their own whiteness and how it implicates them in white power structures. These narratives would have also helped me to process my own reactions to white students' denials, suggesting ways of responding and strategies to deploy. Indeed, critical narratives by black men and black women philosophers that delineate classroom dynamics, and professional institutional dynamics more generally, are crucial, particularly where these dynamics are mediated by and structured by whiteness. Such experiences can function to dispel the illusion that within so-called intellectually pristine classroom spaces a black philosopher is perceived by white students in the same way they perceive a white philosopher.

More critical narratives are needed by black philosophers to generate pedagogically honest and challenging discussions about how racial and racist epistemic and axiological assumptions in classroom spaces negatively impact black bodies. I am told, though, that such *publicly* revealed narratives can prove devastating to one's philosophy career. How can this be so in our so-called postracial moment? Indeed, it was shared with me that some black philosophers feel intimidated by white backlash regarding revelations about the negative and problematic ways in which whiteness functions in both the classroom and the profession. If true, and I have no reason to doubt that it is, this fear needs to be urgently addressed, especially given the assumption that philosophy is a field concerned with issues of "truth" and "justice." The importance of these narratives is that they will help to reveal the hypocrisy that exists within the professional field of philosophy and the fact that the field continues to be not only monochromatically white but also shaped by white racist hegemony and white policing of bodies of color.

Classrooms are microcosms of the larger social order and reflective of powerful problematic racist stereotypes and assumptions. In philosophy classrooms, and in the academy more generally, black bodies enter those spaces against the backdrop of various racist constructs. After all, black males have been stereotyped as violent thugs and hypersexual fiends. D. W. Griffith's *Birth of a Nation* (1915) helped to install the black male body as a predacious animal, lusting after white female bodies.[1] Indeed, according to this filmic racist narrative, the Ku Klux Klan became the white heroes needed to restore white law and order. *Birth of a Nation* functioned as a Manichean trope for white saintliness/goodness against the dark and evil black male body. Black female bodies have been stereotyped as welfare queens and irresponsible, negligent mothers who suffer from hyper-fertility.[2]

As Dorothy Roberts writes, "American culture is replete with derogatory icons of Black women—Jezebel, Mammy, Tragic Mulatto, Aunt Jemima, Sapphire, Matriarch, and Welfare Queen."[3] These icons are not just nominal; it was believed that black women's moral degeneracy was passed down through them. Again, Roberts writes, "For three centuries, Black mothers have been thought to pass down to their offspring the traits that marked them as inferior to any white person."[4] Despite their intellectual accomplishments, black women are seen as "prostitutes," deemed vulgar and immoral and reduced to their "sexually insatiable" black bodies. Anita Allen relates, "Two very prominent philosophers offered to look at my resume (I was flattered) and then asked to sleep with me (I was disturbed)."[5] Furthermore, Adrian Piper notes that black women have a great deal to get over when they enter a philosophy department because they are perceived as maids and prostitutes. Again, Anita Allen: "My dissertation adviser was the famous utilitarian moral philosopher Richard Brandt. I was sitting in Dick's office one day when he reached over and grabbed my chin. He tilted my face up toward his face and said, 'Anita, you look like a maid my family once had.'"[6] Asked about encouraging more black women to enter the profession of philosophy, Piper said, "I think about this a great deal and I think that the problem about getting Black women into the profession is that if you tell them what it is really like, no rational black women would want to go into it."[7] And as Lionel McPherson notes, "The philosophy profession—in composition, sensibilities, and content—is a racially hostile environment, even if that hostility typically manifests itself as benign neglect. No black person who takes himself or herself to have viable alternatives, and common sense, would go down this road."[8] In short, black philosophers, both male and female, often enter academic spaces as problem bodies,[9] bodies that are sites of a "tangle of pathology,"[10] faced with deep racial hostility and often uncertainty.

My objective in this chapter is to delineate and highlight, indeed, deploy, aspects of bell hooks's understanding of education that frame the critical pedagogical ethos that I attempt to create and enact in philosophy courses that are predominantly white. The chapter functions precisely as a slice of that critical body of work that I desired as I began teaching at a predominantly white institution. I am specifically interested in how hooks's critical pedagogy helps to frame my pedagogical engagement with predominantly white students in teaching courses in philosophy where the central philosophical theme is race. This chapter will prove indispensable for black philosophers who attempt to tackle philosophical issues related to race and whiteness in predominantly white universities.

In my philosophy classrooms, I have attempted to create spaces that are "unsafe"—that is, spaces that do not perpetuate, in this case, the normative status of whiteness. Thus, in my classrooms I openly mark whiteness—"Look, a white!" And despite the difficulty, I also help to nurture the sort of critical space for whites to do so as well.

If to create a "safe" space within the classroom is to elide white privilege, then such "safety" is actually an affront to both justice and the exercise of critical intelligence deployed toward the aim of emancipation. There is an important bridge between modalities of teaching that respect and care for the souls of students *and* modalities of creating the necessary conditions where engaged learning has a profound and personal impact, an impact that will often result in states of unhappiness,[11] feelings of disappointment in oneself and in society. By "unhappiness," I don't mean that my pedagogy is to encourage a depressive form of nihilism. Rather, the objective is to create a sense of creative discontent; it is to instill a sense of freedom to question assumptions that have shaped students' identities and lives in ways that have made them complacent and uncritically satisfied, giving them a false sense of "happiness," one that conceals complacency and mediocrity.

Within the context of the classroom, hooks provides a succinct delineation of her critical pedagogy:

> The classroom, with all its limitations, remains a location of possibility. In that field of possibility we have the opportunity to labor for freedom, to demand of ourselves and our comrades, an openness of mind and heart that allows us to face reality even as we collectively imagine ways to move beyond boundaries, to transgress. This is education as the practice of freedom.[12]

For hooks, then, the classroom is a location of possibility, a site that has the potential for change and transformation. As a site of possibility, as hooks understands it, the classroom is a space of fluidity, transgression, movement, challenge, growth, and metastability.

Hooks suggests that it is within the field of possibility that we have the occasion to *labor* for freedom qua collective transformational possibilities. Hence, the classroom can function as an important matrix of possibility for the occasion to labor and work for freedom. "Laboring for freedom" is probably the last thing that students think of when they enroll in a course. After all, their sense of themselves as "free" and "autonomous" is something that the ideology of liberalism has already taught them. My sense is that by "laboring for freedom" hooks presupposes that there are expressions and layers of freedom that must be fought for to be achieved, that the self is a continuous project that must be made aware of the multiple ways in which it is in a state of un-freedom.

Laboring for freedom in the classroom suggests effort, work, endurance, diligence, and an awareness of incompleteness, that more work needs to be done on the self. Indeed, stressing the significance of laboring for freedom in the classroom implies the reinforcement of new and radical ways of interrogating and conceptualizing what *ought* to take place there. And while learning new facts is certainly necessary in a classroom, it is not sufficient in terms of demanding of ourselves and our comrades an openness of mind and heart. Demanding of ourselves *and* our comrades speaks to the emphasis that hooks places on the importance of relationships. It is important that openness of mind and heart be a mutual experience, one shared by members of the classroom. Openness of mind and heart creates the possibility of being touched by the other, transformed by the other, even as one maintains a healthy sense of criticality and distance. It is within a community of others that the self is challenged and transformed, that we are taken "out of ourselves,"[13] that the sense of self-certainty might be challenged and shattered. Within such a community, students are encouraged to appreciate the ways in which they are connected to others, the ways in which knowledge is a cooperative project.

For hooks, it is not enough that we open our minds; it is also important that we open our hearts. There are no doubt many who would argue that this sounds too "soft," too romantic, too Pascalian. In this view, the heart has no place where rigorous thought and dispassionate argumentation are required or even demanded. However, hooks is calling into question the assumption that learning is primarily an intellective process, one that is emotionless and free of feelings and thereby free of ambiguity. As a philosopher, I have noticed that many colleagues bring various unquestioned pedagogical assumptions to the learning process and to the classroom. For example, they tend to privilege the mind over the body. The body is viewed as an impediment to knowledge. The body is identified with passion, suffering, the erotic, and is deemed unwieldy. Thus, as philosophers we are often expected to enter our classrooms as disembodied, as abstract minds, as spectral beings. But for hooks, "Entering the classroom determined to erase the body and give ourselves over more fully to the mind, we show by our beings how deeply we have accepted the assumption that passion has no place in the classroom."[14] She links the assumption of a split between the mind and the body to "the philosophical context of Western metaphysical dualism."[15] To strive for wholeness—a mode of being and pedagogical engagement that does not fragment the self—in the classroom is thus to challenge deep and perennial philosophical narratives that tend to bifurcate the self and perpetuate the assumption that learning and knowledge are divorced from the "messiness" of the body.

The silent hegemonic norms of the profession of philosophy do not appear to be concerned with our integrity and honesty of heart, the upsurge of passion and suffering that we often feel as we grapple with ideas, the integrity of our spirits, our sense of wholeness, our sense of embodiment and finitude, and the feeling that we are ensconced in the mundane matters of quotidian life. Such norms support pedagogical assumptions that make us alien to ourselves. Their buttressing breeds self-alienation and dishonesty, and encourages the creation of a chasm between theory and practice. In fact, the intellect becomes privileged over ethical practices vis-à-vis questions of personal integrity and a deep commitment to processes of self-confrontation and self-transformation. While the academic scholar might have no sense of genuine compassion and care for others, he or she might possess a publication record that is extraordinary, one that reflects well on the department and on the university.

Hooks argues that the intellectual quest for wholeness has "been replaced with notions that being smart meant that one was inherently emotionally unstable and that the best in oneself emerged in one's academic work."[16] While the so-called genius may be emotionally unstable, he or she can still think with extraordinary intellective power and lucidity. It is not the "bizarre" behavior and emotional instability of the genius that matters; it is his or her pristine mind. After all, or so the view goes, geniuses are supposed to be peculiar. In fleshing out the implications of this pedagogical outlook, hooks writes, "This meant that whether academics were drug addicts, alcoholics, batterers, or sexual abusers, the only important aspect of our identity was whether or not our minds functioned, whether we were able to do our jobs in the classroom."[17]

For hooks, engaged pedagogy is very demanding; it "means that teachers [professors] must be actively committed to a process of self-actualization that promotes their own well-being if they are to teach in a manner that empowers students."[18] By self-actualization, hooks has in mind the idea of someone who is engaged not only in auto-critique, self-exploration, and interior healing but also in outward movement toward the other, someone who is willing and eager to transform the other and be transformed by the other in rich and positive ways. In other words, self-actualization, while *centripetal*, is not hermetically antisocial. Self-actualization, while *centrifugal*, does not lose sight of the importance of silence and the need for being alone, for self-examination. This "inward-outward" dynamic is not contradictory, then, but fundamentally dialectical. Hooks maintains that self-actualization is "the coming into greater awareness not only of *who we are* but our relationship *within community* which is so profoundly political."[19]

Hooks writes, "In the United States it is rare that anyone talks about teachers in university settings as healers. And it is even more rare to hear anyone suggest that teachers have any responsibility to be self-actualized individuals."[20] It was the Vietnamese Buddhist monk Thich Nhat Hanh, both teacher and activist, who influenced hooks's notion of the teacher as healer. Hooks's discourse of healing, however, is not grounded in mysterious incantations. By healing, in stream with Thich Nhat Hanh, she suggests working toward a form of wholeness, a concept that also connotes restoration, integrity, and processes of overcoming/transcendence. The teacher/ professor as healer is therefore one who strives to encourage wholeness. As healers, teachers/professors encourage educational experiences (etymologically, a "leading out") that lead students to seek greater levels of self-exploration and integrity, which means encouraging them to bring their entire selves—raced, gendered, classed, and so on—to bear on the learning process. Hooks is critical of the view that race, gender, sexual orientation, class, and the like are deemed nugatory to the learning process. In this view, such aspects of the self are usually deemed nonconstitutive and so can be and ought to be abandoned at the classroom door. "The self was," hooks argues, "presumably emptied out the moment the threshold was crossed, leaving in place only an objective mind."[21]

There are philosophers who seem to believe that "real" philosophy dispenses with the body. In fact, they hold the position that philosophy is a "pure" mode of inquiry, a practice that ought to be taught with a deep sense of seriousness and a commitment to abstraction and conducted in terms of a form of intellectual stoicism. Prostrating themselves before the all-discerning light of *reason* is their pedagogical purpose, while they sing a requiem to the death of embodied passion. In fact, I have met philosophers who seem to believe that philosophy should not be fun. Laughter is an indication of too much play and too little "serious" thinking. As hooks points out, those of us who attempt to exemplify in our practices new and progressive forms of pedagogy must worry about how we deal with the ways in which our colleagues perceive us. She writes, "I've actually had colleagues say to me, 'Students seem to really enjoy your class. What are you doing wrong?'"[22]

When I teach, particularly courses dealing with issues around race, it is not that reason has somehow died at the door; rather, I must bring the entirety of myself to the classroom. I bring the self that is emotive; the self that is genuinely *happy* to teach courses that matter to students as they negotiate the existential trenches of life; the self that has been wounded by racism; the self that has biases yet to be explored; the self that is attuned to the subtlety of racism; the self that is capable of effectively dealing with heated controversy over longstanding race-related issues; the self that might become the unintended or intended target of racism in the classroom; the black self on whom racist stereotypes are projected; the self that must be ready for racist remarks exchanged between students and the self that must be prepared to help students think critically through such exchanges; the self that must create balance when critical dialogue borders on the precipice of turning into a blaming game; the self that is ecstatic when it sees real transformation take place in the classroom; the self that must and often does provide a safe space for tears; indeed, the self that, at times, also feels hopeless in the face of so much racism in and outside the classroom.

To provide a space for tears in a classroom is important to any pedagogy that engages students at the very core of how they understand themselves, particularly when it comes to issues of race and racism. During a conflictual discussion about my style of pedagogical engagement, a style that apparently was somewhat abrasive for some in the audience, a white woman philosopher said to me, "Bringing tears to the eyes of white people is something your work aims to do and for which you want to be able to take credit."[23] Her words implied that I somehow reveled in the fact that students, particularly white students, cry in my philosophy courses. Her claim, which felt more like an accusation/critique, implied that I derive some sort of pleasure from this, a kind of ego boost.

She could not have been more incorrect. My objective has been to provide the space for vulnerability. There is no *aim* to bring tears to the eyes of white people/students. The tears, and there have been some, may result from some white students' sense of impotence in the face of racism, guilt, feelings of shame, and perhaps the sudden anxiety felt in the face of radically new forms of self-recognition. In short, while I provide a context for tears and dare to speak fearlessly and with unflinching honesty, there is no *aim* as such to elicit tears. I would argue that what I do in the classroom has meta-philosophical significance. In order to engage race and racism critically in a philosophy classroom, it is important that one changes the medium itself—the way both philosophical discourse and philosophical performance are enacted. So my objective is to reimagine and perform what philosophy might look like—its aim and style. It is necessary to rethink the ways in which philosophy speaks to the mind *and* the heart.

I recall once that an African American student's voice cracked as she explained to her predominantly white classmates that she was weary of all their denials. Their denials communicated the message that her experiences of white racism were false, imaginary. The violence of white denial had already reared its ugly head. As Zeus Leonardo and Ronald K. Porter write, "If we are truly interested in racial pedagogy, then we must become comfortable with the idea that for marginalized and oppressed minorities, there is no safe space."[24] In short, then, "mainstream race dialogue in education is arguably already hostile and unsafe for many students of color whose perspectives and experiences are consistently minimalized. Violence is already there."[25]

My African American student was unambiguous: "I'm tired of all of you [white students] saying that racism doesn't exist anymore!" Her protestation functioned to mark the proverbial elephant in the room. Airing a powerful stench of mendacity, she was able to unveil and identify, in the classroom, the site of collective denial. In the *singular*, she dared to identify the *collective* culprit: "Look, a white!" By doing so, she disrupted the assumptions that framed what was seeable. She introduced a counter-gaze, a counter-epistemic position that was not afraid to nominate the real problem.

There was silence in the room, a sort of awkwardness of not knowing what to do next. I actually see this awkwardness as indicative of pedagogical success, not failure. My African American student's white peers looked away, some down to the floor, others staring off, seemingly oblivious. She then cried, her tears visible. Her tears spoke to personal experiences of racism in the face of so much explicit and implicit denial. Pedagogically, I allowed the silence to function as a teachable moment. I allowed it to linger in the room so that all of us present might feel the weight of the moment, to become cognizant of her passion, her honesty, and her suffering, to feel the immediacy and urgency of how racism was real for this black female student. I did not intervene, not wanting to detract from the intensity and density of the moment.

There was a time when I would have been pedagogically immobilized had a student begun to cry in my class, especially as I teach philosophy, but I had already created the pedagogical conditions for this sort of emotional response on her part, conditions that allow students to bring their complex emotional selves to class. After this single experience, many of the white students began to listen in ways they previously had not. They listened to others with greater animation. Many of my white students who had seen themselves and the world as color-blind and postrace were faced with this anomaly. The weight of the experience challenged their thinking about ways in which they had failed to take racism seriously.

Even if only for a moment the cracking voice and tears touched the normative core of a group of white students and challenged their assumptions regarding their own sense of themselves as "good whites" and our society as "postracial." My African American student's tears and the initial response from my white students confirmed for me that spaces within the classroom must pedagogically nurture students and encourage them to bring their entire multitudinous selves—their angry selves, their fragile selves, their painful selves, their racially prejudiced selves—as they struggle with issues of race and racism in the classroom. If the entirety of the self is left at the proverbial door, processes of self-interrogation and healing will find it that much more difficult to occur within the context of a classroom.

When I shared this story with a black colleague, he thought that my student's tears were "a rather pathetic display of the Black need for white acceptance and approval, a legacy of slavery that runs deep in the Black psyche."[26] He was simply wrong, totally missing the dynamics that can result from classroom discussions that dare to be honest and unsafe. The tears had to do with black frustration regarding white denial. This is different from a display of (genuflecting) dependence regarding the need to be recognized by white people. It was not as if this black student lacked self-esteem. She showed righteous indignation and anger in the face of denial from her white classmates, students with whom she had to share an entire semester, perhaps even four years. She courageously and boldly engaged in an act of naming their indifference/denial. In this case, her tears were not to be taken as a sign of weakness but as deep frustration aimed at the ethical failure of white students to come to terms with their privilege/racism. Her frustration was a sign of agency, not kowtowing to white power and approval. She could have simply walked out of the classroom, refusing to engage with white students who continued to deny either explicitly or implicitly the veracity of her experiences with white racism. Had she done so, I would have understood.

Christine E. Sleeter talks about one of her cultural diversity courses, in which almost all the enrolled students turned out to be white that semester, despite the racial diversity of the student body at her university. Students of color had decided not to take the course. She writes, "The few students of color who initially enrolled dropped the course, explaining to me that it would be too frustrating to spend all semester being one of the only voices of color in a sea of 'white talk,'"[27] which "serves to insulate white people from examining their/our individual and collective role(s) in the perpetuation of racism."[28]

Pedagogically engaging issues of race and racism calls for deeper levels of analysis; it involves exploring aspects of the self that often operate beneath the radar of conscious reflection. The transformation of consciousness is not limited to pedagogies that stress the mere manipulation and mastery of concepts. Rather, it is linked to a form of critical pedagogy that provides "students with ways of knowing that enable them to know themselves better [that is, more complexly and more deeply] and live in the world more fully."[29] Emphasis is also placed on what one *does in the world*. Hooks does not reject the love of ideas, but she links this love to "the quest for knowledge that enables us to unite theory and practice."[30] In this way, "the classroom becomes a dynamic place where transformations in social relations are concretely actualized and the false dichotomy between the world outside and the inside world of the academy disappears."[31] Hence, self-actualization in relation to issues of race and racism is not simply about one's ability to comprehend concepts in the confines of a classroom. According to hooks, the world outside and inside the walls of the academy constitute a continuum. While it is important for her that practices of freedom take place in the classroom, spaces that often teach conformity, such practices must extend beyond. Healers, in this case both teachers/professors and students, are not navel gazers, but are committed to social praxis. In short, we must act and reflect "upon the world in order to change it."[32]

One of my white undergraduate female students wrote a very insightful paper she entitled, "Racism: Etched into Our Souls." After discussing ways in which racist effective history deeply shapes who we are, she explored the question of how we might "de-etch" (her term) the racism that is so etched into our souls and into our society. The word "etch" is etymologically linked to a word meaning "to eat." This is a powerful metaphor. In short, my student was interested in ways that whites internalize racism and how they might find ways of refusing "to eat," to ingest, its madness and disease. Of course, there is another sense in which we "etch" our own perceptions onto the Other and thereby frame them and socio-ontologically freeze them according to our desires and fears, imprison them, confiscate their integrity, and "eat them," making them into a version of ourselves, reducing their otherness to the *same*.

While my student did not pick up on the rich metaphorical implications of the process of etching, she did emphasize the importance of both reflection and practice. Her paper was *not* about what we *think* but about what we have *become* in our souls as a result of our consumption, so to speak, of racism and how this negatively affects our entire society. She wrote that "unless we are constantly participating [a clear signifier of practice and action] in the battle against racism it can never be overcome." She thus stressed not only the importance of fighting against racism at the level of direct participation/action but also the importance of caring for the soul. This student, perhaps one of a few, picked up on the significance of how racism actually militates against spiritual well-being and how it destroys the soul.

My class had read the works of critical whiteness theorists whose primary objective was to heal their "soul wounds" caused by the internalization of racist outlooks. Perhaps exposure to these experiences will enable this student (and others) to maintain fidelity to the idea of the intellectual as one who seeks wholeness/care of the soul, particularly wholeness vis-à-vis combating the internalization of racist outlooks through diligent efforts of deracination and self-interrogation, despite how such efforts are fraught with so many difficulties and shortcomings. Sharing information about her disappointment during her actual experience of college in terms of the teaching profession, hooks notes, "It was difficult to maintain fidelity to the idea of the intellectual as someone who sought to be whole—well-grounded in a context where there was little emphasis on spiritual well-being, on care of the soul."[33]

Those students who do strive for more than "academic excellence," defined as the accumulation of facts and the ability to reiterate those facts on command, function as threats to teachers/professors who see it as their job to produce good functionaries, who would prefer to keep academic spaces free of too much controversy, too much pain, too much interrogation, too much dialogue, too much funk, too much risk, creativity, and imagination—elements that are crucial and indispensable for self-flourishing and wholeness. Critically engaging in questions of race and racism in the classroom is risky. In fact, one of my white male students shared with me that, as he was buying a book for one of my courses, another white student said, "I see you're taking Dr. Yancy's course. You know he hates white people." My student disclosed that he was perplexed, somewhat amazed, and simply dismissed the comment, as he had already taken a course with me and so had the opportunity to experience my pedagogical approach firsthand. My assumption is that this sort of risk—the risk of being labeled a hater of white people—is not faced by white professors who critically engage race and racism. Hence, being black or a professor of color who critically explores whiteness/racism has its attendant risks.

Hooks notes, "Not surprisingly, professors who are not concerned with inner well-being are the most threatened by the demand on the part of students for liberatory education, for pedagogical processes that will aid them in their own struggle for self-actualization."[34] From her own *personal experiences*, which she deploys as a source of positional knowledge that speaks to the interiority of her suffering and joy, hooks notes, "Most of my professors were not the slightest bit interested in enlightenment. More than anything they seemed enthralled by the exercise of power and authority within their mini-kingdom, the classroom."[35]

For teachers/professors who see their role as epistemic autocrats, as it were, there is very little or no room for a sense of epistemic shared space with their students and within their classrooms. Those who would dare insightfully question the teacher/professor, revealing gaps, inconsistencies, conservatism in the latter's knowledge, are deemed troublemakers, marginal, confused, naïve. As in a political autocracy, authority is expressed top down, and there is often no room for forms of epistemic diversity, particularly as this might engender dissent, critical discussion, and the spirit of interdisciplinarity. Hooks believes "that our work [as teachers/professors] is not merely to share information but to share in the intellectual and spiritual growth of our students."[36] An engaged pedagogical space, then, is one where a plurality of voices are valorized, where students are participants in the space of transformative speech and action, where they are not threatened to engage the teacher/professor through the process of elenchus.

Important here is that students are not passively waiting to consume knowledge from the lips of those who deem themselves gods. Hooks's emphasis on a shared space of pedagogical engagement includes inviting students to shape the content and outcome of the learning process. She notes, "On another day, I might ask students to ponder what we want to make happen in the class, to name what we hope to know, what might be most useful."[37] In this single act, hooks effectively challenges the teacher/professor as epistemic autocrat and positions her students as cocreators in the learning experience. By encouraging students to participate in this fashion, she deploys a profound pedagogical intervention, calling forth her students as subjects and agents. Hooks engages in a form of hailing whereby students are given the opportunity to respond in ways that provide them a sense of profound inclusion and historical agency. She creates a space of "we-learners" and "we-knowers," a space where roles are creatively fluid, not calcified and rigid. Indeed, through her pedagogical openness to sharing major classroom decisions, she demonstrates a profound respect for her students as independent thinkers, thinkers with complex and nuanced embodied voices, voices that are not afraid to disagree or "back-talk."

Within the engaged pedagogical spaces that hooks envisions, "back talk"[38] loses its signification of impudence or sassiness. Indeed, she emphasizes the "complex recognition of the uniqueness of each voice and a willingness to create spaces in the classroom where all voices can be heard because all students are free to speak, knowing their presence will be recognized and valued."[39] In recognizing each and every voice, and affirming it in the classroom, hooks is critiquing privileged educational institutions where students feel *entitled* to speak, "that their voices deserve to be heard."[40] This is in contrast to students from working-class backgrounds who attend public institutions. Hooks is particularly invested in those student voices that are marginalized because "professors see them as having nothing of value to say, no valuable contribution to make to a dialectical exchange of ideas."[41] Hooks wants to encourage a dialogical space where students are able to see themselves as "speaking subject[s] worthy of voice."[42] As speaking subjects worthy of voice, it is not enough that students name their personal experiences. Rather, they must also cross-examine the experiences of others (students/

teachers/professors) and respond in critically engaged ways "to knowledge presented."[43]

Given hooks's notion of a mutually engaged pedagogy, students share in classroom power, help shape the direction of the classroom discussion, and make significant contributions to epistemological issues (what is known, what is knowable, what is valued as knowable) and socio-ontological issues (who am I, what structural mechanisms partly constitute who I am, what I desire, and how I/we see myself/ourselves). Hooks shares that on entering "the classroom at the beginning of the semester the weight is on me to establish that our purpose is to be, for however brief a time, a community of learners *together*."[44] It is this goal that positions hooks as a colearner. Yet she is cognizant of the power that she holds and does not claim outright equality but that "together we are all equal here to the extent that we are equally committed to creating a learning context."[45]

For hooks, power is not intrinsically negative. In fact, she had to transcend her fear of power—that is, forms of coercive power and abuse that she had witnessed exercised over those who lacked power. Instead, the meaning of power "depended [on] what one did with it."[46] In this sense, education as the practice of freedom and transgression is incompatible with despotic rule. It is not contradictory, according to hooks, for students to demand knowledge that is meaningful to their lives and yet refuse to accept the guidance of their teachers/professors. Hooks writes, "This is one of the joys of education as the practice of freedom, for it allows students to assume responsibility for their own choices."[47]

For hooks, a liberatory education is one that encourages excitement and transgression. I have met philosophers who appear to think that the practice of philosophy was never meant to be exciting, never meant to challenge the boundaries of Western canonical purity, and never meant to link philosophical practices explicitly to issues of power, sexism, classism, and racism. Challenge the foundations of Greek philosophy through alternative stories that link Greek thought to earlier African influences, and one's counter-narrative is said to be apocryphal. Have the fortitude to raise the issue of how Immanuel Kant's racism influences his ethics, and one's inquiry is dismissed as a form of reductionism. Raise the issue of the existence of black philosophy, and one is assured that philosophy transcends issues of race.

Even as *white* bodies dominate the profession and generate ideas that speak to their social existence, philosophy as a view from nowhere is defended and preserved with tooth and nail, although, I would argue, in bad faith. It is within such contexts that certain forms of creative thought are deemed a threat. So-called safe classrooms are those that suppress serious and probing questions that interrogate "sacred" boundaries. Safe classrooms are those that do not interrogate the lack of self-transformative practices; that do not interrogate pedagogical approaches that refuse to value the whole person in terms of her multiple standpoints and how these standpoints shape knowledge claims. Indeed, safe classrooms are those that teach us to conform through false choices. We are also taught *how* to pose questions, *how* to remain "calm" when discussing ideas, *how* to impress those in positions of academic authority, *how* to speak academese, and how to gesticulate and engage in body postures that signify power and authority and academic and cultural refinement.

Not only am I *excited* by ideas, but I also *feel* the transformative dimensions of wrestling with them. Furthermore, this excitement is deeply *embodied*; it is not captured in a "pure" moment of abstract contemplation, but induces shuddering and ecstasy. Within this context, ecstasy also signifies transgression, that sense of standing outside of one's self, moving against old embodied practices, reaping the *pleasure* and *passion* of self-flourishing, and *becoming* more than what is dictated by the status quo. Hooks notes, "Even though many viewers could applaud a movie like *The Dead Poets Society*, possibly identifying with the passion of the professor and his students, rarely is such passion institutionally affirmed."[48] She observes that "students are desperately yearning to be touched by knowledge, [but] professors still fear the challenge, allow their worries about losing control to override their desires to teach."[49] Hence, not only do teachers/professors who encourage academic lockstep surveil students, but they also engage in destructive forms of self-censorship for fear of caring "about teaching in uniquely passionate and different ways."[50]

I recall a black student of mine who was very worried about my safety and job security because I dared to ask white students to raise their hands if they thought of themselves as racists. Of course, I always make a point of asking my male students a similar question: "So, are there any males in here who see themselves as sexists?" There are those rare moments, in both cases, when hands go up. And while we later collectively discuss what is meant by racism and sexism, I am impressed with the boldness and honesty of those few students who initially raise their hands, and their risk of self-ascription amid their peers. I recall what one white female student confided in me after class: "The [white] girl next to me was like, 'Did you *hear* the question he asked?'" This student had a different take. She said she felt completely comfortable with the question that I posed.

What troubled me, though, was my black student's perception of the power of universities and how that power can affect my attempt to teach in uniquely passionate and different ways. Embedded in her concern was the recognition that there is something threatening about posing questions that are direct and that shake students out of their intellectual and personal comfort zones, especially when it comes to race. By implication, though sadly, her point was that many universities do not truly value practices of freedom or are at least equivocal about them. Also, as she spoke, there was a moment of implicit mutual recognition of a shared historical memory: I am a black male teaching a course filled predominantly with white students in a large, predominantly white university. And while I feel comfortable with the pedagogical style that I have adopted, the legacy of racism in America informed my black student's fears and shaped our mutual understanding. Yet this pedagogical style of speaking and being—which actually creates an important sense of community and a space of mutual trust within my classrooms—has a way of cutting through individual and collective denial around highly charged issues of race and racism. As Patricia Williams argues, "Creating community . . . involves this difficult work of negotiating real divisions of considering boundaries before we go crashing through, and of pondering our differences before we can ever agree on the terms of our sameness."[51] She sees "the discounted vision of the emperor's new clothes [as] already the description of corrupted community."[52]

Fear and forms of control that do not empower students and teachers/professors belie educational practices of freedom and militate against forms of communal learning that valorize honesty and parrhesia, or fearless speech. For hooks, a learning context is not one where teachers/professors use "the classroom to enact rituals of control that [are] about domination and the unjust exercise of power."[53] Engaged pedagogy creates conditions that enhance self-reflexivity and critical thinking; indeed, it explores the limits of self-reflexivity in terms of social location, and it complicates the meaning of "critical" in critical thinking. According to hooks, "Engaged pedagogy has been essential to my development as an intellectual, as a teacher/professor because the heart of this approach to learning is critical thinking."[54]

Because critical thinking can be perceived as threatening in pedagogical spaces that demand and sanction conformity, within those spaces it is discouraged and policed. Ann Berlak argues that "teachers, like the police, are servants of the state."[55] And if this is true, teaching to transgress must challenge the ways in which larger apparatuses of political control are linked to educational institutions, and, by extension, classrooms that attempt to domesticate[56] students and teachers/professors alike. The deeper political implications raised here are reflected in hooks's observation that her "commitment to engaged pedagogy is an expression of *political activism*."[57] Hooks argues that it is because "our educational institutions are so deeply invested in a *banking system*, teachers are more rewarded when we do not teach against the grain. The choice to work against the grain, to challenge the status quo, often has negative consequences."[58] For her, to teach against the grain speaks to the desire and practice of engaging *with* students to nourish counter-hegemonic practices and modes of being. This is not a simple matter of possessing a "contrary" attitude. After all, having a contrary attitude does not ipso facto mean that one *yearns* for change, that one actually engages social reality in order to overturn systems of oppression that submerge modes of critical consciousness. Hooks's notion of working against the grain is inextricably linked to Brazilian activist, theorist, and educator Paulo Freire's conception of problem posing, a pedagogical approach that "involves a constant unveiling of reality,"[59] one that "strives for the emergence of consciousness and critical intervention in reality."[60]

Despite her critique of the sexist language in Paulo Freire's liberatory discourse, hooks is, in stream with Freire, critical of the banking system of education (a term that Freire, to my knowledge, coined). Indeed, she notes that her experiences with Freire "restored [her] faith in liberatory education."[61] Freire's critical insights provided hooks with the support that she required to confront critically "the 'banking system' of education, that approach to learning that is rooted in the notion that all students need to do is consume information fed to them by a professor and be able to memorize and store it."[62]

It is important to remember that Freire's pedagogy, with its stress on political, educational, and existential liberation, was developed in a Brazilian context, where he (and other subaltern peasants) experienced oppression and hunger. In fact, Freire was imprisoned and exiled for his decision to teach the silenced to transgress and engage in practices of freedom. Undergirding his critical pedagogy is a philosophical anthropology that frames his theorizing of the importance of the existential and historical complexity of human reality and how this complexity sheds light on other sites of oppression and domination. Coming out of a rural southern experiential background, hooks gravitated toward Freire's language of transgression and liberation as she was beginning to grapple critically with "the politics of domination, the impact of racism, sexism, class exploitation, and the kind of domestic colonization that takes place in the United States."[63]

Hooks discerns, in the United States, what Freire refers to as "attitudes and practices, which mirror oppressive society as a whole."[64] It is these attitudes and practices that are characteristic of the banking system of education. I list five here:

1. The teacher teaches, and the students are taught.
2. The teacher knows everything, and the students know nothing.
3. The teacher thinks, and the students are thought about.
4. The teacher talks, and the students listen—meekly.
5. The teacher chooses and enforces his or her choice, and the students comply.

In the banking system of education there is no calling out to the other, no movement toward the other (the student) as an agent with her own ideas and insights. The teacher/professor rejects education as a mutual process of *becoming*. As Freire argues, "The teacher presents himself to his students as their necessary opposite; by considering their ignorance absolute, he justifies his existence."[65]

Given the insidious ways in which institutional and embodied racism thwart thematization and examination, the ethos of the banking system of education in the United States—where issues of racism are displaced onto "those white supremacists" and where students are made to feel they are "good whites" because they have never lynched a black body or owned any blacks as slaves—is complicit in the prolongation of *un*critical practices of liberation that sustain the hegemony of whiteness.[66] For Freire, those who are committed to the practice of freedom must reject "the mechanistic concept of consciousness as an empty vessel to be filled."[67]

White students who have been fed on the ideological pablum of the banking system come to see themselves as "good whites" without racist blemishes. Partly this is because they have been told, *have had information deposited*, that racism has ceased to exist in our contemporary moment. The "banking system of education (for obvious reasons) attempts, by mythicizing reality, to conceal certain facts which explain the way human beings exist in the world."[68] According to Freire, it "emphasizes permanence and becomes reactionary."[69] He sees this system as isolating "consciousness from the world,"[70] thus militating against, in my view, whites' engaging in the dynamic process of problem posing, as opposed to being *reactionary*.

According to Freire, "In problem-posing education, people develop their power to perceive critically *the way they exist* in the world *with which* and *in which* they find themselves."[71] In the case of whites, they often exist in profound states of bad faith regarding their white privilege, inhabiting spaces of world-making efforts that are fueled by racist hegemony and spaces where whiteness functions as the transcendental norm. Thus, I see problem posing as a form of demythologizing vis-à-vis whiteness. What whites had not seen as a problem at all—their white privilege—comes to stand out through problem posing. Freire notes, "That which had existed objectively but had not been perceived in its deeper implications . . . begins to 'stand out,' assuming the character of a problem and therefore of challenge."[72] He continues: "Thus, [white] men and women begin to single out elements from their 'background awareness' and to reflect upon them. These elements are now objects of their consideration, and as such, objects of their action and cognition."[73] Ann Berlak construes this process in reference to figure/ground perceptual organization. She argues that, "For most [white] students who come into class, a meritocratic framework is ascendant; it is the 'figure,' and white supremacy [whiteness] is the pale and mostly invisible 'ground,' or background."[74]

Through the work I do in the classroom, in stream with hooks and Berlak, I try "to accomplish a reversal."[75] This is not easy, especially as white students have come to identify whiteness with what it means to be human or what it means to be American or simply a person. In short, their whiteness has become invisible. And just when the possibility of a slippage is on the horizon, just when there is the possibility that their whiteness begins to "stand out" as a problem to be dealt with, society reinforces whiteness as normative, pushing it further into the background. In my classes that deal with race and racism, then, a site where I actively *name* whiteness, there is often tension.

The majority of my white students are not prepared to take the journey involved in exploring what it means to be white, in rethinking issues around whiteness, power, and meritocracy, and the subtle ways in which white racism is expressed through embodied practices and uninterrogated values and ways of looking at the world. And just when those who are willing to begin problem-posing their whiteness, where whiteness as a set of historical and institutional practices begins to emerge as a *problem*, larger social practices and norms (outside the classroom) reinforce their situation as normative, unproblematic. That deepened sense of active and engaged consciousness that *we* were able to effect in that *collective* pedagogical space, within the limits of specific temporal constraints, resigns itself, becomes passive and receptive to interpellation that hails the white self, hails white consciousness, forcing "accommodation to the normalized 'today.'"[76] Of course, there are other times, through critically engaged *dialogue*, mutually shared *naming* ("Look, a white!"), that my white students begin to problem-pose their whiteness, thus creating a *lived* phenomenological sense of lack, a liminal moment when they recognize that whiteness, as the transcendental norm, not only distorts reality but limits how they see themselves. For example, one white undergraduate student of mine, after taking a course that I designed entitled "Film and Race," wrote the following in one of his papers:

I enrolled in this course strictly to fulfill a lingering philosophy requirement, and thought that I might as well see a few movies while
I was at it. I am pleased to say, the course far exceeded these meager
expectations. I was frequently challenged by our film-based discussions and readings throughout the semester, being forced to consider
alternative perspectives and viewpoints. I learned quickly that the
images in films always have a context, and should never be taken at
face value. I was forced to reevaluate many of my personal beliefs and
assumptions regarding race, some of which were more than surprising. It is safe to say that my journey through this course was not always a comfortable one (never have I been exposed to such parrhesia
in the classroom) but it was certainly enlightening.

Through critical dialogue around film, through collective sharing and honesty, this student came to shift both his perspective about the importance
of the course and his consciousness about whiteness. He came to *name* his
engagement with the course differently. He came to recognize aspects of his
whiteness through the medium of critically engaging issues of whiteness/race
through film. He also learned to problem-pose and to appreciate "a lingering
philosophy requirement" that shifted his assumptions about the pleasures
and self-transformative rewards of doing philosophy through deep and honest dialogue.

The banking system would not have provided the conditions necessary
for the level of insight, transformation, naming, and disclosure demonstrated by my student's paper. The course actually encouraged the student
to rethink his assumptions, to be surprised (and perhaps even shocked) by
them, to inhabit a space and place that was *not comfortable*. But this is what
it means to engage in practices of freedom. "Whereas banking education
anesthetizes and inhibits creative power, problem-posing education involves
a constant unveiling of reality."[77] I recall another white student saying to
me once after class that he would never look at the movie *King Kong* (and
certainly not the racial semiotics of "beauty" and the "beast") in the same
way. I have had white students say to me, "I can't stop seeing racism since
your class." Freire says, "Once named, the world in its turn reappears to the
namers as a problem and requires of them a new *naming*."[78]

In another course that I developed entitled "Race Matters: Philosophical and Literary Perspectives," one white male student, after responding to
my invitation to engage in fearless speech and an open naming/nomination
of his racism, shared with the class that he had been harassed by a group of
African American males about his sexual orientation. He explained to the

class that as they taunted him, he said to himself, "I might be gay, but at least I'm not black." One could see the reluctance on his face, the shame. Yet he spoke. He was cognizant of the risk of vulnerability and verbal reprisal. There were at least three black students in the class. The disclosure was clear. "While I might be gay and looked down upon by many in society, at least I'm superior to you, at least I'm better. Compared to me, you're nothing." As with my African American female student, I did not want to interrupt the silence. At that moment, it was enough that he *named* his racism without condemnation from others. He decided to take a risk and to do so fearlessly. Creating a space for taking risks of this sort is designed to "promote [not] hostility but growth."[79] And we listened with courage—a process that I like to think of as *fearless listening*.

On another occasion, a white female student shared that while she and her boyfriend were walking down the street, her boyfriend saw a black female from behind and turned to her and asked, "Now, why don't you have an ass like that?" Without skipping a beat, she responded, "At least I have real hair." Instead of critiquing him for his sexism, she resorted to a racist retort, characterizing and stereotyping the black female as aesthetically fake by presuming that she was wearing hair extensions—that is, "phony hair." One could visibly see the disappointment and discomfort on her face. In these cases, whiteness did not remain the insipid and invisible "ground"; whiteness *became* the figure—a reversal had taken place. By risking, this student was able to take responsibility for her whiteness. As Leonardo and Porter write, "After many years of experience in the university setting, we have learned that this apostasy—of creating risk as the antidote to safety—leads to more transformative learning opportunities."[80]

In the "Film and Race" course, I made sure that my students posed their own whiteness in relation to the movies that we watched. They found the racism that they witnessed on-screen deeply problematic, and many of them communicated feelings of embarrassment, implying a feeling of being uncomfortable in their skin. They were able to see the link between whiteness performed on the screen in the form of innocence, purity, paternalism, hatred, and power vis-à-vis blacks (and other people of color) and then further link the filmic space of white semiotics with their own whiteness, closing the gap between "those whites" and "us." This sort of consciousness is possible when "safety" in the classroom is defined by values that emphasize a nonpenalizing openness. In fact, according to hooks, "It is the absence of a feeling of safety that often promotes prolonged silence or lack of student engagement."[81] Concretely, this openness means that various subtle and at times not so subtle levels of white racism can be expressed. For example,

I recall one white male student, when asked if he believed race to be real, exclaimed, "Yes. Why do you think blacks dominate the NBA?" Another white male student, frustrated with the ways in which racist systemic institutional structures continue to position him as racist, even as he struggles to fight against his own racism, said, "If society will continue to position me as a racist because I'm white, why don't I/we just become racists?"

A white female student once wrote in a paper that white men are discriminated against because black men have larger penises. Apparently, she actually believed that white men were a disadvantaged group because their penises (or so she believed) were smaller. These moments can become difficult, triggering frustration, bewilderment, and anger. But as Freire says, "How can I dialogue if I am closed to—and even offended by—the contribution of others."[82]

In my "Film and Race" course, by defending and practicing an open and engaged pedagogy, I was (we were) able to create a subversive academic space. On this score, silence, in this case, is nonsubversive; it helps to maintain the status quo. If to be silent is a form of pedagogical safety, then there can be no growth. The classroom is a place where mutual recognition and respect must be demanded. "Anger, hostility, frustration, and pain," according to Leonardo and Porter, "are characteristics that are not to be avoided under the banner of safety."[83] I frequently shared with my students just how impressed I was with their critical engagement with the filmic texts and how particularly fortunate I felt to have so many students who demonstrated so much passion, candidness, and openness to take risks. As hooks notes, "Conditions of radical openness exist in any learning situation where students and teachers celebrate their abilities to think critically, to engage in pedagogical praxis."[84] My aim was not to engage my students in theory to make them "more brainy." Rather, I engaged them in what hooks calls "the production of theory as a social practice that can be liberatory."[85] Hooks shares that she "came to theory because [she] was hurting . . . [and that she wanted] to grasp what was happening around and within [her]."[86]

I encourage my students to think about their engagement with theory (or the need to engage theory) as an exercise in living, as part of an *existential* project; that theory might assist and be assisted by the complex struggles, fears, and pains that we all experience. I do not make an idol of theory or philosophy in my classes. However, I do make sure to emphasize how the funkiness of existential pain, suffering, and other *lived* experiences can and do impact theory and humanize it. I attempt to explain to my students that academic spaces are often artificial, spaces where they become intoxicated by the "brilliance" and clever minds of their professors. Some of them are temporarily transported to an ethereal place where abstract minds engage in "immaterial" discourse. Perhaps this is why I like to remind my students of the reality of dread, of death, of the tragic existence of those who often live just within blocks of such bastions of so-called higher learning. *Turn around. Look at your classmate. No, really look. One hundred years from now, none of us will be here. Where we will be, I can't say. That is a question of faith. But let's make a difference now in the short time that we have.*

In courses where I explore whiteness, my white students have begun to engage ideas, experiment with ideas, and theorize social behaviors (their own and others') around the theme of whiteness beyond the classroom. Then again, my aim is precisely to encourage them to nurture practices of freedom that extend beyond the confines of our collective academic space. I emphasize a noncompartmental approach to thinking and doing, creating an organic link between reflection, everyday life practices, and habituated modes of being. My approach to teaching the value of philosophy stresses that an engaged form of *collective* elenchus can create conditions that help to make us better human beings. My hope is that such conditions will inspire the white students I teach to think of themselves as historical beings, not simply "in" and "of" history but *makers* of, and *agents* in, history. This raises profound issues regarding the importance of responsibility in relation to white privilege.

While it is often difficult, my objective is to encourage my white students to comprehend the ways in which their consciousness has been shaped by various historical practices and norms. In fact, even more difficult is getting them to begin to think about their consciousness and practices as *contingent*. I encourage them to see themselves as neither complete before they enter the historical scene nor complete after they enter it. It is important that they begin to see themselves "for whom immobility represents a fatal threat,"[87] particularly as whiteness is invested in maintaining not only institutional power but somatic power as culturally inscribed in white bodies. This understanding of human reality is consistent with a problem-posing pedagogy. As Freire notes, "problem-posing education affirms men and women as beings in the process of *becoming*—as unfinished, uncompleted beings in and with likewise unfinished reality."[88] My aim is to encourage them to see themselves beyond the security of "some such thing in general,"[89] so there is the desire that they become critically subjective about their being-in-the-world, but that they never lose sight of how their subjectivity is historically situated. And because whiteness is insidious, it is important that they understand the indefatigable diligence involved in continuously engaging one's whiteness.

There is no single action that will rid one of racism. It requires constant readjustment of the self vis-à-vis complex forces. As Søren Kierkegaard says of the uncertainty of death, "To think this uncertainly once and for all, or once a year at matins on New Year's morning, is nonsense, of course, and is not to think at all."[90] To think about race only when passing black bodies or other bodies of color on the street is not to make *whiteness as raced* an object of critical consciousness; indeed, it is not to think critically about whiteness at all.

As a white person, Peggy McIntosh came to realize that she "had been taught about racism as something which puts others at a disadvantage, but had been taught not to see one of its corollary aspects, white privilege, which [put her] at an advantage."[91] She defines white privilege as "an invisible package of unearned assets which [she] can count on cashing in each day, but about which [she] was 'meant' to remain oblivious."[92] Again, this raises the issue of the importance of responsibility as it relates to white privilege. After discussing McIntosh's understanding of privilege and racism in structural terms, as something that whites inherit without asking for it, one white male student of mine said, without any hesitation, that he agreed with her. I was somewhat skeptical of the alacrity of his response. I reminded him that part of McIntosh's definition of privilege involves forms of white *domination* of people of color. The truth then appeared. "Well," he said, "I'm not sure about that!" He accepted the de facto truth about white privilege but as something that was wrong with "the system"—that structure *out there*—without thinking more deeply about the ways in which this privilege has implications for the oppression and anguish of others. The language of domination had implicated him in the lives of others in ways that his understanding of white privilege did not. He did not want to tarry with the idea of himself as someone who participates directly or indirectly in the domination of others. Yet white privilege is not privilege at all unless it has negative and problematic implications for the lives of those who are not white. "For describing white privilege," as McIntosh argues, "makes one newly accountable."[93] My student embraced his white privilege without any sense of its negative implications for people of color and without any sense of accountability.

Before I introduce the work of McIntosh to my white students, they are convinced that who and what they have become have absolutely nothing to do with their whiteness. The few African American students in these classes are able to articulate fairly convincingly how "blackness" functions as an obstacle to them in a world where whiteness is hegemonic and a site of privilege. The white students have learned to cut whiteness off from its historical formation, its colonial history, its history of terror, and its current hegemonic practices. Whiteness, in their eyes, is therefore incidental to their identity.

This way of thinking about their identity "downplay[s] the necessity of keeping alive [or even developing] a subversive memory of critique and resistance by precisely evading the role of history in the production and meaning of whiteness."[94] Frances E. Kendall shares a time that she was a guest speaker in a predominantly white class. She had gone there to discuss whiteness and its impact on her life as a white woman. She writes:

> Most of the students were either listening or pretending to, but one young woman appeared agitated. Suddenly she burst out, "I don't want you to see me as white!" I was puzzled; she had very white skin and red hair. I wasn't sure I could see her as anything else. "How would you like me to see you?" I asked. "I want you to see me as Jane!"[95]

Using this example, I encourage my students to think about the ways in which differently raced bodies are able to conceptualize their identities as "singular" and atomic (nontransversal): "I am Jane!"

After thinking in greater detail about whiteness as privilege, and the ways in which white privilege is conferred beyond one's intentions, my white students come to recognize Jane's demand as a form of bad faith regarding her whiteness. For that reason, I encourage them to engage in the process of renaming Jane as *white* Jane and by doing so repositioning her in the context of effective white racist history, a lens through which Jane is rendered visible: "Ah, yes, *look, a white!* The *white* Jane who passes herself off as a racially neutral identity/self; the *white* Jane who has both the power and the privilege to bracket her identity as white and to presumptively suspend the affordances of her whiteness." Of course, this marking also has the impact of effectively shifting white students toward a more critical lens in terms of how they begin to think about the ways in which they have attempted to evade their own whiteness.

I recall one student of mine who complained, "I think that we've talked enough about whiteness." He implied that once "the basic premise of whiteness," so to speak, is learned, things become a bit redundant. I addressed this by pointing out that most of the white students in the course had come from predominantly white backgrounds. In fact, many of the white students in my courses had gone to schools where there was only one person of color or had come from neighborhoods where no people of color resided. "For the last twenty-one years of your lives," I explained, "you have not had to think about your whiteness, to name it, to make it an object of critical consciousness. We meet for a little over one hour, two times a week, for about four months.

I can assure you that we have only scratched the surface of whiteness." It is as if this student had reduced whiteness to a few basic concepts that once memorized were enough. For those other whites in the classroom who may have found it difficult to explore their whiteness or who thought it strange and awkward to talk about whiteness in the first place, this student's comment may have provided an easy way to rationalize moving on to another subject—a form of rationalization that can be linked to a deeper apprehension of confronting their responsibility in sustaining white racist practices. The reality is that the process of understanding their whiteness—to say nothing about the extraordinary attempt to "undo" it—will take these students a lifetime.

I have often wondered to what extent my being a black male mediates the responses of my white students. If I was a white professor engaging students in the process of discussing whiteness critically, would my one white student have said the same thing, and if he had, would it have been motivated from the same place? Does my black body create levels of defensiveness in my white students that a white body would not? For example, I can imagine a male student saying to a woman teaching a course on gender, "Haven't we discussed patriarchy long enough?" When my white student commented that we had discussed whiteness long enough, my sense was that this functioned as a site of evasion. In the current scenario, maleness as gendered and as a site of power is also evaded. I recall asking my students what was so historically unique about the Obama-Clinton race. Without pause, many of them said race and gender. After a critically engaged discussion, they came to see that they had *marked* blackness and femaleness in ways that they had not marked whiteness and maleness in previous elections. Indeed, they came to see that presidential elections had always been about race and gender (that is, unmarked *white men*).

Again, however, does my black body make a difference? I think so. Yet that I am black[96] and that there are a few other nonwhite bodies in my classrooms provides an important counter-voice to an otherwise majority white class attempting to think critically about whiteness. Most of the white students in my courses not only have not thought critically about whiteness, but they also have not engaged in critical discussions about race more generally, and certainly not with blacks and other nonwhites or with a teacher/professor who is black. Hooks pulls from her personal pedagogical experience to demonstrate how the black gaze might mediate white students' responses:

In these classrooms there have been heated debates among students when white students respond with disbelief, shock, and rage, as they listen to black students talk about whiteness, when they are compelled to hear observations, stereotypes, etc., that are offered as 'data' gleaned from close scrutiny and study. Usually, white students respond with naïve amazement that black people critically assess white people from a standpoint where 'whiteness' is the privileged signifier.[97]

At one level, I think that white students react this way because of their belief in meritocracy and the assumption that they are just like black people when it comes to chances for success, when dealing with police officers, when out shopping, and so forth. Indeed, many, from my own experience, seem to think that racism exists because *we* (black people) will not let go of the past. If blacks would only let go, they would see that racism no longer exists except perhaps as an aberration. Hooks suggests that white students' "rage erupts because they believe that all ways of looking that highlight difference subvert the liberal belief in a universal subjectivity (we are all just people) that they think will make racism disappear."[98]

Perhaps more is at stake, however. At the beginning of the semester, I enter introductory philosophy classes filled with white faces. Many students may wonder just who this person is who is about to teach *us* about one of the most elite and white of subjects—philosophy. After all, most of them have been taught only by white teachers/professors up to this point. And while most of them can name just a handful of white male Western philosophers, the idea of a black philosopher is just too hard to wrap their minds around. Within the framework of their limited experiences, they have not witnessed blacks engage the likes of Plato or Descartes. Indeed, they may not have had any contact with blacks in positions of responsibility and authority. I recall one black female student who, fearing that she would bring undue attention to me, struggled to articulate before the entire class just how happy and proud she was that she was sitting in a class with and learning from a *black* professor who teaches philosophy. Imagine a white student saying this to a *white* male professor of philosophy.

Nevertheless, as I enter these spaces I wonder if my white colleagues feel students' looks of surprise, maybe even doubt. "Perhaps he got the rooms mixed up." There is a deeper racist narrative that undergirds these looks, even if my students are unaware of its origins.. There is the unstated assumption that black people are intellectually incompetent, perhaps charlatans. And when it comes to talking about whiteness (*their* whiteness), "many of them are shocked that black people think critically about whiteness because racist thinking perpetuates the fantasy that the Other who is subjugated, who is subhuman, lacks the ability to comprehend, to understand, to see the working of the powerful."[99] As hooks notes, though, for years black people, "acting as informants, brought knowledge back to segregated communities—details, facts, observations, and psychoanalytic readings of the white Other."[100]

Imagine the difficulty of cutting through not only their assumptions about black bodies, and *black male bodies* in particular, but also their initial reaction to the presence of a black body talking to them about whiteness as a form of power, privilege, and historical terror, particularly as my white students want to sugarcoat that history (not just its contemporary manifestations) and blame those who are its victims, those who look like me. And while I am the object of their gaze, and perhaps even of their amusement (like a monkey riding a unicycle), I bring a counter-gaze, a demanding gaze, an inviting gaze, an understanding gaze. It is a gaze that encourages them to travel, to move into a space of uncertainty, to fracture just a little bit, to rename familiar experiences, to dialogue, to transgress, to show trust, a form of "trust [that] is obviously absent in the anti-dialogics of the banking method of education."[101] If I am successful, my white students come to value a form of double consciousness, one that militates against silence and encourages efforts at embodying the fruits of "action-reflection."[102]

When my white students show no interest in exploring whiteness, its historical construction, its myth making around origins, its power, hegemony, and privilege (perhaps even refusing to do so), I convey to them that they have decided to settle for less, that they have decided to remain unfinished as human beings. In fact, if *I* refuse to develop a critical consciousness regarding sexism, patriarchy, and problematic social and historical constructions of masculinity, then I also fail to explore ways in which *I* might become more, ways in which *I* might unbecome. *I* must make sexism and patriarchy (and other normative practices that privilege me) an object of *my* cognition—to the extent this is possible. My own sexism is something that I openly share with my students. Why should only they confess? As hooks notes, "When education is the practice of freedom, students are not the only ones who are asked to share, to confess."[103] As a way of having students express levels of vulnerability, teachers/professors must also disengage the façade that we have no history and that problematic historical practices are not, indeed, in us. For hooks, "When professors bring narratives of their experiences into the classroom discussions it eliminates the possibility that we can function as all-knowing, silent interrogators."[104]

I too must develop "conscientization" (Freire's term for critical awareness). As Freire argues, "Problem-posing education is revolutionary futurity."[105] As an expression of hegemony, oppression, and exclusive transcendence, whiteness, on this score, thwarts the expression of human potential. When whites refuse to interrogate whiteness as expressed institutionally or through their own embodied practices, they remain static. When white philosophers speak as all-knowing voices that exclude and relegate to silence and insignificance non-Anglo/non-European philosophical voices, they exemplify misanthropy. Freire asks:

> How can I dialogue if I always project ignorance onto others and never perceive my own? How can I dialogue if I regard myself as a case apart from others—mere "its" in whom I cannot recognize other "I"s? How can I dialogue if I consider myself a member of the in-group of "pure" men, the owners of truth and knowledge, for whom all non-members are "these people" or "the great unwashed"?[106]

When white teachers/professors engage white students in African American literature courses, for example, without encouraging their white students to question how such literature speaks to their own whiteness, whiteness remains sustained as silent background. This silence evades important ways in which African American literature critically engages whiteness and how it shifts attention toward intra-textual and extra-textual white racist practices. White students approach African American literature as "different," "exotic," perhaps as having to do with "the great unwashed." Such a colonizing hermeneutic approach secures white identity and shifts white students away from the important work of self-examination and praxis.

White teachers/professors who are guilty of this silence around whiteness, and how African American writers telescope whiteness within the purview of their critical subjectivity, contribute to maintaining the status quo, fail to transgress, fail to engage in practices of freedom, and "fail to acknowledge men and women as historical beings."[107] According to Michael Apple, "What counts as 'official knowledge' consistently bears the imprint of tensions, struggles, and compromises in which race plays a substantial role."[108] To recognize that one's disciplinary legitimating practices, and one's style of pedagogical engagement, are fueled by racial and cultural hubris and hegemony is threatening. This leaves one vulnerable not only to the charge of lacking self-critical engagement but also possibly to the more toxic charge of ideological obfuscation with intent.

Hooks is cognizant of how easy it is to avoid important discussions around race and racism, how, in this case, *white students* resist shifting ways of engaging ideas and how they attempt to reinscribe the status quo. She provides an example involving African American women's literature. Hooks is aware that her white students hold varied political postures. "Yet," she notes, "they come into a class on African American women's literature expecting to hear no discussion of the politics of race, class, and gender."[109] The implication is that in other literature classes, classes where white male literati "played in the dark," whiteness remained the unnamed, the unmarked, the transcendental norm. Hooks continues:

> Often these students will complain, "Well I thought this was a literature class." What they're really saying to me is, "I thought this class was going to be taught like any other literature class I would take, only we would now substitute black female writers for white male writers." They accept the shift in the locus of representation but resist shifting ways they think about ideas.[110]

Shifting the locus of representation without changing the ways in which students engage ideas only reinscribes unexamined normative assumptions and reinforces intellectual rigidity. For example, to teach a course in Africana philosophy, it is not enough to substitute black for Anglo-American and European philosophers. Rather, it is important that students comprehend and appreciate the ways in which Africana philosophy, which in many ways functions as a *resistant* disciplinary matrix, interrogates the *raced* epistemological, ethical, and sociopolitical assumptions embedded in Anglo-American and European *Weltanschauungen*. In this way, ideas are engaged (not flattened). Students begin to interrogate ideas, to shift how they think about ideas, through an appreciation of how ideas are reconfigured and rethought in a framework in which *standpoint* is important in terms of how ideas are approached, valued, and theorized.

Hooks knows the importance of creating and using space creatively. During those times that I spend with my students, I attempt to create a space within which they might be, as Pema Chodron metaphorically says, *pushed over the cliff*.[111] Hooks felt deep kinship with this insightful metaphor as she "sought teachers in all areas of [her] life who would challenge [her] beyond what [she] might select for [herself], and in and through that challenge allow [her] a space of radical openness where [she] is truly free to choose—able to learn and grow without limits."[112] Loving wisdom, it seems to me, is an intimate engagement. After all, it does involve love or a profound sense of kinship. Etymologically, passion is linked to suffering. To engage one's identity and being-in-the-world through the *passionate* deployment of critical interrogation can cause suffering, great disappointment, and creative vertigo. Such states are not to be thwarted but encouraged. The objective here is not to fall into a state of epistemic nihilism or deep abiding depression. Loving wisdom in this context points to the sense of humility and appreciation for the sheer complexity of the self and the distal experiences that have helped to constitute the self that one must now confront, understand, and attempt to think about and engage differently. Suffering, in this case, results from the sense of *undergoing* the experience of coming face to face with one's finitude and incompleteness.

Through my pedagogical practices, through words and deeds, theory and practice, I invite my white students to take a collective leap, one informed by a passionate and critical drive to push the limits of *what* they know and *how* they come to know what they know. I invite them to suffer, to bear the burden of finding out that they have been wrong about the world and about themselves. I try to create a space where my white students become more "watchful" and more self-reflexively aware (despite the fact that these processes can be compromised by the insidious nature of whiteness) and where the "unconscious," that opaque "other" to the white self,[113] that stranger within, is challenged and becomes better if never totally known.

3

Looking at Whiteness

The Colonial Semiotics in Kamau Brathwaite's Reading of The Tempest

My Turn to state an equation: colonization = "thingification."
—Aimé Césaire, *Discourse on Colonialism*

At times this Manicheism goes to its logical conclusion and dehumanizes the native, or to speak plainly, it turns him into an animal. —Frantz Fanon, *The Wretched of the Earth*

When Christopher Columbus first came to the Caribbean islands, he encountered human beings whom he chose to apprehend as different (enslavable, conquerable) rather than as people (humans) who warranted the same respect and honor he would give to any European stranger who spoke a different language than he. —Steve Martinot, *The Machinery of Whiteness*

European colonialism is an unequivocal expression of white supremacy. In its global reach, in its expansionist drive, it created a "world of difference." European colonialism made a difference in terms of not only how the world became the "property" of whites but also how the world, its peoples, became *different* qua inferior "things" to be usurped and exploited. White colonial desire and hegemony opened up, as it were, a field of difference, hierarchically arranged, with the colonized at the existential bottom rung of civilization and the colonizers at the apex. Within this hierarchically arranged colonial space, the colonial gaze, structured through the white colonial imaginary, learned "to see the world wrongly, but with the assurance that this set of mistaken perceptions will be validated by white epistemic authority, whether religious or secular."[1] Indeed, according to Charles Mills, white supremacy, which is based on an inverted epistemology, results in massive forms of hallucination. "There will be white mythologies, invented Orients, invented Africas, invented Americas, with a correspondingly fabricated population, countries that never were, inhabited by people who never were—Calibans and Tontos, Man Fridays and Sambos."[2]

One might say that the colonial adventure resulted in the creation of *distances* between the "normal" (the colonizers) and the "abnormal" and "bizarre" (the colonized). As the world began to narrow under colonial domination, then, a colonial philosophical anthropology installed distinctions and vast distances at the site of the *anthropos*, specifically in terms of those who were recognized as humans/persons as opposed to subhumans/subpersons. As Abdul R. JanMohamed notes:

> If . . . African natives can be collapsed into African animals and mystified still further as some magical essence of the continent, then clearly there can be no meeting ground, no identity, between the social, historical creatures of Europe and the metaphysical alterity of the Calibans and Ariels of Africa. If the differences between the Europeans and the natives are so vast, then clearly . . . the process of civilizing the natives can continue indefinitely.[3]

In this chapter, I explore colonial whiteness through the work of the prominent Caribbean poet and literary figure Kamau Brathwaite,[4] specifically in his reading of Shakespeare's *The Tempest*. What makes Brathwaite's reading so insightful is the way in which he invokes a symbolically and hermeneutically rich political semiotic field to explore the far-ranging historical and political implications of Prospero's white colonial order of things. After all, Prospero is part of the colonial imaginary; he is both product and vehicle. He has come to see the world wrongly.

To conceptualize Brathwaite's exegetical project within political semiotic analysis alone, however, would completely overlook his use of a framework of magical realism, which has the capacity to create a gestalt shift in the reader's perspective. In this way, specifically with respect to *The Tempest*, new realities and connections begin to emerge and seemingly disparate elements begin to come together, generating new and deeper narrative juxtapositions and tropes that depict broader meanings in Prospero's imago of Caliban and Sycorax, who is Caliban's mother. Brathwaite not only disrupts certain forms of normative historical writing (staying true to the "facts") via his deployment of magical realism; he also collapses images and narratives that bring readers face to face with the reoccurring same. His narratives collapse space and time and bring what appear to be different events into a contiguousness that unveils and highlights a particular aspect of the world.

The objective of this chapter is to provide a provocative description of Brathwaite's reading of how Caliban and Sycorax are deemed "ontological deformations" vis-à-vis Prospero's white colonial imaginary/white colonial gaze. Brathwaite exposes colonial whiteness as *missilic*, a profound term denoting that whiteness knows no bounds in terms of its destructive ontology as it relates to those who have become the "objects" of its aim. The concept of a "missilic consciousness" telescopes the ways in which white colonial consciousness profoundly shapes how the world is perceived in terms of that consciousness. In this view, the world and its nonwhite inhabitants are perceived as *targets*. Prospero's missilic consciousness, his white colonial gaze, is always already shaped through a larger (white) racist epistemic regime in which the colonized body functions as an ersatz entity, an entity whose construction dialectically fixes the white body as positive, superior, and normative. As suggested, Brathwaite's hermeneutic framework uncovers deeper historical continuities of the white master self,[5] its hegemony and procrustean tendencies. Prospero functions both as a process of historical reality as European colonialism and racial empire building and as a tropological site that finds expression throughout the history of various configurations of white power, hegemony, and terror. To capture the unique rhythm and content of Brathwaite's writing style, it is useful to explore his work in a way that reflects and mimics it.

Where is the best place to begin a narrative, a telling of a history that is so incredibly large, so incredibly bloody, cruel, divisive, and pernicious? Perhaps, like Brathwaite, who integrates history, magical realism, a complex political semiotic field, and fragments of his historical identity, I should begin with my own fluid, historical identity. To trace what Brathwaite refers to as the vectors of "missilic consciousness" and the negative and devastating impact of this consciousness on non-Western cultures, it is apropos to begin with *process* and *movement*. On this score, *I am* (though not in the Cartesian garden-variety sense of "I," which borders on solipsism) a process, a process in the middle (passage) of a larger story of diasporic people whose plot was/is/shall be constantly unfolding. Black people of African descent have a rich narrative that is loop-linked to the past, present, and future simultaneously. In this sense, then, the black self that I am is both a site of possession and dispossession. I am autonomous, and yet the meaning of my being transcends me, reaches into a distal past that claims me—heteronomously.

One cannot begin from an existential and historical *here* without invoking a surplus of significations. The black body, my very black body, is a signifier (a historically fluid hypertext) of pain, joy, movement, crossings, mutilation, tears, European expansionism, Elmina Castle, creolization, syncretism, colonialism, the whip, the rope, and the so-called New World. The black body invokes the names and themes of Nat (Turner and Cole), Sojourner Truth, Harriet Tubman, and Mary Prince, "Lift Every Voice and Sing," gospel music, to enact a "good spell," Tituba, Champong Nanny or Grande Nanny, the field holler, James Brown, the ontology of the blues, the improvisational dimensions of jazz expressed existentially, reggae sounds, Bob Marley, Bessie Smith, the Lindy hop, and hip-hop. These are all loop-linked to, and subtended by, Sycoraxian endurance, as Brathwaite would maintain. Sycorax, for Brathwaite, functions as both a particular site of embodiment and as a dynamic metaphysical force that moves across both space and time. He conceptualizes her as a postcolonial heroine to multiple subaltern voices; she is a site of healing and empowerment, one who gives voice to the silenced, to the marginalized.

For Brathwaite, Sycorax and Caliban are targets of Prospero's hegemonic and divisive consciousness. And while it is true that both have become the objects of colonial lies and mythopoetic constructions, "Sycorax," according to Brathwaite "can function as a sort of hidden mother."[6] Hidden, and self-submerged, she fades "into the background in order to change things from within."[7] Like Maryse Condé's depiction of Tituba, Sycorax continues to work her magic of healing and revolution. Tituba says:

> For now that I have gone over to the invisible world I continue to heal and cure. But primarily I have dedicated myself to another task. . . . I am hardening men's hearts to fight. I am nourishing them with dreams of liberty. Of victory. I have been behind every revolt. Every insurrection. Every act of disobedience.[8]

Sycorax travels with Harriet on the Underground Railroad, moving all the way to Canada once the Fugitive Slave Law is passed in 1850; her voice is heard in Frederick Douglass's powerful oratorical skills; she stands with Malcolm X as he looks white hatred in the face; she is there fighting along with Cinque and Sam Sharpe. Of course, this way of understanding Sycorax is consistent with Caliban's understanding of her, which calls into question the "positivistic" conceptualization of Prospero's understanding of nature, and his relegation of all non-Western communities of intelligibility to super-stition and exotica. Caliban points out Prospero's image of the earth as governed by a set of values predicated on commercial aims to subdue the earth, to exploit its resources, and drain it of its life. Like Caliban, the earth is treated as an object *for* Prospero's use. The earth, like the black body, is to be dominated by a superior (read "white") consciousness. The earth, especially those "strange" and "exotic *dark* regions," signifies that which is to be force-fully taken—raped.

Thinking through the racial and gendered implications regarding those "strange" and "exotic *dark* regions," Lola Young writes, "Through the sexu-alization of the feminized African landscape, lying passively on its (her) back displaying naked splendor and availability (for penetration and conquest), the white male unconscious can indulge itself in fantasizing about his assault on, his merging with the forbidden object of fascination and desire."[9] On a Hegelian reading, Caliban, like Africa, is a site of raw material waiting to be exploited and controlled through the racist intentional structures of Euro-pean consciousness.[10] In the science fiction film *Avatar*, Pandora, a planet inhabited by the Na'vi, is in danger of being "ecologically raped" by those who show little or no respect for life, the complexity of different planetary ecosystems, or different cosmological worldviews and ways of being-in-the-world. Like Africa according to Hegel, Pandora is absent of *Geist*. In short, the Na'vi have become targets of interplanetary colonization. Primarily white business power brokers—driven by a missilic consciousness—target the planet for colonial usurpation.

In Aimé Césaire's *A Tempest*, however, Caliban, referring to his mother, counters Prospero's white epistemic myopia and arrogance when he says:

> Dead or alive, she was my mother, and I won't deny her! Anyhow, you only think she's dead because you think the earth itself is dead. . . . It's so much simpler that way! Dead, you can walk on it, pollute it, you can tread upon it with the steps of a conqueror. I respect the earth, because I know that Sycorax is alive.[11]

Caliban understands that Sycorax continues to exist; he knows that her be-ing continues to endure through a variety of interconnected manifestations. One might say that life on the planet Pandora is Sycoraxian; it is synergistic, everywhere linked. Indeed, as Caliban reminds us, Sycorax is the site of mul-tiple, intertwining phenomena:

> *Sycorax. Mother.*
> *Serpent, rain, lightening.*
> *And I see thee everywhere!*
> *In the eye of the stagnant pool which stares back at me,*
> *through the rushes,*
> *in the gesture made by twisted root and its awaiting thrust.*
> *In the night, the all-seeing blinded night,*
> *the nostril-less all smelling night!*[12]

When one works within such interpretative spaces where the "real" and the "magical" become blurred, where dependence on a mimetic language is inadequate to re-present the dreamlike space of multiple images/personages/symbols/signs/semiotic fluidity, *Chronos* time is of no use. Brathwaite is working with a conception of time that "operates at any point in 'time' and in its own space, as in a dream. So that Richard Nixon is Julius Caesar, presiding over national scandals and his wife (Caesar's wife) can discover herself in a black glittered television star."[13]

Cogito ego sum is too epistemologically and ontologically thin for the historically convoluted self that I am/because we are. More like a wave than a particle, I, like Brathwaite, am a black child of predecessors who survived the Middle Passage, that physical, spiritual (triangular) movement through which the children of Sycorax survived. Her deep roots have proven heavy laden with fruit, though Lady Day's "strange fruit" continues to haunt us. I invoke her name: SYCORAX! Through the power of *Nommo*, the spoken word, she emerges (reemerges) through a "collective consciousness" and unconsciousness of a people marginalized, oppressed, brutalized, beaten, terrorized, castrated, lynched, raped, silenced, fractured, Othered, and torn apart from their land, from their loved ones, and, indeed, torn apart at their limbs.

In Greek mythology, Procrustes, son of Poseidon, forced travelers to fit into his bed by either stretching their bodies or hacking off their legs. This procrustean theme is a harsh reminder of the vicious butchery of King Leopold II of Belgium, who ordered black bodies to be cut, hacked, and torn in order to feed his greed for rubber. Imagine having to look at the severed limbs of your children. Nsala, a Congolese father who lived in the district of Wala, knew what it was like to sit, emotionally catatonic, and look at the severed hand and foot of his five-year-old daughter, Boali, who was a victim of the Anglo-Belgian missile, that invasive power, that site of white expansiveness and explosive penetration.[14] The hands of innocent children were viciously severed, and black women's bodies raped, because of *mercantilism*, an instantiation of missilic consciousness, an economic system, a postfeudal system of governance, a white philosophical orientation, a form of relational distortion, that increases a nation's power and monetary wealth through the formation of trading monopolies without regard for the earth or human life, in this case black life. Leopold's Belgium was such a monopoly. Against European greed for rubber, black lives were deemed nugatory.

Of course, we cannot forget American and British sites of mercantilism; they too needed fuel: copper, cobalt, diamonds, gold, and tin. Brathwaite's equation is informative: "Missilic Europe + the alterRenaissance = Mercantilism."[15] The mercantile missile murdered 10 million or more Africans in the Congo alone. This was the result of a powerful missile, an ICBM (intercontinental ballistic *madness*). It was also the result of materialism, a driving force of the mercantile missile, involving not only European greed but also "the corruption of the tribe by bribe."[16] Brathwaite writes:

> Mercantilism is the ideology/philosophy/praxis dev by the W Euromissile (later ERA) as it devs from 17th cent nation state ("rise" of Money Econ etc) into its capitalist/industrial/imperialist fuel-consuming mode following the postColumbian discovery of SOUTH American gold (dorado!)(mineral fuel) & the dev of Plantation slavery (man & vegetable fuel) from the 16th C into the (fossil & nuclear fuels of the) present—the apotheosis of the missile.[17]

Mercantilism "missilically" seeks its target and at "ground zero" explodes into existential chaos and crisis. Out of this chaos and crisis, however, Sycorax emerges in the guise and presence of Patrice Lumumba. And, like Sycorax, Lumumba in the Congo became the *target* of a deadly object, a fuel-seeking projectile, delivered by Prospero's consciousness, a consciousness informed by values that seek to colonize, to rule, to dictate, to *name and define all things* from its center of geopolitical control. Prospero's consciousness has created a world of iconic/paradigmatic[18] representations that materialize into *missile*-like structures that seek out and destroy/control/invade. The bullet (the one that took the life of King—not Leopold but Dr. Martin Luther, Jr.), the cannon, the rocket, the atomic bomb, weapons with multiple warheads—these are the artifacts of missilic consciousness, the handiwork of Prospero's greed for power and centralization.

Brathwaite is familiar with "the missilically armed Sagittarian Horseman."[19] The horse is both sign and symbol, emblematic of power and hierarchy. In Austin Clarke's *The Polished Hoe*, Mary-Mathilda, the enslaved black woman on the colonized island of Barbados, graphically describes the feeling of being owned, of feeling inferior, of being examined, *as if for the taking*, in relation to her white master's position on his horse. Describing Mr. Bellfeels, the white master, or the master self, Mary says, "He could see my face, because he was looking down."[20] "Looking down" is suggestive of one who gazes with superiority. The expression also connotes a spatial relationship of literally "standing over." Moreover, "looking down" suggests the activity of gazing at the genitalia. After Mr. Bellfeels touched her as a young girl with his riding crop, Mary recalls what it felt like: "That smell of leather. And the feel of leather of the riding crop, passing over my dress, all over my body, as if it was his hand crawling over my body; and I was naked."[21]

The point here is that epistemic violence—a certain way of know-ing black women/young black girls even before actual physical rape—was already operative. She was learning to internalize the *knowledge* that she was property. Her status of being *owned* was articulated through Bellfeels's rid-ing crop. From his position sitting on his horse (one might say his "throne"), he made his power/"superiority" felt and known. Brathwaite speaks of the "horse-ikon" when he writes:

> This conversion/conversation was therefore a symbol (version) of the new "universal" human concern; of having the humility, for instance, of getting off your horse (or orse or arse), which was a sign of Euro-pean "superiority" in the Caribbean (as was the case for feudalism everywhere): the horse=knight=chivalry: like now car=richness=boss (very much a part of our inherited tradition). But you just can't talk or take a man to Christ from top a horse. It's too high, too restless and it snorts.[22]

Brathwaite is aware of how certain icons/ikons/paradigms reflect certain forms of consciousness and how certain forms of consciousness affect cer-tain forms of human relationality. On a postcard, for example, he sees (seer) a European city skyline in its paradigmatic missilic form. The concept of landscape becomes "manscape," revealing something about a culture's para-digms. On the postcard, the buildings, like the Eiffel Tower in Paris, are pointed upward as if ready to launch.[23] Brathwaite writes:

> *Note the continuation of*
> *paradigm from Assyrian*
> *Sagittarius*
> *Thru Euro Gothic spires*
> *Big Ben*
> *Eiffel*
> *The Empire State Building*
> *Manhattan + skyscrapers*[24]

Also on the postcard is the image of the sun, a circular structure, which ap-pears, in juxtaposition to the missilic structures, as a target, a bull's-eye. For Brathwaite, the circle paradigm of Africa is diametrically opposed (in struc-ture, in consciousness, in spirituality, in motion) to European missilic struc-tures, structures that appear to be designed to take flight: ten, nine, eight, seven, six, five, four, three, two, one. *Blastoff. Blasted. Blasphemous.* Notice that there is a backward countdown, as if in temporal *retrograde*, perhaps a form of spiritual and moral diminution. Contra-diction. Counter-speech. A lie. Counter-speech/act. We are moving in that highly symbolically charged space that Brathwaite refers to as "alterRenaissance."

Brathwaite describes the circle symbol as Africa's chief subsistence source and model:

> The drums are round, its dancers dance a circle; the villages and their houses: also round, though this shape is changing (superficially?); though the compound, don't you see, remains; and the elders sit in their circle and the farm. Surround the villages in dispositions like wheels; and time is a wheel: ancestor, spirit, child.[25]

Hips moving in circular rhythm, rap artists doing verbal battle in a circular cipha, black women catching the spirit in the encircling arms of the congregants, the ring shout, the nonhierarchical (nonmissilic) performance of improvisation. These are embodied spaces that are spiritually charged, kinetic, moving, swaying, wavelike, tidal-like, call and response–like.

Christopher Small says that there is something about (Euro-American) classical music that imitates the process and structure of industrialization: both emphasize fragmentation, linearity, power hierarchy, and so on. For him, this "manner of performance . . . affirms and celebrates the values of the industrial state in all its singleness of vision."[26] There are many offshoots of this motif of verticality: commoner, proletariat, lumpen-proletariat, serf, slave, disempowerment, "thing," and reigning white consciousness.

Verticality as power ran through the veins of Columbus/King Leopold/ Vasco da Gama/Marco Polo/Cesare Borgia/Julius Caesar/Augustus/Sir John Hawkins/Bernard Drake/Hernan Cortez and others. It is a dream—the dream of absolute vertical power—from which America and Europe have yet to awaken. It is a dream steeped in procrustean narcissism. This dream of cultural universality not only has created a destructive form of self-conceit and myopia; it has also led to the missilic devastation of those who do not share it.

Christopher Columbus, like the Roman Empire, like European and American imperialism, had a form of consciousness that sought fuel and power, that did not hesitate to fit those who did not look like him or talk like him into his own narrow xenophobic and misanthropic *Weltanschauung*. In short, non-Europeans were Othered, considered dispensable, and deemed *not human* or infrahuman. European *universal* humanism failed along the axis of ethical practice. Thus, an alterRenaissance took place—an alterhumanism. As Aimé Césaire writes, "And I say that between colonization and civilization there is an infinite distance; that out of all the colonial expeditions that have been undertaken, out of all the colonial statutes that have been drawn up, out of all the memoranda that have been dispatched by all the ministries, there could not come a single human value."[27]

The construction of "the human" was shaped by a white "oracle" voice (one that presumes to speak the history of human reality from beginning to end), a voice that defined the *anthropos* and the nature of reason along a geo-ontological axis of Western white values and hegemonic, imperialistic power. For Robert J. C. Young, "The formation of the ideas of human nature, humanity and the universal qualities of the human mind as the common good of an ethical civilization occurred at the same time as those particularly violent centuries in the history of the world now known as the era of Western colonialism."[28] European civilization was deeply complicit in the violent negativity of colonialism and played a crucial part in its ideology. In this process of alterRenaissance, the "human" became *particularized* to (defined by) Euro-missilic ways of being, and Euro-missilic ways of being became *universalized*. In his preface to Frantz Fanon's *The Wretched of the Earth*, Jean-Paul Sartre is critical of the hypocrisy and empty ideological titillation of Western humanism:

> Let us look at ourselves, if we can bear to, and see what is becoming of us. First, we must face that unexpected revelation, the strip tease of our humanism. There you can see it, quite naked, and it's not a pretty sight. It was nothing but an ideology of lies, a perfect justification for pillage; its honeyed words, its affection of sensibility were only alibis for our aggressions.[29]

This same procrustean motif is enacted by Prospero in *The Tempest*. According to Brathwaite, Prospero, too, embodies the values of the missile; he, too, conquers the unfamiliar, forcing those who are indigenous into ontologically rigid roles: evil witches, bestial monstrosities. While Prospero constructs his identity and forms of consciousness as universal, Sycorax and Caliban are rendered particularistic, delineated according to the European imago of the black. Sycorax and Caliban become sites of teratology. There emerges a Manichean racist world. Like Europe, which targeted/targets Africa, transforming/deforming/destroying the latter's living geo-psychic constitution and its ecosystems, Prospero targets Sycorax with the aim of rendering her utterly submerged, invisible, voiceless. Within this context of the universal versus the particular, it is important to point out that the Enlightenment might also be described as an *alterEnlightenment*.

It was the German philosopher Kant who described the Enlightenment's organizing motif as *Sapere aude* ("Dare to know"). However, he never conceded the capacity ("to know") to blacks of African descent.[30] Even if they dared to know, they would have failed. The point here is that, for Kant (the Enlightenment philosopher par excellence), reason was an attribute of European man/*anthropos*. In an internal critique of Kant's philosophical system, Henry Louis Gates writes:

> Did Kant stop being a racist, stop thinking that there existed a natural, predetermined relation between "stupidity" and "blackness" (his terms) just because he wrote *Foundations of the Metaphysics of Morals*? Hardly! Indeed, one might say that Kant's *Observations on the Feeling of the Beautiful and Sublime* function to deconstruct, for the black reader, Kant's *Foundations*, revealing it to be just one more example for the remarkable capacity of European philosophers to conceive of "humanity" in ideal terms (white, male), yet despise, abhor, colonize, or exploit human beings who are not "ideal."[31]

One is forced to ask of the Enlightenment: Whose reason? Kant's reason? Prospero's reason? Sycorax's reason? Caliban's reason? Europe's reason? Africa's reason? In practice, the age of reason for Europe became the age of forced *irrationality and unreason* on non-Europeans.

This places us back in the missilic, the psychic terrain of Prospero. In Brathwaite's reading, Prospero embodies the values of the missile. His immediate impulse is to *conquer* the unfamiliar (think here of the conquistadors or, rather, of "Columbus's long-time cousins"),[32] to force human persons to conform to his white colonial desires, thus preventing the possibility of a *circle* of acceptance, leading instead to a missilic invasion, a territorial usurpation, an explosive diasporic shattering/scattering. Like a missile, Prospero *targets* Sycorax/Caliban/the indigenous nonwhite body. "Targets" is important, for it suggests *deeds*, which are within the realm of the ethical and the relational. The ethical requires the recognition of the not-self as another self, a self due equal respect qua self/person.

Even more radically, perhaps "the stranger" is a *corrective* to who/what some of us think we are. Prospero failed to see himself as the stranger in Caliban's eyes. He also failed to allow Caliban's presence to create a shift in his identity. This dyadic relationship calls for mutual recognition, perhaps a *tidalectics*[33] (back-and-forth, recursive movement) of recognition, which will perhaps allow for the dynamics of a radically different form of sociality and intersubjectivity between Prospero and those he colonized. By *targeting* Sycorax, which involves a discourse of missiles, launchpads, ridicule and criticism, condemnation through name-calling and misnaming, Prospero has already undermined the possibility for mutual respect; he has already limited the imaginative space of the possible in the creation of a mutual (positive) constitutionality between himself and those indigenous to the island. He is on the island as a colonizer. He deems himself sovereign. He is the so-called biologically and ontologically fittest; he is the *Summa*.[34] W.E.B. Du Bois was aware of how American and European whites aspired to be "super-men and world-mastering demi-gods."[35] Whiteness is at the highest rung of "the ladder of the angel-mix."[36]

Prospero wants to impose a closed system[37] of thought, action, and value on those he deems Other, the ersatz. His presence, his being, governed by symbols of soaring expansionism—the missile—creates a state of "progressive disequilibrium."[38] To move beyond his own site of power, his cultural centeredness and white hierarchical consciousness, it would benefit Prospero to engage in a process of negative capability,[39] which involves the willing suspension of various inherited prejudices, judgments, and the like. In this way, Prospero might attempt to disrupt his own aggressive self-aggrandizement and his cannibal-like possession of "exotic" minerals and dark flesh for fuel. Perhaps he could suspend his recurring dream/nightmare of Rome. Empire. Leviathan. 1492. The eagle: a bird of prey and the iconography of the Roman empire and America. Projectiles of penetration and invasion, laced with the poison of colonial myths and ideology. Destination: more territory. At least this is what Captain Kirk told us.

Still dreaming of El Dorado. Such dreams have a way of blinding their dreamers. One wonders if Christopher Columbus ever opened his prayer book, allegedly given to him by Pope Alexander,[40] for advice as he missilically launched his ships into distant lands, only to cause profound levels of disquiet, physical and psychological trauma, death, inhumanity, and progressive disequilibrium. The Arawaks were decimated. The native women felt they must kill their own children so as to keep them forever safe from Columbus's malevolent deeds. Or what of those who had their noses cut off by Columbus's entourage of hired killers? What of those innocent babies whose heads were bashed against walls as their parents watched? Ask Bartolome de las Casas—he recorded many of these inhuman deeds.

In *The Tempest*, "Christopher Prospero" rules over the island. He has power over both Caliban and Ariel (who is one of his agents) through his magic. As if they were living on a plantation, which is an "overseas (colonial) fuel-base,"[41] they serve him; they are his colonial objects. Prospero's colonial-plantation consciousness is made evident through his use of various forms of representation and control. Ariel and Caliban are treated as *things* to be manipulated. Prospero uses his magic as a whip. He *is* whip, missile, projectile, and gun. The copula "is" suggests a strong identity relationship; it suggests a movement from *person* to *thing*. Indeed, Sartre characterizes the colonizer as undergoing a process of transmutation from the for-itself to the in-itself. Consistent with Brathwaite's understanding of Columbus *as* a gun, Sartre writes, "This imperious being, crazed by his absolute power and by the fear of losing it, no longer remembers clearly that he was once a man; he takes himself for a horsewhip or a gun."[42] This has important existential implications for how the human subject is able to hide from his/her own freedom and responsibility. This is the space that Simone de Beauvoir calls "the serious man," a space of dishonesty that involves ceaselessly trying to deny one's freedom.[43] To be a "horsewhip" or a "gun" speaks to self-thingification or the thingification of another human being, which leads to a form of distorted relationality. As Césaire notes:

> No human contact, but relations of domination and submission which turn the colonizing man into a class-room monitor, an army sergeant, a prison guard, a slave driver, and the indigenous man into an instrument of production. My turn to state an equation: "colonization = thingification."[44]

And there is Brathwaite's observation regarding the multiple transmutations of the human: "Man into slave slave into chattel chattel into thing thing into no thing no thing into nutten."[45] In short, the colonized are reduced to nonbeing, nothing, *nihil*.

Prospero's demigod status is imparted through his ability to control the lives of others. He reveals his vanity and narcissism through his magical power, by his delight in it. He also delights in his power to *name*. Caliban and Sycorax function as "tabulae rasae" on which Prospero writes their lives and identities in *his* vocabulary. This, after all, is what colonialists do. The aim is to create a split, a massive rupture in the consciousness of the colonized through which they begin to see themselves through the eyes of the white colonizers. The French did it with/to Sarah Bartmann, the so-called Hottentot Venus, making her into something that she could not recognize. "Because, you see, part of the unwhole system of control was to make people (*us*) believe that we were European: but altered and fragmented out of any paradigm that you, in Europe, would recognize as 'real.'"[46] If only Toni Morrison's fictional character Pecola Breedlove could have done without those *bluest* eyes. Decolonization. "The middle passage in reverse."[47] Malcolm X understood the importance of this "reverse." Fanon did. So did Larry Neal and the critical cadre of the Black Arts Movement (BAM). Philosopher Alain Locke understood this with his conceptualization of the New Negro. Reverse the historical script.

Prospero's power to *name* is evident in his references to Caliban, whom Prospero refers to as a "thing of darkness."[48] He is "not honored with a human shape."[49] He is a dull thing that is kept in service.[50] He is deemed the source of evil.[51] He is a villain.[52] Caliban is also said to be by nature evil, a savage, without meaning or language, and to have come from a vile race.[53] He is a hewer of wood[54] and no doubt a servant of servants. This is the discourse of the colonizer, one who brings "enlightenment" (or is it alterEnlightenment?) to the land of "uncivilized savages," those prone to bestial violence, primitive forms of communication, sexual licentiousness; those who are devoid of complex intellectual processes befitting a "real" (read "Euro/Anglo") human person.

One wonders to what extent an Elizabethan audience's ego maintenance was parasitic on the teratological, bestial, and hypersexual depiction of Caliban. Joane Nagel discerns more racist fodder for Elizabethans, writing, "Early in the seventeenth century, William Shakespeare refers to Othello's embraces as 'the gross clasps of a lascivious Moor.'"[55] Given the white racist imaginary, a "lascivious Moor" no doubt functions as a tautology. And Fanon situates the lustful Caliban motif vis-à-vis the white nation-saving Prospero motif in the context of North American racism: "Toward Caliban, Prospero assumes an attitude that is well known to Americans in the southern United States. Are they not forever saying that the niggers are just waiting for the chance to jump on white women?"[56] In the spirit of Toni Morrison's conception of American Africanism, a term she deploys to cover the various ways in which African people and people of African descent have come to embody "the range of views, assumptions, readings, and misreadings that accompany Eurocentric learning about these people,"[57] one might argue that Caliban became a trope for a certain "rawness and savagery, that provided ground and area for the elaboration of the quintessential [Elizabethan] identity."[58] After all, in the European imaginary, non-Europeans were but satellites, moons that maintained their orbits because of Europe's gravitational pull.

As a centralized and centralizing force, Europe created a *socio-epistemic* cartography, as it were, that demarcated those who were fit to be used as fuel (the primitive, satellite *targets*) from those who were to partake of the fuel (the white, civilized *missiles*). For example, the European racist "sciences" of physiognomy and phrenology (Prospero's discursive framework), with emphasis on the prognathous jaw of Negroes, were said "to support" the primitive nature of African people. In short, the black, who was used as fuel after the extermination of the Amerindians,[59] one of the *targets* in the scientific discursive universe of European missilic alterEnlightenment, was constructed as an object of meticulous scientific "truth." Examining the so-called Negro anatomy, the French physician Pruner-Bey observed (notice the attempt to map fundamental/essentialist differences):

> The intestinal mucus is very thick, viscid, and fatty in appearance. All the abdominal glands are of large size, especially the liver and the supra renal capsules; a venous hyperaemia seems the ordinary condition of these organs. The position of the bladder is higher than in the European. I find the seminal vesicles very large, always gorged with a turbid liquid of a slightly greyish colour, even in cases where the autopsy took place shortly after death. The penis is always of unusually large size, and I found in all bodies a small conical gland on each side at the base of the fraenum.[60]

As Jan Nederveen Pieterse (1992) argues, "Anthropology, as the study of 'otherness,' never disengaged itself from Eurocentric narcissism."[61]

One significant point here is that those who have been marginalized and stigmatized by Prospero's/Columbus's power to name and control have had to create new languages, new discourses, new frames of reference, new ways of *being-in-the-flesh*, new ways of defining home, and new ways of remapping their identities (a counter-Euro cartography). Perhaps this is why Brathwaite refers to Caliban as a "would-be rebel/against the plantation."[62] In *The Tempest*, for example, Caliban fails to reverse his consciousness.[63] Has he no other frame of reference? Is he not able to *X-out* (*X-it/Ex-it*) the plantation system/self? Caliban does not appear to engage in any attempt to rupture in any serious fashion the plantation system or its logic so as to move from a closed to an open system.[64] He has not yet become self-conscious. He is still living his existence in black according to the projections created through the white imaginary; he has not found (or *become*) an alter/*native* to Prospero's alterRenaissance.[65] Just as obsequiously as he serves Prospero, Caliban refers to Stefano and Trinculo as gods.[66] As Brathwaite sees this:

> *If Caliban instead of falling for Miranda had cleaved toward the mother*
> *If Caliban instead of learning how to curse in pidgin had listened to his*
> *   mother's voice; if he could speak to her in their* language
> *He might have had a better chance when the chance for revolt came his*
> *   way; might not have made himself a such poor fish when Stefano*

and Trinculo came along; would not have made them gods, had he come near his mother's immanence.[67]

Césaire's version of Caliban is of one who has moved beyond a plantation/colonized consciousness. Indeed, the black body's resistance is captured through the voice of a *transformed* Caliban[68] as he refuses to live by the dehumanizing imago. Césaire's Caliban has become cognizant of the source of his double consciousness; he is now able to nihilate the given of Prospero's world and to resist the lived experience of corporeal malediction. At the level of the gaze, he challenges the relational asymmetry of which he has been a victim. In the process of defying this relational asymmetry, Caliban engages in an act of counter-hegemonic marking, and in a profound reversal of the gaze—"*Look, a white!*"—Caliban's act of nomination ("I see you for what you are, Prospero!") uncovers an assemblage of lies, deceptions, and colonial trickeries.

> *Prospero, you're a great magician:*
> *you're an old hand at deception.*
> *And you lied to me so much,*
> *about the world, about myself*
> *that you ended up by imposing on me*
> *an image of myself:*
> *underdeveloped, in your words, undercompetent*
> *that's how you made me see myself!*
> *And I hate that image . . .*
> *But now I know you, you old cancer,*
> *And I also know myself!*
> *And I know that one day*
> *my bare fist, just that,*
> *will be enough to crush your world!*
> *The old world is crumbling down!*[69]

Perhaps Prospero thinks that he can more effectively target Sycorax through the control of her son. Perhaps, as long as he keeps Caliban politically unconscious, he can possess some aspect of her. Although Prospero is cunning in his efforts at constructing a world within which the racial Manichean divide appears as a "naturally given" state of affairs, his cunning cannot ensnare Sycorax. She has already gone underground, submerged. She resides in that space of fecundity and growth. She has long immersed her roots in the ground, bringing forth change like the force of a harmattan. She is invisible, though not like Ellison's invisible man. "SHE IS A SUBMERGED MOTHER."[70] Indeed, "She represents the sub/maroon."[71] Target Caliban, cut him down, and she continues to grow. Target, usurp, and invade her island/land (left to Caliban), and she finds another home. Rape her, and she heals from the trauma. And like Celia, a young black girl enslaved by an abusive white "master," she may eventually catch you unaware.[72] Hang her by the neck, and she speaks through other metaphors: Billie Holiday's strange fruit. Name her Isabella Baumfree, and she renames herself: Sojourner Truth. Divide her family, and she retains her memory, passing down stories within stories like Nana Peazant, the knower of African retentions in Julie Dash's film *Daughters of the Dust*. Movement. Fluidity. Kinesis. She is immanent in a people in *process*, indomitable, forever remaking, renarrating who and what they are. Attempts to trap her in Prospero's derogatory discourse ("foul witch," "hag") fail. She transcends the colonial discourse of Prospero/Columbus/Cortez. Sycorax will find a word warrior through whom to speak her Caribbean and African spiritual and cultural roots. But Prospero is persistent. Brathwaite writes:

> *white oracle*
> *white order*
> *white ruler*
> *white ships*[73]

And I would add this:

> *white robes/hoods*
> *white lies*
> *white terror*
> *white ignorance*
> *white denial*
> *white arrogance*
> *white complicity*
> *white privilege*
> *white power*
> *white narcissism*

Prospero, as suggested previously, continues to dream of Rome. He has never quite recovered from its collapse. Ever since, he has been attempting to *Roman*ticize the world. Making false promises (perhaps *Roman*tic ideals) about abundance and the "infinite" resources stored in the earth. Francis

Bacon was seduced by this ideal. Expanding/penetrating inward. Expanding/penetrating outward. All spaces (inner and outer) are seen as available for the taking, the exploiting. *Star*ship Enterprise: "To Enter." "To invade." "To take." To take what? To take the *prize*!!! Yes, Enter + Prize = To colonize. The only difference is that Captain James T. Kirk, Captain Jean-Luc Picard, and Captain Kathryn Janeway had to follow, or so they were told, the prime directive. Not so with Prospero/Columbus/Cortez. If only *universal* humanism had functioned as a prime directive for the crews of the Niña, Pinta, and Santa Maria. Missilic movements. Torpedo-like; Star Trekking through indigenous spaces. White expansive consciousness is restless. Prospero continues unsatisfied. Rome. Roaming. Spreading like a virus and leaving death and destruction in its path. For Brathwaite:

> The thing about Europe in the Caribbean, in the New World, imperial over/seers & seas; the reason why that occidental (far from accidental) culture formed itself into a missile (seek explore destroy); it is because an alteration of consciousness . . . took place from the moment when Christopher Columbus successfully crossed Atlantic Ocean: bring with him them no Botticelli no Beethoven no no Michelangelo Da Vinci Descartes Newton La Fontaine. In fact no body but those guns his faith.[74]

We are back to Columbus as a missile/gun. He came to "the Americas" (1492) with his "missile probing" and eventually created fragmentation,[75] pain, death, trauma, and extermination. Movement: from the port of Palos to *The Empire Strikes Back*. Christopher Columbus set out from Spain to look for gold/fuel. The missile, as Brathwaite observes, is the "ikon of Europe's imperialist psyche and technology."[76] One knows what happens once a missile finds its target: *ex*plosion, which is a process of moving outward from the source of the detonation/thunder. After his first trip to the Caribbean, Columbus's missilic consciousness was revealed: "I could conquer the whole of them with fifty men and govern them as I pleased."[77] The reader will note that this statement belies the "universal humanistic" rhetoric of the Renaissance.

For his second trip to the Caribbean (1493), Ferdinand and Isabella provided Columbus with more men, seventeen ships, "cannons, crossbows, guns, cavalry, and attack dogs."[78] Columbus is indebted to Marco Polo, another missilic figure, a seeker of fuel, who returned from China with an abundance of gun power. Brathwaite writes, "Marco Polo overland to china; the portuguese by stepping stone to africa; Columbus to san salvador;

looking for power, for powder, gun/power; converting the grain to gain, unholy grail."[79] This makes for the emergence of more deadly projectiles/missiles. Was it not feudalism that was toppled by the cannon, and the cannon responsible for the establishment of nation-states? Did Polo see this coming? Could he have seen the causal links: gold, materialism, greed, mutilation, extermination? Prospero now possesses jumbo nuclear ("new-clearer") weapons. Can Polo wash his hands of the blood? Too late to cry about a lack of prescience; Columbus has already embarked on a mission to destroy any alter/natives with his exportation of missiles of death.

But "why was this Renaissance so un/exported? Why only gun and sword and flame the fragmentations we are speaking of?"[80] Brathwaite answers:

> the rocket missile at its apogee: re-entry: the metal burn against earth's
> atmosphere begins. To counter this the missile must reverse itself:
> *that* alteration of its axis: *so that it enters at its widest thickest*
> *bluntest back or bottom:* its basest forward *as it were*
> And that is how I see Europe's trajectory into the New World certainly
> into the New World plantation[81]

Note Brathwaite's use of the term "basest." The missile's basest part is not only its bottom;[82] it is also the part that is vile, low, or lacking in higher values (such as the value of *universal* humanism). Another way to articulate this is that the base of the missile transformed "the psyche of its navigators into this new base-born, monopolistically materialistic culture of mercantilism-colonialism-imperialism-total-fuel-consumption syndrome—soil w/out soul and you know the rest as omened by Shakespeare's *Tempest*."[83]

Things have never been the same. Columbus came back with his *base* in front of him, telling the natives to kiss his arse. When a native Arawak refused to do this or committed a minor offense, Columbus/the Spanish "cut off his ears or nose. Disfigured, the person was sent back to his village as living evidence of the brutality the Spaniards were capable of."[84] Of course, the Arawaks did not stand a chance against missiles. Columbus had his horses, cannons, crossbows, and the twenty attack dogs, "who were turned loose and immediately tore the Indians apart."[85] (Ask white racist Theophilus Eugene "Bull" Connor; he knew about those attack dogs. Back in his time, though, they called them "Nigger dogs." Here we are moving in that magical-realist dimension in which space and time are collapsed, where Columbus *is* "Bull" Connor.) There were Spaniards who hunted the natives for sport and "murdered them for dog food."[86] The desire for mammon ruled. This desire had its dire consequences: natives killed themselves in mass suicides, many suffered from malnutrition, massive depopulation occurred, native female sex slaves, ages nine to ten, were in demand by the Spaniards, genocide/sidearm. Pow! Pow! Pow! Pow! Not many POWs, though. Whether in Haiti, the Bahamas, Puerto Rico, the Canary Islands, Cuba, Guadeloupe, or Antigua, mammon trumped universal humanism. Whether in Mexico, Peru or Florida, the conquistadors/conquerors enslaved the natives of these lands, using their bodies and land as fuel. The explosive fallout of Columbus's missilic "progress" became infectious:

> Other nations rushed to emulate Columbus. In 1501 the Portuguese began to depopulate Labrador, transporting the now extinct Bo-ethuk Indians to Europe and Cape Verde as slaves. After the Brit-ish established beachheads on the Atlantic coast of North America, they encouraged coastal Indian tribes to capture and sell members of more distant tribes. Charleston, South Carolina, became a major port for exporting Indian slaves. The Pilgrims and Puritans sold the survivors of the Pequot War into slavery in Bermuda in 1637. The French shipped virtually the entire Natchez nation in chains to West Indies in 1731.[87]

When the food supply runs out, however, it is time to travel, to move "forward," farther, in search of food/fuel, leaving a trail of *under*develop-ment. The missile consumes all. It is never satiated. Caliban—and the land left to him by Sycorax—was not enough for Prospero. The Carib was not enough. "Because the Indians died," according to James W. Loewen, "Indian slavery then led to the massive slave trade to the other way across the Atlantic, from Africa."[88] Brathwaite writes, "For missile Europe labour had become a fuel: first Amerindia (fragmented designation) and after their extermination, the darks from darkest Africa; readily steadily easily available hundreds thousands hundreds thousands hundreds thousands thousands millions: converted workforce."[89]

But where is Sycorax? Submerging/submerged. Surfacing/surfaced. Mov-ing in and out tidalectically. *Like breathing.* Orality. Voicing when necessary. Silent when needed. "Sub/marooned" warrior(s), who knew when to come out and when to go back into hiding. Sisyphean movement is too monoto-nous, too nihilistic. When it comes to Sycoraxian undulation, her movements are life sustaining. *Like breathing.* She is forever adjusting, responding to the crucible of historical time and place. Prospero's power cannot deracinate her from the ground/groundation. She slipped right by Columbus. You've heard her voice: *reggae sounds.* After she escapes one crisis, she waits for the next, ready to reemerge. You have to look carefully, though. There she is: *Mary Prince*. No, wait, there she is: *Malcolm X*. But look again: *Kwame Nkrumah*. Sycorax is always already in the process of *becoming*. Being is too static. Non-being is too empty. Becoming is her mode of ontology. This "becoming," as Brathwaite reminds us, is not to be equated with the

> *"success" of dialectics: synthesis. For dialectics is another gun: a missile:*
> *a way of making progress:*
> *forward*
> *but in the culture of the circle "success" moves outward from the centre*
> *to circumference and back again: a tidal dialectic: an ital dialectic;*
> *continuum across the paristyle.*[90]

In search of more fuel, after devastating the psychophysical balance in the Caribbean, the missile mouth was headed to Africa, to that dark mysterious continent, that place that Hegel said was devoid of *Geist*/Spirit. Once the Euro-travelers, fuel eaters, made it to their destination, with their *basest* part first, they enslaved, exploited/exploded/exported the black "exotic" inhabitants. Indeed, they excised them from their geo-ontological *lived* space of social and familial interaction, cognition, and worship. Trapped by a form of worship/*war*ship that denied them human status, Africans were packed into suffocating decks below ships whose destinations were unknown. Again, Sycorax submerges. She can wait to reemerge in a post–Middle Passage, post-traumatic, post-plantation articulation. Of course, she can fade into the background so as to instigate change from within. She can be on a plantation and engage in acts of "infra-politics," breaking tools, burning food, and so forth. She can be that enslaved black woman who is raped by her white "master" and thrown into a state of silence, only later to find strength to rearticulate her identity in her imagination, the possible, far removed from the inertia of traumatic memory. She can also be that voice on the slave ship that refuses to yield, that prays in its native tongue, calling on the Orisha—from the Yoruba pantheon. Missilic imperialism attempts to *militate* (a discourse of warfare) against the upsurge of "subaltern" knowledge, an episteme that is indispensable for an enslaved and brutalized people who desire to move toward some form of "wholeness" or narrative coherence, particularly once the invasive missile has delivered its explosive payload, resulting in scattered fragments of identity.

Within those dark holds at the bottom of the ships, black bodies were kept in the "dark." Hortense Spillers writes:

Those African persons in the "Middle Passage" were literally suspended in the "oceanic," if we think of the latter in its Freudian orientation as an analogy for undifferentiated identity: removed from the indigenous land and culture, and not-yet "American" either, these captive persons, without names that their captors would recognize, were in movement across the Atlantic, but they were also nowhere at all. Inasmuch as, on any given day, we might imagine, the captive personality did not know where s/he was, we could say that they were the culturally "unmade," thrown in the midst of a figurative darkness that "exposed" their destinies to an unknown course.[91]

The number of black bodies demanded by this cannon culture might shake even Caliban into self-consciousness. Europe brought its own *racial* version of the "black death" to Africa. The four thousand brought to so-called New Spain (1518) and the first twenty at Jamestown (1619) were only the beginning. Brathwaite writes:

First 10, then 20; first 20, then 200; first 200 then 2000; first 2000, then 20,000 . . . africans, slaves, lucumi, tears . . . 200,000, 300,000, 400,000, a million . . . tears, tears, lucumi . . . a million, 2 million, 3 million, 5 million . . . *materialism* . . . building hotels, plantation houses, brothels . . . 10 million, 20 million, 25 million and 30 million . . . flight flight fuel tears . . . tears tears lucumi . . . 30 million, 40 million, 50 million . . . the draining of the lake of mexico, destruction of the fountains of the youth . . . *lucumi* . . . tears . . . to feed the hungry missile mouth . . . *lucumi* . . . *tears* . . . *tears* . . . where are the bison of the prairies, the water spirits of the pacific Indians; where are those 50 million Africans, torn out of tongue, torn out of mother, torn out of soil and soul?[92]

Dreaming of Rome, mourning its collapse, its disequilibrium, the white/ Euro-missilic mode of comportment moves in the direction of expanding its neo-Roman power base, to increase its wealth, to fatten its pockets, and to bring symbolic balance back to the days when Augustus was the *center* of power. In a world where nothing but power matters, where fuel and more fuel is the organizing motif, where the missile is the icon through which (anti) social relationships are constituted, and where materialism rules, humanism has become indefinitely deferred. Keep in mind Brathwaite's equation: "Missilic Europe + the alterRenaissance = Mercantilism." A missile is designed to destroy. That is its *telos*. A missile, when it is aimed at its target, is neither philosophical nor ethical. It simply does its job.

Recall that it is Simone de Beauvoir's "serious man" who acts like a missile, a thing, as if he lacks all freedom and responsibility. In *Feeding The Ghosts*, by Fred D'Aguiar, a powerful fictional narration of an event that took place in 1781, Captain Cunningham, who is in charge of the ship *Zong*, heading back to England, makes the purely (*mercantile*) calculative decision to throw 131 physically ill Africans (men, women, and children) into the ocean to die. He calculates that if he throws about a third of the infirm overboard he will earn a profit from the remaining Africans who are not (as yet) sick. Cunningham asks his crew, "Are we to make a loss or a profit?"[93] Although his crew initially hesitates, with his first mate Kelsal finding the magnitude of the plan difficult to absorb, they decide that it is profit they desire. Referring to the enslaved Africans as "cargo," they begin to jettison them.

As men, women, and children are thrown into the ocean, "Captain Cunningham mark[s] the strokes in his ledger and nod[s] with satisfaction."[94] As the children are being thrown overboard, for profit, for mercantilism, to feed the missile mouth, anger and heartrending screams come from the deck below:

> Mothers shouted to children to show the evil men that they were not sick but healthy; to struggle and scream. Men banged their chains on the decks and shouted in Yoruba, Ewe, Ibo, Fanti, Ashanti, Mandingo, Fetu, Foulah, at the crew to leave the children and take them instead. Mothers pulled out their hair, fell into dead faints, wished for death to take them now, now, now, since life could never mean a thing after this. And cried with dry eyes and hardly a breath left in them.[95]

No matter how often I read this passage, I feel an uncontrollable surge of profound sorrow. Think of all of those millions of Africans who died during the Middle Passage. Thrown out to sea/see Yemaaja. Many jumped overboard. Perhaps some even flew back to Africa, or so their indigenous stories tell.

The point here is that when Prospero *targets* Sycorax, or when Columbus targets the Caribbean, or when King Leopold II targets the Congo, or when Vasco da Gama targets India, or when Cortez targets the Aztecs, each is ruled by a set of missilic values: horsepower, materialism, mercantilism, profit, fuel, mammon, gold, money, power, El Dorado, expansion, invasion, death, destruction, obliteration, erasure, imperialism, usurpation, colonization, territorialism, gun power, cannon power, nuclear fission, the power of 1 centillion exploding stars (10^{303} or 100 groups of three zeroes after 1,000). Prospero forgets, as does Columbus, that he is a man. He is the man who mistook himself *not* for a hat but for a missile (one for Oliver Sacks to think over). His very being is a weapon, which means that his *telos* is to destroy, to obliterate.

As a weapon of mass destruction, Prospero/Columbus/Polo/Cortez/Leopold/da Gama have become transmuted into their own icons, giving these icons white flesh so as to walk among the living. But they have become *things* that call themselves (super) human when in fact *they have become* Euro-humanism's opposite; they have become *altered in their rebirth*. Reborn without those spiritual elements. One might call it a "breech birth presentation." Kelsal! Kelsal! This was the call/breath of Mintah,[96] holding Kelsal to his Euro-Renaissance, his *renaistre* (etymologically, "to be born again"). Who will convince Columbus's white offspring/offshoots[97] to struggle against inhumanity, to struggle against disequilibrium, to struggle against their *basest* part? As the white master missilic self is effectively resisted, it rearticulates its power, its hegemony, and its basest part, "only to return with greater intensity."[98] How do we stop this expanding white master self from returning with greater force in order to sustain its power to define and control the nonwhite Other? After all, the white master self's assertion is really a modality of maintaining its fantasy of stability and ahistorical supremacy. Without the negative construction of the Other, the white master self stands on the brink of ontological evisceration. Perhaps without the nonwhite Other, the white missilic self would self-destruct. Toni Morrison knows the "buffering" function of black people in North America. They constitute the wretched, the damned of the earth, and through this buffering whites gain "superior" status:

> If there were no black people here in this country, it would have been Balkanized. The immigrants would have torn each other's throats out, as they have done everywhere else. But in becoming an American, from Europe, what one has in common with that other immigrant is contempt for me—it's nothing else but color. Wherever they were from, they would stand together. They could all say, "I am not that." So in that sense, becoming an American is based on an attitude: an exclusion of me.[99]

Morrison also recognizes the destructive and implosive possibilities inherent in a society that scapegoats other people. The societal and intrapsychic price of a collective (white) identity purchased through the degradation of those deemed "inferior Others" situates white identity on the edge of disintegration. In this case, without black people (without those about whom whites can say, "I am not that"), what becomes of whiteness? Ontologically, it appears to fall flat.

4

Looking at Whiteness

Whiting Up and Blacking Out in White Chicks

Hollywood spreads the fictions of whiteness around the world.
—**Hernan Vera and Andrew M. Gordon,** *Screen Saviors*

As long as race is something only applied to non-white peoples,
as long as white people are not racially seen and named, they/we
function as a human norm. Other people are raced, we are just
people. —**Richard Dyer,** *White*

To look directly was an assertion of subjectivity, equality.
—**bell hooks,** *Black Looks*

Consistent with the other chapters in this text, the objective here is to *name* whiteness, to mark it, to undo its invisibility, to share a critical way of looking, and thereby encourage a new way of discerning and hopefully a new and unflinching way of bringing attention to what has become normative and business as usual. While certainly a comedy, and some would argue a potboiler, the movie *White Chicks* takes seriously the critical capacity of the black gaze to tease out the subtleties of whiteness and thereby reflect whiteness back to whites themselves. It is argued that this film, directed by Keenen Ivory Wayans and written by Keenen and his brothers Shawn and Marlon (the latter two playing the main characters) has the power to produce "the shock of being seen."[1] In this case, it is whites who are seen. On this score, the Wayans brothers resist the hegemony of the white gaze through filmic agency. By not only enacting and performing whiteness but also mimicking predominant racist images of the black body,

A previous version of this chapter, coauthored with Tracey Ann Ryser, was published as George Yancy and Tracey Ryser, "Whiting Up and Blacking Out: White Privilege, Race, and *White Chicks*," *African American Review* 42, nos. 3–4 (Fall/Winter 2008): 1–16.

the Wayans brothers are able to create an effective space of opposition and critique. Even the title of the film—*White Chicks*—engages nomination that frames and clearly delineates its theme of interrogation. The Wayans brothers are, in essence, saying, "Look, a white!"

The themes explored in this chapter constitute only a select few of the many important themes generated within this filmic text. One underlying premise that informs the scholarship in this chapter is that *White Chicks* constitutes an important popular cultural site that speaks to complex silent assumptions embedded in the white American imaginary in relationship to issues of race. While critical of the class and essentialist presuppositions behind the expression "urban black behavior," it is argued that the Wayans brothers enact and, indeed, exaggerate various stereotypical forms of black behavior in order to interrogate the white imaginary. This does not mean, however, that they buy into a thin, noncomplicated understanding of "blackness." In fact, the Wayanses complicate the stereotypes precisely through their exaggerations. Such exaggerations function as a subtext that illustrates their sense of self-reflexivity regarding white myths vis-à-vis the black body. And while the white imaginary is no doubt inflected by class and other nonracial registers, the film's characterization of whiteness as a signifier of power and privilege is one that captures social ontological manifestations of whiteness across nonracial variables.

Under the influence of European travelogues and colonial films and white philosophers, anthropologists, ethnographers, and fiction writers in the eighteenth and nineteenth centuries, the West came to understand nonwhites as inferior Others. More specifically, as I argued in Chapter 3, the construction of whiteness functioned epistemologically and ontologically as a prism through which the Other was constructed and rendered subhuman. The Other (Caliban, the so-called Hottentot Venus, and so on) was deemed inferior in virtually every way—intellectually, morally, aesthetically, and culturally. The Other was constructed as savage, uncivilized, barbaric, evil, lustful, *different*, and *deviant*. Whiteness, on this score, served as a metanarrative in which nonwhites functioned as "possessions" to be exploited and used in the service of white people. "In the white mind, racial others do not exist on their own terms but only as 'self-objects' bound up with the white self."[2]

Winthrop Jordan points out that the Great Chain of Being, or *scala naturae*, became the ordering hierarchical structure in an age when the West was obsessed with scientific discovery and exploration; it "served as a powerful means of organizing the facts of the natural world."[3] Nonwhite bodies constituted part of this world; they were constructed as part of the chaotic and exotic natural landscape in need of being ordered, properly identified and categorized, and subdued by those (whites) who thought of themselves as the very expression of a teleological order that privileged whiteness as the quintessence of beauty, intelligence, and cultural and historical progress. As V. Y. Mudimbe notes, "Evolution, conquest, and difference become signs of a theological, biological, and anthropological destiny, and assign[ed] to things and beings both their natural slots and social mission."[4] Anthropological descriptive discourse, "with its roots in the exploration and colonialism of the rest of the world by the West, is the discourse of the [white] self. It defines itself primarily as the study of the other, which means that its selfhood was not problematic."[5] In the context of this ontologically truncating white epistemic order, forms of "knowing" that distort and deform, the nonwhite body became a fantasy of white mythos and desire. This body was rendered devoid of voice and interiority. More specifically, the *black* body came to represent the epitome of hypersexuality, savagery, and immorality. What remains problematic is that while blacks in the United States have fought to combat the internalization of themselves as savages and brutes, white privilege and hegemony continue to exist.

Historically, film has been a powerful vehicle in which white ideological frames of reference have been buttressed and perpetuated. It can be argued that "Hollywood movies are one of the main instruments for establishing the apartheid mind-set that leads people of all colors to automatically consider white to be superior."[6] Through the process of controlling and manipulating the images of black people and policing their bodies, black people became the "looked at," not "the lookers." Whites became the gazers, those who controlled what was seen and how it was seen. D. W. Griffith's *Birth of a Nation* (1915), for example, focuses "upon the racialized body, an Other whose race is an immediate marker of a problematic difference."[7] This film not only made more money than any other in the silent film era, but it also became "one of the seminal American films of the twentieth century in terms of codifying the sincere fictions of the white self on the screen."[8] The white gaze, in *Birth of a Nation*, depicted the "truth" of the sexually rapacious black body, which was constructed as something to be feared and controlled by white nation builders and keepers of white purity. It is no surprise that *Birth of a Nation* is claimed "to have inspired a new wave of terror by the Ku Klux Klan."[9] It explicitly expressed the racist distortions of a collective white unconscious writ large—on filmic display.

While most films tend to reinscribe white normativity and power, some actually go as far as to challenge antiblack racist stereotypes and directly confront white privilege and the power of the white gaze. *White Chicks*

(2004) is one such movie.[10] It is similar to *Some Like It Hot* (1959), *Tootsie* (1982), *Mrs. Doubtfire* (1993), and others, where the central comedic theme centers around men disguised as women. However, unlike these films, *White Chicks* deploys this theme to present a serious unearthing of race relations in America. It constitutes a counter-gaze, one that attempts to render visible the often invisible normative power of whiteness.

As Jean-Paul Sartre notes, "When you removed the gag that was keeping these black mouths shut, what were you hoping for? That they would sing your praises?"[11] Sartre was aware that "the white man has enjoyed the privilege of seeing without being seen."[12] Indeed, in the historical context of the power of the white gaze, blacks were deemed devoid of critical subjectivity; it was claimed that they were devoid of a perspective on the world, including a perspective on their own lives. This meant that blacks also lacked a critical perspective from which to examine and critique whiteness. Bell hooks notes, "White people can 'safely' imagine that they are invisible to black people since the power they have historically asserted, and even now collectively assert over black people, accorded them the right to control the black gaze."[13]

There is, however, no historical inevitability that necessitates the accrual of white hegemony and the power of the white gaze to position and subordinate nonwhites. White power and privilege are fundamentally contingent. The scopic hegemony of whiteness is grounded in structural, historical, and material processes of subjugation, dispossession, and imperial invasion. As a perceptual practice, the white gaze is predicated on contingent and value-laden historical practices. In short, it is a historically embodied and habituated phenomenon. Linda Alcoff states that "what is true is what is visible" and that "the realm of the visible, or what is taken as self-evidently visible . . . is recognized as the product of a specific form of perceptual practice."[14] As a form of *perceptual practice*, directly challenging the socially constructed privilege and power of the white gaze is a possibility. One way of doing this is to render whiteness visible, to uncover and deconstruct its normative and "unconditioned" status and thus reveal the ways in which it is invested in maintaining its invisibility so as to cling to its power.

White Chicks is a gold mine of critical reflections on race because it puts whiteness and blackness on display and resurrects the basic elements (though with a different aim) from the minstrel show, which monopolized the entertainment industry of the nineteenth century when overt racism was a matter of course. White actors "blacked up" their faces with burnt cork, using white or red makeup to enlarge, in a grotesque fashion, their eyes, lips, and nose. To be successful, blackface minstrels had to be able to sing, dance, and, most important, *perform* what they stereotypically understood to constitute blackness. Thus they exaggerated a southern Negro dialect and grossly caricatured so-called Negro mannerisms.[15] As white America laughed at the minstrels' antics, racist stereotypes of blacks were being firmly entrenched in the American consciousness when the white body appropriated the black one.[16]

Patricia Williams notes that America has historically had a near-fetishistic obsession with what she calls "racial voyeurism," which became all too visible during the O. J. Simpson trial.[17] The problem with this white voyeurism is that it tends to place the Other at a "condescending distance."[18] In fact, minstrelsy placed the black body perfectly at a distance. The white minstrel enacted distorted images of the black body that permeated the white racist social imaginary. In this sense, the minstrel was able to perform the "black body" as an object of ridicule, with the white audience manifesting a form of "fascinating cannibalism."[19] Like the white ethnographic gaze that was fascinated by the so-call primitive, white onlookers were fascinated by the "accuracy" of the performed white-body-in-black, eager to consume such racist depictions—depictions that were actually projections from their own consciousness—which allowed whites, "mostly white workers," the opportunity to create an important racial distance between themselves and those dark, inferior Others. Such depictions reinforced the dynamics of the white gaze across white class divides. Minstrel shows "were popular with middle class and elite whites, including U.S. presidents such as John Tyler and Abraham Lincoln. Before and during his White House years, Abraham Lincoln was fond of minstrel shows and the 'darky' joking of white performers."[20]

Whites of all classes consumed the images that they themselves had regurgitated. In short, they internalized/ingested what they themselves externalized or "vomited." This is a peculiar case of chewing the cud, although in terms of complex social and racial dynamics. It is important that newspapers and magazines also participated in the distortion of black bodies, with cartoons and drawings of black people accompanied by negative descriptions. As Joe R. Feagin writes, "Cartoons accented 'ugly' (to whites) physical characteristics: distinctive hair, skin, lips, and odor. Such physical traits were commonly linked to palpably tangible, visual, and emotional ways and were commonly linked to other negative images of black Americans, including alleged hypersexuality."[21]

White Chicks deploys a "reverse" minstrel show technique. Instead of whites "blacking up" to ridicule the oppressed Other, black men (Shawn and Marlon Wayans) "white up" to reveal and critique various instantiations of whiteness. In *White Chicks*, however, to "white up" is not to violate the dignity of white people (as in the case of blackface minstrelsy) or to lampoon them with sharp racist vitriol. The film does not attempt to define white bodies in terms of a racist ideology that defined black bodies as racial essences. Black bodies in Hollywood cinema were historically portrayed as "eternal, unchanging, unchangeable."[22] As James Snead writes, "One of the prime codes surrounding blacks on screen, then—one much at variance with the narrative codes that mandate potential mobility for other screen characters—is an almost metaphysical stasis."[23]

White Chicks uses the black body, and the black-body-in-white, as an instrument of humor and mimicry in complex and subversive ways. Whiteness is thrown up against a black background, where it becomes the object of scrutiny. While the Wayanses, disguised as white women, acquire a power position in their "reverse minstrel show" performances, what remains obvious is that *white women*, not white men, are the object of ridicule and critique. However, *white men* continue to possess most of the political and economic power in America, so it might be argued that, while wealthy white women are the main characters through which whiteness is critiqued, white men slip through the filmic counter-gaze of the Wayans brothers and this slippage serves to reassert white male domination.

Thus, even though theirs is an incomplete critique of the racism of white males, the Wayanses effectively address issues of racism and whiteness head-on. Through humor, they are able to ease viewers into that space of recognition where whiteness qua *difference* emerges. This, after all, is what must be done when it comes to sites of power. The objective is to bring those sites of power, in this case whiteness, out of the background and make them part of the foreground. The Wayanses challenge the status of whiteness as the transcendental norm, a norm that functions as the *condition of the possibility* for "seeing" blackness as different and whiteness as the same. In this way, the Wayans brothers are in stream with what Patricia Williams calls "creating community"—a process by which the eradication of racism must begin with the "most difficult work of negotiating real divisions, of considering boundaries before we go crashing through, and of pondering our differences before we can ever agree on the terms of our sameness."[24]

Williams argues that one of the greatest impediments to negotiation and change regarding racism in America is that whites simply do not see themselves as raced and marked. Indeed, for them "the majoritarian privilege of never noticing themselves was the beginning of an imbalance from which so much, so much else flowed."[25] Because the Wayanses literally paint their skin white, dutifully and strategically *marking* it, they effectively make whites recognize that whiteness does show itself, that it, too, is an identity marker that has a history and performative elements that can be identified. *White Chicks* challenges viewers to tackle the issue of race by forcing it to emerge from the space of uncomfortable silence, where it usually "tends to be treated as though it were an especially delicate category of social infirmity . . . like extreme obesity or disfigurement"[26] or "some sort of genetic leprosy or a biological train wreck."[27] Unlike the movie *Crash* (2005), in which racism is so pervasive that the systemic power of whiteness is obscured, *White Chicks* reveals the social and interpersonal anatomy, so to speak, of whiteness so as to subvert its normative status and privilege. The movie dares to mark that which masquerades as unmarkable and unremarkable. In doing so, it demonstrates its epistemic credibility vis-à-vis the ways of whiteness.

As explored in Chapter 2, Peggy McIntosh argues that white privilege is an "invisible package of unearned assets which I can count on cashing in each day"; she refers to this as a "knapsack of special provisions, tools, maps, guides, codebooks, passports, visas, clothes, compass, emergency gear, and blank checks" utilized on a daily basis in the white's lived experience.[28] This privilege "simply *confers dominance*, gives permission to control, because of one's race or sex."[29] McIntosh also points out that "whites are taught to think of their lives as morally neutral, normative, and average, and also ideal, so that when we work to benefit others, this is seen as work which will allow 'them' to be more like 'us.'"[30]

In a world where race is real as *lived* and where people of color are denied the sort of power and prestige that whites are born with, whites often remain unaware of their fortune, and when confronted with the possibility of continued inequality, they all too often repeat their belief in meritocracy.[31] After all, this belief helps many whites to ethically deal with the social failures that people of color experience; it allows them to flee any responsibility. The belief in meritocracy allows whites to obfuscate the ways in which their whiteness has social, political, psychological, and economic dividends. Under the illusions of meritocracy, people of color fail because they have failed themselves.

White Chicks begins with FBI agents Kevin and Marcus Copeland (Shawn and Marlon Wayans, respectively) in the process of foiling a drug sting. Humiliated and desperate to show themselves as competent agents, they decide to volunteer to escort two wealthy "white chicks," Brittany and Tiffany Wilson (Maitland Ward and Anne Dudek, respectively) to the Royal Hampton Hotel. The Wilson sisters plan to spend Labor Day in the Hamptons, where only the "hottest people" (read white and wealthy) gather. They hope this year to make the cover of *Hamptons Magazine*. The FBI has received a tip that the sisters are targets of a kidnapping.

As FBI agents, the Wayans brothers challenge the racist belief that black male bodies are always already on the wrong side of the law. Yet they are aligned with the dominant white society ("the man") that employs them.

By crafting themselves as FBI agents, they render their black bodies harmless and capable of fulfilling their comic role. After all, they work with the judicial system that attempts to bring order and control to society and to protect whiteness from the dangerous Other lurking in the shadows. Thus their black bodies qua dangerous and brutal are partly neutralized. They are an appendage of the legal system (the white body politic). They are also "safe" because they are depicted as constantly making stupid mistakes and as the misfits of the agency, which places them in a lower power position than their white, competent male peers. Judith Butler addresses the problematic positioning of the black body as it relates to the brutal beating of Rodney King, particularly in terms of how the video that showed the beating was interpreted—as King being the aggressor. She notes that the black body is interpellated through a racist lens and is "circumscribed as dangerous, prior to any gesture, any raising of the hand and the infantilized white reader is positioned in the scene as one who is helpless in relation to that black body."[32] The police beat King because that is their job—to "protect whiteness against violence,"[33] and since King's body is black, he is always already a threat.

Despite the power and prestige that accompany the Wayans' characters' position as FBI agents, although lower than that of their colleagues, the film highlights how their blackness marks them as "anonymous" Others vis-à-vis whiteness. For example, when they are sent to escort the heiresses from the airport to their hotel to protect them from being abducted, Kevin and Marcus are reduced to stereotypes and thereby erased in terms of their individuality. They are treated as "the black help" as they greet the sisters, with Brittany saying, "We already gave to the United Negro fund."[34] Despite the brothers' initial attempt to reveal themselves as agents, the sisters have foreclosed the need for them to speak for themselves. As black bodies, they have already been assigned a meaning.

Kevin and Marcus attempt to clarify matters by mentioning that they have come to escort the women to the hotel, but the sisters immediately identify them as chauffeurs and accordingly treat them as inferiors. The brothers are immediately tasked to carry the luggage, to pack the car, and to clean out Baby's (the dog's) filthy carrying case. Marcus is even forced to sit in the back of the car with the luggage to make room for the dog because "Baby got to ride in the car seat"[35] to be comfortable. Not only is this a throwback to a moment in American history when blacks were forced to sit in the back of buses, but even the dog's comfort trumps the comfort of the black body. Thus, the black body's integrity and dignity are under erasure in the white value structure of the Wilson sisters. Although the audience knows that the black men are FBI agents, they are able to witness the presumptive privilege and arrogance of whiteness. And while class is operative here—after all the Wilson sisters are heiresses—the presumptive privilege of whiteness, indeed its solipsism and narcissism, is by no means restricted to wealthy whites when it comes to the disparaging treatment of black bodies.

Another moment of white privilege and power is rendered visible toward the beginning of the movie, when the Wilson sisters threaten to lodge a complaint against Kevin and Marcus because of the former's "reckless" driving that lands them in a car wreck—a wreck that occurred because the pampered, bejeweled dog scampered across the top of the dashboard. Just as they fail to acknowledge their white skin privilege and its implications for perpetuating racial injustice, the sisters refuse to concede their part in the wreck and transfer all responsibility and blame onto their black "servants." Having constructed Kevin and Marcus as working for a company no doubt owned by whites, the Wilsons threaten them. This scene is particularly forceful as it underscores the historical power relationship that white women have had with black men, particularly in terms of how this power was shaped around the issue of the myth of the black male rapist. It does not in any way treat the complexity of the intersection between race and sexuality, but the history is invoked by the illocutionary threat. On the surface, the threat's effectiveness is related to the inferior roles into which Kevin and Marcus have been forced, roles that clearly implicate race. Brittany threatens, "I am going to call your boss. No, I'll call the owner of the company. No! I'm going to write a letter."[36]

Concerning white privilege, McIntosh notes, "I can be pretty sure that if I ask to talk to 'the person in charge,' I will be facing a person of my race."[37] Brittany is basically saying that as a white woman she will report the incompetence of these two black men to their presumed (white) superiors. The threat of a letter speaks to Brittany's understanding of who the real power holders are and that power is unequally distributed along racial lines, where whites are those who possess the only real power in America. Also, the threat of "writing a letter" is coded as a move that wealthy whites make to exert their power. While class privilege is no doubt operative here, the Wilson sisters' disparaging treatment of Kevin and Marcus reflects the reality of antiblack racism. Kevin and Marcus respond to the threat with genuine trepidation because they recognize that it is not an empty one: these women have real power and privilege not only because they are wealthy but also because they are *white women*. The FBI agents' black skin can only place them at a disadvantage.

Partly convinced by Kevin and by their own narcissism that the minor scars incurred from the car accident are hideous and that they should not be seen in public, the brothers make the daring decision to masquerade as Brittany and Tiffany Wilson in order to discover who is trying to kidnap the girls—appropriating whiteness to achieve their ends. In "whiting up," there is a doubling of thematic perspective of black consciousness vis-à-vis whiteness. In other words, whiteness is now rendered visible not only through the eyes of the Wayans brothers in their capacity as writers of *White Chicks* but also through the enactment of whiteness from the standpoint of the characters of Kevin and Marcus as black men, adding nuanced detail to match the specific racist and class behavior of the Wilson sisters. As they whiten up, the brothers not only spray paint their bodies but also adopt white scripts in the form of white language, behaviors, judgments, and gestures.[38]

As "Brittany" and "Tiffany," Kevin and Marcus perform whiteness in ways that do not reduce to mere caricature. Their performance of whiteness reveals its sense of entitlement, its solipsism, and its duplicity. For example, the letter-writing threat is repeated when "Brittany" (Kevin whitened up) is asked to show her ID at the hotel reception desk. Kevin (as Brittany) looks down at his ID, and his nonwhite face stares back at him. It is at this point that Kevin enacts a white racial script. He begins a tirade, showing his ("her") indignation for having been asked for a credit card and ID, a common enough situation when one is checking into a hotel, especially one in the Hamptons. Kevin says, "Credit card? ID? I'm so fricking pissed.[39] I want to speak to your supervisor. Better yet, I'm going to write a letter."[40] Getting a pen and paper, Kevin comically begins this fictitious letter writing by speaking the opening of the letter aloud and slowly for effect: "Dear Mr. Royal Hampton. I am a *white* woman in America."[41]

While the audience knows that "Brittany's" only ID is that of the black man hiding behind the white mask, Kevin deploys whiteness and is given the keys and a VIP pass to the weekend's fund-raising and entertainment. If Kevin and Marcus had been masquerading as nonwhite women, this situation would have ended differently, with both "women" being escorted out of the building. The message is clear: to be white in America is to possess a form of property—white skin privilege—that bolsters one's sense of self and one's sense of ontological expansiveness, which involves a feeling of entitlement such that "the [white] self assumes that it can and should have total mastery over its environment."[42]

What is so fascinating about the actors' performance of whiteness is that they must perform it dialectically. Whiteness gains its ontological purchase through the construction and degradation of nonwhiteness. Thus, to "authenticate" their whiteness, they must enact a form of white solipsism whereby the nonwhite is erased and devalued, reduced to a form of nonbeing. This perspective is unique, though, for not only can they enact white solipsism, but they know, as black men, what it is like to be the object of it. Performing their whiteness as if white people are the only people who matter and exist, "Brittany" immediately responds to a man of color (who is actually a Latino FBI agent) by calling him José. The agent says, "The name is Gomez."[43] "Tiffany" simply instructs him to take Baby and clean out the bag. As they treat him as a mere servant, effectively erasing his sense of dignity and individuality, Tiffany says, "And teach him how to say, '*Quiero* Taco Bell.' Thanks a lot, Rico Suave." Brittany quickly adds, "Thanks, Julio."[44] In each case, the man of color is misnamed, relegated to insignificance, and reduced to a stereotype.

The sense of antiracist duplicity is effectively demonstrated when the N-word is introduced. In the middle of the film, when Kevin and Marcus have successfully deceived everyone and have been fully embraced by the Wilson sisters' rich female friends, they are all on their way to the mall when one of the women changes the radio station after "the Wilson sisters" fail to remember the lyrics to Vanessa Carlton's "A Thousand Miles." A rap song comes on in which "Feel a nigga" is constantly repeated. Brittany and Tiffany, claiming that the song is really hot, begin to sing along, an act that their white friends appear to find abhorrent:

GIRLFRIEND: Guys. I can't believe you said that.
TIFFANY: Said what?
GIRLFRIEND: The "N" word.
BRITTANY: So? [*brief pause*] Nobody's around.[45]

They all look at each other, as if mulling some momentous decision. It is a tense moment. The space of silence for a few seconds allows the audience to consider the word "nigger" in terms of its deep and problematic racist history. It functions as a crucible to determine the racism or antiracism of the white women, who smile and then begin to rap in unison: "Don't try to act like you don't feel a nigga." As when laughing at a racist joke when in the presence only of other whites, no one argues against the use of the term *nigga*, each implying that she is in no way uncomfortable with her racism as long as it remains out of earshot of blacks. The implication is that when whites perform antiracist gestures around people of color, such "moral" gestures are, in essence, merely ad hoc.

In some sense, "Brittany's" reassurance that "nobody's around" (that is, there are no *blacks* around) puts the white women at ease in revealing their racism. This speaks to how little respect they have for the other's possible moral indignation toward the use of the N-word. What is also ironic is that each one knows all of the lyrics in the rap song, thus belying their initial sense of moral shock when it is sung by "Tiffany" and "Brittany," which highlights the superficiality of their aversion to the word and their antiracist duplicity. "Whiting up" affords Kevin and Marcus not only the perfect opportunity to catch the kidnappers but also the rare opportunity to observe whites in a specific form of "white bonding"[46] when unaware that they are in the presence of blacks.

One has to stop and pose the question: How many whites actually use the N-word when not in the company of blacks, especially those who otherwise deem themselves antiracist? This scene highlights the importance of suburban/upper class white appropriation of black cultural productions—an additional interpretation that reveals the potential layers of interpretive possibility in *White Chicks*. Thus it points both to the antiracist duplicity of the white women in the car and to white privilege whereby upper-class young white women can playfully engage "blackness" without actually facing the existential hardships and angst of what it means to be black within the context of antiblack racism. One can "musically slum," as it were, without physical proximity to black bodies.

White Trophies and Black Male Sexuality

The relationship between white female bodies and black male bodies, particularly in terms of sexual intimacy, is highly explosive. Black male bodies have been constructed as violent, dangerous, and sexually rapacious. Indeed, American and European history is replete with myths regarding black male sexual potency and the myth of the innocent, vulnerable white female body as the target of black men's uncontrollable sexual potency. Hegel argued that the Negro is frozen in time, mere animal man, without history, and preoccupied with the *sensuous* world, not the realm of abstract representation.[47]

In 1903, Dr. William Lee Howard argued that the "African's birthright was sexual madness and excess."[48] In this white mythological view, the black male body by its very nature is bestial and sexually insatiable and must be controlled, policed, and, at times, if necessary, castrated. Gail Bederman notes that "throughout the South black men were regularly tortured and lynched for consorting with white women, and that even Northern whites feared that black men lusted irrepressibly after pure white womanhood."[49]

White Chicks engages this volatile history in effective ways through the character Latrell Spencer (Terry Crews), who is a black professional basketball player obsessed with white women. As has been argued, the Wayans brothers reflect whiteness back on the white viewers of their film in the form of being seen. In the case of racial-sexual images of black masculinity, the theme is mainly explored through the stereotype of Latrell and to a lesser extent through the assumptions of the film's whites. The effort to show the white audience to themselves, creating the filmic possibility for self-reflection, is tied into the Wayans brothers' presentation of Latrell in exaggerated and full stereotypical display, as it were. The message is subtle: "*I* see how *you* see me. Now, watch me *perform.*"

The performance, however, is designed to show white people something about themselves. The assumption is that these exaggerations effectively communicate to the white audience a moment of self-recognition. While this approach through exaggeration may risk the possibility that some whites will fail to understand the message, indeed, that they will believe that *White Chicks* only confirms their suspicions about the sexually rapaciousness of black male bodies, this should not come as a surprise given the insidious nature of whiteness and the historically ingrained perceptual practices of white bodies. And while it is argued in this chapter that the Wayans brothers' use of hyperbole is an effective mode of critiquing and countering the white gaze, one might also argue that the Wayanses invest too much faith in the hypersexual and hyperbolic stereotyping of Latrell as a site/stratagem capable of turning the white gaze on itself.

At one level, the Wayanses stereotype Latrell's relations with white women to the point of hilarity. At another level, they effectively spoof the history of white America's myth of black men and their alleged obsession with white women. Given that Latrell becomes obsessed with "Tiffany" (whom we know to be Marcus), there is a sense in which the taboo against miscegenation is not actually threatened, though there is an implicit play on the homoerotic.[50] After all, Tiffany is not a real white woman and is thereby not in danger of being sexually "sullied" by a black man. Nevertheless, the Wayanses creatively exploit Latrell's interactions with "Tiffany" in ways that insightfully delineate various subtle and not so subtle racist motifs.

There are moments when Latrell's relationship with "real" white women shows up deep fantasies and fears around the bountiful "sexual virility" of the black male body—even to the point of playing on the theme of that body's sexuality as a site of sadism—and the aggressive sexual appetites of white women who desire to *play in the dark.* In *White Chicks*, white women's desire for the black male body invokes masochism and the white man's greatest fear. So, while Latrell is racially caricatured as a black male, his performance operates at the level of mimicry that speaks to the lies of whiteness vis-à-vis the Black male body.

When Latrell makes his debut in the film, it is at a party where almost all of the guests are white and wealthy in this exclusive, predominantly white Hamptons community. One of the white men passing by says, "Great game last night, Latrell." Latrell replies offhandedly, "That's what I *do*, baby."[51] While his comment reveals a level of confidence as a professional athlete, it might be argued that it has deeper ontological implications regarding issues of essentialism. *"That's what I do"* may indicate a definitive ordering of Latrell as the very essence of athleticism and hence his reduction to his body, to sensuality and aggressivity. Because his athletic career marks him as *the* performing black body, he is also connected to American slave history in which blacks are reduced to their bodies in the form of laborers and toilers. Not only is Latrell physically large; he is also a black man and sexually obsessed with white women. It might be argued that he exists triply in his forebodingness. Of course, in the Hamptons, he is the exotic Other. According to Frantz Fanon, the black athlete "through time has become singularly eroticized"[52] and the black male in general has been mythologized into representing a "penis symbol" that causes the white man to experience feelings of "impotence" and "sexual inferiority."[53]

Latrell steps into the role of the lustful black man within seconds after arriving at the party. With a look of voraciousness in his eyes, he says, "Man, it may be summertime in the Hamptons, but it is snowing up in here."[54] Immediately afterward, making a clear reference to snow (a trope for white women), he sees "Tiffany" and declares, "Now that's what I'm talking about. A white girl with a black girl's ass. I'm taking that home to Mama."[55] Latrell, no doubt because of his prior success with white women, is certain that this particular white girl is *his*. After all, his plan is to take *that* home to Mama. Race and aesthetics are invoked in this scene. In this case, not only is she white, a "genuine" trophy; she also has the distinction of having a black girl's ass. As viewers, we are made to understand that this juxtaposition is anomalous yet something to be desired. But to get the joke, we, too, must be familiar with the "anomalous" juxtaposition. Hence, this alludes to our own assumptions regarding what constitutes *the* distinguishing features of a black female body as opposed to a white female body, which further implicates us in problematic forms of essentialism.

Latrell's desire for a white woman with a black girl's ass valorizes whiteness but reduces black women to the *value* of their asses. To be a *white* woman is sufficient for Latrell, but having a *black* girl's ass is a black man's ultimate dream. He gets not only the best of whiteness, the quintessence of beauty and social power, but also the "very best" that black women have to offer—their asses—which is clearly a form of reductionism. He has the "best" of two worlds: the social, aesthetic, and economic power that comes with whiteness and the sexually primitive steatopygic attribute of the black female body.

Confident that no white woman will refuse him, Latrell makes his move on "Tiffany": "Pardon me. Santa must've come early this year because you are first on my Christmas list. I want to know, are you naughty or nice?"[56] Undaunted by Tiffany's refusal—she places her hand in his face in an unambiguous gesture of rejection—Latrell says, "I take that as naughty." In short, he projects his own desire onto her, effectively rejecting her agency to say no. Given the *size* (a multiple entendre) of his sexual appetite for white women, no is simply not an option. He then evokes the myth of the black male's genitalia by saying, "You know what they say: when you go black, you're going to need a wheelchair."[57] Presumably, this line, despite its reference to a wheelchair, is designed to convince white women to have sex with him. A second later, when a white blond-haired woman in a wheelchair greets Latrell and eagerly attempts to talk to him, she is quickly and dismissively wheeled out of view by Latrell's attaché. As she is forcefully pushed out of sight, she says, "Okay, call me later."[58]

This scene is brilliant in its mimicking of the myth of the black penis. Latrell does not repeat the familiar saying, "Once you go black, you never go back." Instead, he flaunts his sexual sadism with his reference to a wheelchair. This line is an important moment of recognition by the Wayans brothers. Through exaggeration, they return, in mocking fashion, the myth of the black male as a beast, a monster, who is so stereotypically *large* that he promises to paralyze, at least temporarily, white women who have sex with him. As is the case with Caliban, in Chapter 3, the theme of teratology vis-à-vis the dark Other emerges. The scene also calls into question the myth of the black male as predator through the white woman in the wheelchair. It is she, after all, who desires more of the forbidden and ominous black penis. She wants to be hurt. In fact, at the end of the movie, once Kevin and Marcus have subverted the attempted kidnapping, the real Wilson sisters, now out of danger, are seen walking with their arms around Latrell. With a curious yet unmistakable desirous look on her face, one sister asks, "A wheelchair?" Latrell says, "Yes, but the feeling will come back. I promise."[59]

Here is a clear image of the black male body as literally a source of pain but nevertheless eagerly desired. Important here is how the Wayans brothers turn the racist white imaginary on itself through Latrell. As one white woman once said to Fanon, "I used to think about (imagine) all the things they [Negro men] might do to me: and that was what was so terrific."[60] The very thought of being temporarily confined to a wheelchair after coitus points to the distorted white imaginary of the black male body as a paradoxical site of the "terrific" and the terrifying, the pleasurable and the violent. "Terrific" signifies something splendid and yet something that causes terror. The term captures the historical ambiguity around the black body under the white gaze.

The technique of embodying racist myths to the point of mimicry and critique is reminiscent of an unforgettable scene in Ralph Ellison's *Invisible Man*. The black protagonist tells the story of his grandfather who, on his deathbed, advises: "I want you to overcome 'em with yeses, undermine 'em with grins, agree 'em to death and destruction, let 'em swoller you till they vomit or burst wide open."[61] Underlying his grandfather's exaggerated grins and no doubt buffoonery is a hidden script of resistance. Latrell, a veritable sexual *Ubermensch*, overcomes and undermines the stultifying confines of racist stereotypes, exploding the myth of the sex-crazed black male by rendering it ridiculous through exaggeration. There is, of course, as suggested earlier, the risk that many whites will interpret these antiracist oppositional performances as simply confirming their racist beliefs, thus further ensnaring them in their own stereotypical notions of blackness.

The paralyzing black penis is well worth the time that white women will be confined to a wheelchair. In short, they become the willing white masochists, those desiring to be physically traumatized by the black male, the oversized black Mandingo, who is the very construction of the white imaginary. Since Latrell is a "successful" black male, it might be argued that he serves as an "inside" critique and joke for black audiences in terms of the stereotype and reality regarding "successful" black men's relationship to white female sexuality. Nevertheless, I argue that Latrell functions as the quintessential embodiment of the black male body as mythologized through the white imaginary. He is the embodiment of white male fear. Latrell is the unquenchable black penis eager to introduce white women into a sexual universe for which the white male "does not have the key, the weapons, or the attributes."[62]

For the white imaginary, this particular myth is not restricted to so-called successful black male bodies. Rather, it is the black male body qua threatening black penis that constitutes the threat. In fact, for Latrell, a regular condom is insufficient; the joke is that he needs a shower curtain.[63] Thus, it is the white woman who *wants* to be subjected to "wild," "dark," and "primitive" sex, seeing the white male as sexually inferior and in this way communicating to him that his self-image as a protector of white women's purity is a farce created to protect his own self-inflicted sexual anxiety and fears and his sense of disempowerment in relationship to the black male body.

Given his dark and foreboding blackness, Latrell embodies the likeness of King Kong, conjuring up the unspeakable sexual mutilation and terror that Kong is capable of visiting on the innocent and pure Fay Wray. There are, after all, undeniable sexual and racial references that shape the movie *King Kong*. Circulating around Latrell and Kong are significant themes such as fear and attraction, miscegenation, temptation, the exotic Other, primitivism, tremendous risk, and especially danger. At one point "Tiffany" even says to Latrell: "Look, King Kong. Why don't you take you and your 1980 pickup lines . . . climb the Empire State Building, beat on your old big monkey chest and jump off?"[64] Though the audience realizes that it is really Marcus insulting Latrell, the analogy to King Kong carries the intended racist sting as it comes from the mouth of a "white" body. As Tiffany insults Latrell, he persists even to the point of being sprayed with mace, after which he says, "She don't know it yet, but that's wifey right there."[65] Despite the mace, Tiffany is white and that is all that matters to Latrell.

This persistence is also demonstrated when Latrell, in a charity auction, wins a date with Tiffany. He gladly donates fifty thousand dollars (in cash) just to take his white trophy out for dinner. Latrell having outbid the others, Heather Vandergeld (Jaime King), who plays the auctioneer (and who happens to be a rival of the real Wilson sisters and daughter of Warren Vandergeld—John Heard—who plans to kidnap the Wilson sisters for ransom because he has lost most of his wealth), says, "Sold, to the big black guy right there. Step right up and claim your prize."[66] As a white woman, Tiffany is indeed a *prize*. Because Heather and her sister Megan (Brittany Daniel) are the nemeses of the real Wilson sisters, there is a sense that Heather takes sardonic pleasure in the fact that Tiffany has just been "sold" to *the big black guy*.

Auctioning off a white woman to a black man cleverly raises politically highly sensitive counterfactual historical implications and constitutes an effective challenge to the historical differential power relationships between antebellum black men and white women. Heather's reference to *the big black guy* also functions as a form of teasing Tiffany about the threat of potential interracial sexual contact with Latrell. In short, the message is that Tiffany is now in danger of having to be romanced by the *big black guy*, and Heather takes delight in this dreaded fate.

Despite how much Tiffany attempts to spoil the date, Latrell is not moved when it comes to coveting his white prize. She demonstrates the worst social graces at the restaurant, from placing her feet on the table and literally biting off a toenail to ordering various dishes smothered in onions, vinegar, extra garlic, and sauerkraut, and stuffing her food down in huge quantities with her hands. Still, Latrell orders oysters, eager to point out to Tiffany that they are an aphrodisiac. Pretending to spill some of the juice from the oysters, Latrell says, "Sorry. My tongue's kind of big."[67] Despite her uncouth behavior and total lack of social etiquette, then, Latrell still desires her, clearly driving home his sexual obsession with the white female body through his overt symbolic gesture (showing the full width of his tongue) of cunnilingus. After all, she is his "miracle whip," "snowflake," "cottontail," and "white chocolate," terms that he uses throughout the movie to describe her. She is, in short, *white*—the site of perfection that excuses all of her major flaws.

In fact, toward the end of the movie, after Kevin and Marcus have exposed Warren Vandergeld as the perpetrator of the attempted kidnapping, Warren Vandergeld aims his gun and shoots at Tiffany, whom he knows to be an agent in disguise. Latrell immediately jumps in front of the bullet. Later, Marcus (still whitened up), kneels down and thanks Latrell, in a deeper-pitched voice, for doing such a brave thing. Latrell says, "I had no choice. I couldn't let them take my one true love away."[68] In the same deeper-pitched voice, Marcus says, "Hey, dude. I'm not what you think I am."[69] Latrell, obviously aware of the change in pitch, is prepared to accept this, making allowances for the fact that everyone has little secrets. Latrell then pauses and says, "Are you telling me that you are not—"[70] Interjecting before he can finish, Marcus says, "Yeah. I'm not a woman."[71] Simultaneously, Latrell says, "White?" Marcus removes his disguise, revealing that he is a black male. Latrell says that he feels betrayed and deceived. As Marcus explains to him that he is an FBI agent, Latrell says, "Negro, please. Didn't somebody tell you this was an all-white party?"[72] Latrell is not angry because he has discovered that Tiffany is a man. Rather, he is furious because he has discovered that Tiffany is a *black* man. Clearly, Latrell manifests a specific form of racialized homophobia. It is not his "manhood" that had been threatened but his sense of "self-worth" that had been guaranteed by the unadulterated presence of whiteness.

Aside from Latrell's unabashed sexual attraction to all things white, the Wayans brothers skillfully construct his black body as a site of white racist stereotypes. Like the Mammy and Jezebel stereotypes, Latrell functions as the brutal black buck, the mythical black male who is big, oversexed, savage-like, and who is forever on the prowl for white women's flesh. He is D. W. Griffith's worst nightmare, the mythic figure[73] and racist trope that gave rise to the white army of "righteousness," the protectors of white purity, and the architects of white order—the Ku Klux Klan. Yet Latrell belies the myth of the black male rapist of white women. For while it is true that he avariciously craves white women, it is through the subversive gaze of the Wayans brothers that we see the insatiable white women who actually lust after him. The representation of Latrell as a big black buck is certainly humorous, but this representation plays on both white fear and white desire.

The first time that Latrell's body is displayed is at the beach in the middle of the film. The camera zooms in on his feet and slowly moves upward to display his big and muscled body in a pair of black Speedos.[74] As Latrell looks out on the white sandy beach covered with white women's bikini-clad bodies, he says, "Let's go hunting."[75] This metaphor constructs Latrell as the experienced and skillful hunter. The white women become prey, mere game, "meat" to be captured and devoured. When Latrell spots "Tiffany" lying on her back on the beach, he walks over and stands directly over her face, clearly displaying his crotch. As the sexually aggressive "black buck," Latrell becomes the feared black body, and yet, because he appears in an approved mode of white representation, whites are put at ease, made comfortable; he is now palatable for white epistemological consumption. Crispin Sartwell notes that "the [white] oppressor seeks to constrain the oppressed [blacks] to certain approved modes of visibility (those set out in the template of stereotype) and then gazes obsessively on the spectacle he has created."[76]

Another time Latrell's body is displayed in the form of a close-up of a wall-sized portrait with a fur blanket thrown over the waist of his otherwise naked black body—a signifier of his primitivism, animalism, and unbridled sexuality.[77] Latrell's body becomes what Patricia Williams calls "a cipher for bestiality."[78] A third time occurs at a primarily white dance club when Latrell is under the influence of a powerful "sex drug," which he mistakenly drank but had intended for "Tiffany," who switched glasses. As he dances in a wild frenzy, his black body is again on display. Shirtless and out of control, he is a signifier of exoticism and sexual madness. Against the backdrop of a rhythmic beat, he moves his black body amid a sea of whiteness. The Wayanses skillfully evoke the familiar white/black binary where blackness is reduced to the corporeal and whiteness elevated to the mind. Within the white-dominated space of the Hamptons dance club, Latrell's behavior is not looked at as the result of something having gone awry. Instead, this is what he *does*. Thus, Latrell is not just a man dancing in the center of the dance floor; he is *every* black man, *every* uncontrollable black body whose meaning is congealed through myths of the dancing, sexually heightened, gyrating black body.

Mimicry, or Reinscribing Race Essentialism

While *White Chicks* deploys mimicry in insightful and powerful ways, there are times throughout the movie when the specter of racial essentialism (and perhaps even the specter of black minstrelsy)[79] appears to emerge, where questions of the movie's complicity in various racialized assumptions regarding the black body ought to be raised. It is difficult to notice those moments that border on essentialism because, as viewers, we already have knowledge that Brittany and Tiffany are "black." Thus, there is the assumption that we already know what black people are like and what they do. The essentialist traps in the movie remain hidden because there is a failure to suspend the assumptions about blackness that we bring to the film. Instead of being critical of such essentialist moments, then, there is a sense of unquestioned expectation. The following are four examples.

One scene is in the car when the rap song comes on. There is instant recognition and aesthetic appreciation on the part of "Brittany" and "Tiffany." Their immediate attraction to rap music as a musical genre does not raise suspicion in us because, after all, they are black. The rap song is coded as black, as if it is an oxymoron for blacks to find rap aesthetically unappealing. However, there is another moment in the film where the Wayans brothers do challenge a form of raced stereotyping when "Tiffany," in an attempt to make herself unappealing to Latrell, intentionally plays Vanessa Carlton's "A Thousand Miles." Because he likes all things white, however, Latrell is impressed by Tiffany's song selection and happily sings along. The scene's interpersonal dynamics assume that Latrell, because he is black, will dislike Tiffany and so ditch her. In fact, the look that "Tiffany" gives Latrell is animated by a sense of disbelief that he actually knows the lyrics and really likes the song. Like "Tiffany," we too are stunned.

Another scene where essentialism emerges is when Kevin and Marcus encounter the real Wilson sisters' white friends for the first time in the hotel. One woman says, "There is something definitely different about the two of you."[80] Kevin and Marcus believe they have been found out. She then says, "Collagen."[81] "Brittany" says, "You little witch. How did you know?"[82] The woman adds, "Duh, it's totally obvious. Your lips went from Cameron Diaz to Jay-Z."[83] Again, because they are black men, left unquestioned are our typological assumptions regarding the black body's physiology. The friend's observation is deemed accurate because the Wilson sisters are in fact black bodies masquerading as white. The white friend simply demonstrates her expertise in race physiology. In some sense, though, this scene leaves the viewer saying, "But, of course, she is correct. These really *are* black bodies. And don't they, as a matter of fact, have big and fleshy 'Negroid' lips?"

Third, there is a scene in which the white friends come over for a slumber party. One of the women is having her hair braided by "Tiffany." After Tiffany is done, the woman looks in the mirror, thrilled by her hair makeover, and says, "I think that you might have been black in a previous life."[84] The subtext of this comment is that only black people know how to braid hair. While this reveals the woman's own racial essentialist assumptions, Tiffany, as we know, is in fact black. The white friend's comment speaks to Tiffany's braiding ability as an anomaly, at least according to the friend's assumption that white women do not possess the ability to braid hair in such a stylish fashion. We might express disbelief in a man braiding hair with such ease and finesse, but we smile to ourselves, realizing that we know something the white woman is unaware of. Forget about a previous life, "Tiffany" is black in *this life*. The suggestion that she might have been black in a previous life because she can braid so well implies that she, whom they all believe to be the *white* Tiffany, in some sense has preserved her "blackness." The racist doctrine of the one-drop rule is implicated in this scene. The rule says that one drop of "black blood" makes one black. In other words, Tiffany cannot possibly be "purely" white, because her braiding ability belies that.

What is also intriguing is that after "Tiffany" hears her comment, "she" says, "Fo' shizzle my Nizzle."[85] In effect, through a form of vernacular urban speech associated with blacks, "Tiffany" is saying, "For sure, my 'nigga.' I was black in a previous life." If this were the real Tiffany, we might say, "Great comeback line" while realizing that she is simply playing with the vernacular styles associated with many black youth. We know, however, that "Tiffany" is black. And it is because of this knowledge that "Fo' shizzle my Nizzle" loses the surprise of a witty comeback. Instead, it is a style of expression that *we know* is associated with black people. So, not only does Marcus perform an essentialist move of sorts (speaking in his *au naturelle* "black-speak," as it were), but we, too, through our lack of surprise over his vernacular switch, essentialize him.

The last example involves a scene where "Brittany" and "Tiffany" and their white girl friends are at a club. Tension quickly mounts when Heather and Megan Vandergeld challenge the Wilson sisters' girlfriends to a dance-off. As they "battle," there are cheers from many others at the club who have formed a circle around the dancers. Both sides prove formidable, though the Vandergeld sisters win. This "win" effectively creates a space in the film for "Brittany" and "Tiffany" to show off their "over-the-top" dance moves. Not only the Vandergeld sisters are left flabbergasted by their moves; "Brittany" and "Tiffany's" friends also look on in astonishment as these two "white" female bodies break-dance and head-spin, bodily articulations that function as codes for poor, urban, predominantly "dark" bodies. In fact, immediately before they perform their dance routine, sending the onlookers into a frenzy, "Brittany" says, "Let's kick it old school."[86]

It is at this point that "Brittany" and "Tiffany" engage in dancing athleticism that take the onlookers by surprise. It is not sufficient that the audience simply knows that "Brittany" and "Tiffany" are black men in disguise, lessening the shock value of their superlative dancing bodies. Rather, we prejudge those black bodies through the internalization of popular cultural representations that send the message that dancing black bodies are tautological, whereas black bodies that cannot dance are oxymoronic.

In fact, we would have been shocked had "Brittany" and "Tiffany" turned out to be lousy dancers. This would have functioned as a powerful didactic and counter-essentialist move, challenging and exploding our assumptions about the black body. As those who see beneath the white masks, we are not surprised or shocked precisely because our "knowledge" regarding the "nature" of Black bodies is foreclosed. We know that *all* black bodies are alike: they can dance, sprint with astonishing speed, and play a mean game of basketball. This entire filmic scenario, where "Brittany" and "Tiffany" save the day through their funky and cool dance moves, reinscribes a form of essentialism couched in the enduring racist ideology that blacks are primitive throwbacks, reducible to wild, sensuous, and *rhythmic* dark bodies that are completely uninhibited and unencumbered by the norms that govern "civilized" white bodies.

White Chicks is a fecund popular cultural site that deals with profound and subtle issues around race. One important assumption that informs this chapter is that popular cultural media such as movies have the capacity to reveal aspects of ourselves that often remain unconscious. Of course, film, more generally, functions as a powerful vehicle through which we literally *see* the contradictions, prejudices, tensions, and complexities embedded in the interstitial domain of our *lived* social reality. As shown in Chapter 1, movies function as sites of interpellation that hail the black body in deeply troubling ways; indeed, they prefigure the meaning of the black body in ways that perpetuate it as an essence. It has been shown that *White Chicks* functions as an excellent and effective filmic medium in terms of which whiteness is *named* and explored as a site of power and privilege. It has also been demonstrated how the movie plays with and mimics various myths around black male "unfettered" sexuality vis-à-vis the historical depiction of white women as the quintessence of sexual innocence. Lastly, despite the critical black gaze that informs the film, it has been argued that there is in it a problematic reinscription of race essentialism.

5

Looking at Whiteness

Loving Wisdom and Playing with Danger

You might easily be annoyed with me as people are when they
are aroused from a doze, and strike out at me.
—Socrates, Plato's *Apology*

Whiteness is not a topic that is usually covered in college
classrooms. It generates uncomfortable silences, forms of
resistance, degrees of hostility, and a host of other responses
that many of us [whites] would prefer to avoid.
—Alice McIntyre, *Making Meaning of Whiteness*

Education can, and should, be dangerous. —Howard Zinn,
"Freedom Schools"

In 2009, during an address on the significance of Black History Month,
Attorney General Eric Holder surprised many when he said, "Though
this nation has proudly thought of itself as an ethnic melting pot, in
things racial we have always been and continue to be, in too many ways,
essentially a nation of cowards."[1] My sense is that black people and other
people of color have shown far more impatience and fatigue than they have
shown cowardice regarding "things racial." After all, black people and people
of color have nothing to lose but everything to gain from a frank and critical
engagement with issues of race and racism. Such engagement is inextricably
linked to questions of unemployment, bank lending practices, homelessness,
poverty, underfunded schools, environmental racism, unfair incarceration
rates, infant mortality rates, current and historically accumulated wealth,
police profiling and brutality, past and contemporary racial stereotyping,
white privilege, and white power. Indeed, "the allocation of resources, with
correspondingly enhanced socioeconomic life chances for"[2] whites and their
descendants, calls for a courageous confrontation of "things racial."

As a nation, we failed miserably to discuss "things racial" during the Gates-Crowley incident in 2009. It was a prime moment for discussing critically the ways in which whites, especially white police officers, come to construct suspicions of black people based on a history of white stereotypes and assumptions. As a nation, we could have had a courageous discussion about perceptions of people of color vis-à-vis white police officers and how those perceptions have been mediated by a real history of white brutality. What needed to be discussed was the sheer "psychological distance"[3] that continues to exist between black and white people. We really do not understand each other, *not really.*

Had Crowley understood Gates—hell, had he understood what it means to be black in America for the vast majority of black people—he would have been far more understanding of Gates's response to a white police officer questioning him about the ownership of his home. Of course, at that moment Gates should have realized the existential gravity of the situation and should not have risked potentially greater danger to his own life. And while I can identify with Gates's outrage, the history of brutalized innocent black bodies at the hands of whites would have, I hope, given me pause. To give a different contextual spin on President Obama's expression, I would say that as a nation we all "acted stupidly"[4] for not engaging this issue with sustained passion and courage, for not seizing the moment to ask difficult and honest questions. At the end of the day, this is not just about the Gates-Crowley dyad but, more important, about the broader complex history of white racist America and its morally abhorrent treatment of black people and other people of color.

Given that I teach at a predominantly white university and given that I teach philosophy courses that deal with the "reality" of race and the structure of whiteness, I stress the significance of courage and passion in the face of "things racial." In fact, I would argue that I have attempted to create *dangerous* spaces within my classrooms. Although I address this issue of pedagogical risk in Chapter 2, I do not include there a specific discussion of the concept of danger as it relates to pedagogy. While the term "dangerous" might sound off-putting, implying something physically or psychologically harmful, I use it to describe the activity of encouraging students to engage in parrhesia, or fearless speech. Fearless speech inevitably involves vulnerability and the possibility of loss—a form of loss that speaks to the possibility of a radically new understanding of the self and the historical forces that have affected the formation of the self, a type of understanding that strives to translate itself into praxes that challenge sites of oppression and dehumanization.

A few weeks into my classes on race, anxiety, misunderstanding, defensiveness, trepidation, anger, and stubbornness are already present. Indeed, at the start of my courses most white students arrive believing that whiteness is something that is irrelevant, a mere accidental phenotypic marker. Some, though, arrive with a willingness to grant at least a modicum of significance to whiteness and how it affects their lives in their relation to people of color. My sense is that by the time they set foot in my classes, the "violence" has already been done; they have already undergone a type of violence of being taught to think of themselves as normative, as human qua human.

Students of color, particularly my African American students, arrive already more than able to name the ways in which they have undergone the violence of relentless assumptions that have identified them as different, deviant, raced. They arrive already knowing what it is like to be profiled, stopped, and harassed because they are black. In short, they know what it is like to have their sense of themselves challenged by white assumptions. Yet *in spite of* this, they have learned to succeed, to sustain a positive sense of who they are, and to survive. My white students arrive already with socially fortified white identities that are certain of who they are, identities that resist being moved, challenged, and addressed by a style of discourse that refuses to be safe, a style of discourse that walks the precipice of danger, on the edge of loss, and on the edge of inviting the real possibility of being wounded and having one's white narcissism, vanity, and presumptuousness shattered.

Loving wisdom is an act of "playing" with danger. By "playing," I do not mean amusing oneself; I mean being daring, audacious, and heroic, though not foolish. Given the history of white racism in this country, black people have always had to walk the precipice of danger. While maintaining bodily survival and psychic integrity, they have had to face existentially catastrophic dangers. I would argue that doing philosophy-in-black can also function as a site of danger. The field of philosophy can cost black people, and other people of color, their psychic integrity. In fact, for some it may very well cost them their identities as black. In a world in which black people are still thought of as bestial and where they continue to signify intellectual inferiority, some black philosophers may opt to be "white," moving within academic spaces, signifying, "I'm not like one of *them*!" Refusing to explore race philosophically, even denying its *philosophical* and *existential* relevance, they lose themselves at philosophical conferences, attending sessions where the "real" philosophical stuff is being discussed, avoiding those who look like them, and always feeling that sense of philosophical nobility granted by white philosophers who have come to see them as honorary whites. My point is that, given Western philosophy's historical status as white and its continued existence as perhaps the "whitest" site within the humanities, the act of "loving wisdom," which, in this case, is really an act of "loving whiteness," may entangle some black bodies in a seductive yet deadly fascination with whiteness that leads to profound acts of self-loathing. The process of interpellation is certainly active: "Hey, you! That's right, *you!* We want you to teach in our department. We'll let you do your 'race thing,' but don't forget about the fundamental orientation of this institution; don't forget about the white bodies and white power that recognized you as 'one of us.' In short, don't forget that we, whites, *hired you.* We want you, because you reflect 'us.'" As Sara Ahmed writes, "Whiteness is what the institution is oriented 'around,' so that even bodies that might not appear white still have to inhabit whiteness, if they are to get 'in.'"[5] One ought to wonder about the specific white normative frame that structures such spaces, its disciplining effects on bodies of color, and how such spaces create conditions for manifestations of bad faith vis-à-vis black people. I wonder how many black scholars feel tremendous pride in the fact that they are hired by whites who see them as somehow better, brighter, and, in this case, more *philosophically* sophisticated than their fellow black colleagues. As white and black philosophers joke, laugh, and touch, the weight of white supremacist history and white bodies that are inextricably shaped by that history are conveniently forgotten. One would rather dream, to remain with that sense of "specialness" that can apparently only come from getting attention from white people.

In my classrooms, loving wisdom risks mutual exposure. The losses that will inevitably incur are not to be mourned but to be celebrated. My classrooms, then, are dangerous because they demand so much at the level of personal integrity, honesty, and exposure while not sacrificing critical engagement. I have been in the company of philosophers who are driven (some perhaps to madness) by what they seem to see as the very aim of philosophy—that is, the capacity to show up the weaknesses of one's interlocutors' positions through a powerful act of refutation. They make a fetish of argumentation and conceal their vulnerability. My point here, of course, may function as a larger indictment of the academy more generally. Even though critical, engaged, and passionate dialogue is indispensable in my classes, my goal has always been to foster intellectually honest and humble human beings.

Again, while critical engagement ought to be nurtured and encouraged, I have witnessed emotionless, "Spock-like" philosophers who thrive on publicly humiliating their interlocutors, who are always ready to display their "brilliant" deployment of rationality, which is synonymous with "instrumental concerns of control."[6] Such philosophers desire to master the art of *silencing*, of controlling the conversation and the mutual flow of agency—they colonize dialogical space, shutting down their philosophical "enemies" and showing them who is superior. The scene is so *cock*sure that it exudes male power bordering on the pornographic. But *reason* need not gloat; it need not be mindful of its "victories." Philosophy is not about technocratic control in my classrooms[7] but about practices of dialogical mutual freedom, dialogical reciprocity, and forms of communicative emancipation that are not afraid to walk the edge of danger or to concede that one was mistaken—indeed, blatantly so. My effort is to actualize continuously, to the extent this is even possible, "the potential for communication to provide liberatory, transformative experiences for [white students], allowing them to [continuously work at transcending] their previously 'fixed' understandings of reality and their acceptance of ideas as 'given' truths."[8]

As a way of challenging my white graduate students, of challenging their "fixed" understandings of their "white reality" and the various ways in which they have not questioned their whiteness as normative, I share with them a narrative of my own sense of awkwardness while walking through academic spaces dominated by white bodies. I have especially felt this peculiar sensation while attending philosophy conferences, those that white bodies typically inundate.[9] And while there is certainly no self-loathing, there is the complex and multifaceted sensation of being drowned in a sea of whiteness. Such narratives enrich the philosophical imaginations of philosophy graduate students, drawing their attention to their own taken-for-granted assumptions about the so-called racial neutrality of space. At these conferences, in every direction, there are white bodies moving and engaging in discourse with ease, with no particular sense of being out of place or not at home. The motif of "home" is important and germane, as it suggests the sense of familiarity, safety, and being among those with whom one shares something intimate, something familial. It is precisely this sense of the familial that I want my philosophy graduate students to mark, just as they might bring attention, perhaps uncomfortable attention, to the fact that only white people show up at their home during Christmas vacation or while attending church.

I explain to them that within such a context they may feel relaxed and unperturbed. Indeed, I argue that the spaces at such conferences, for them at least, are inviting and alluring. To be white in these spaces is perceived as commonplace. One is fully engaged, prereflectively so, with the mannerisms and etiquette of white social bonding. But what is the frame of intelligibility that creates the conditions for the possibility of white bodies inhabiting such spaces, "owning" such spaces—spaces that go unmarked as white? It is in this question that danger lurks. For the question dares to mark a space predicated on a history of exclusion.

I point out to my students that part of the structure of this white *lived* space is that it is structured by whiteness, a norm that has a transcendental feature. I share with them that the historical transcendental normative status of whiteness is *productive* of monochromatic sameness, a sameness that does not call attention to its monochromaticity. Whiteness is *productive* of white identity formation, shaping how one sees and how one *does not* see the world. Whiteness also produces conditions of exclusion, exclusion of people who look like me, and it produces the very conditions for racial difference. What this means, then, is that so-called benign philosophy conferences, places where predominantly white male philosophers come to bond, are actually spaces that have been socially constructed for them. They are reminiscent of Dorothy in *The Wizard of Oz* (1939): "There's no place like home." Indeed, there is no place like home in a context where everything feels safe, familiar, and ready to hand. At philosophy conferences, the white social and communicative space "calls" to white philosophers just as my computer keys "call" to me to tap on them, to complete the operation of typing. My fingers are mobilized by my glance toward the keys.

The point here is that there is a dialectical transaction that is smooth and uninterrupted between my computer and my body. My body and the computer feel as though they are made for each other. We complete each other. So, too, within the context of predominantly white philosophy conferences, white bodies move with ease, they complement and complete each other, they bond with each other. Their bodies are mobilized by the entire scene: tweed jackets, bow ties, pipes, white hair, white skin, books on white philosophers—such as Kant and Hegel written by other white philosophers for white consumption—contorted white faces deep in reflection, looks of perplexity, slight hints of wine and cheese on the breath, and strained eyes red with intensity.

The entire philosophical performance, with all of its props, constitutes a site of effective (white) history, a history that points to a continuous chain of white men "jerking off" with wild gesticulations, hands flailing while delineating some supposedly grand philosophical distinction or while articulating a philosophical system that eventually comes to elide its human face. Trained to do philosophy in such normative spaces (that is, white spaces), young white philosophers (men and women) come to inhabit academic spaces without question, without critical self-reflexivity, without readjusting their white gazes. Cynthia Willett understands how these white spaces work in specific contexts where white philosophers and philosophers of color meet. Regarding the American Philosophical Society, she writes, "This space has been marked as white turf by [white] body gestures and styles of movement that work below the threshold of consciousness."[10]

I have often received uncomfortable looks, perhaps looks of incomprehension, from my white graduate students when I share with them that I feel ill at ease at predominantly white philosophy conferences. It is at this point that I attempt to unsettle their sense of themselves—to throw them head-on into that space of danger, that space of vulnerability—by asking them to reflect critically and honestly on the fact that they have never felt ill at ease at such conferences. The objective is to use that feeling of never being ill at ease to unsettle the violence done, to challenge the interpellative power of whiteness as the transcendental norm. There is often a pause, perhaps an uneasy, indeed, "unsafe," moment of a new neuronal link being configured that their white bodies are *not* prepared to undergo. I encourage that initial feeling of *strangeness*. I want them to question their sense of feeling safe within that space, their sense of being wanted within that space, their sense of being complicit in creating that space.

My aim is to encourage a critical sense of discernment by which my white graduate students begin to comprehend the systemic patterns of privilege[11] that provide appreciably different experiences for whites as opposed to people of color within those philosophical spaces. As they continue to reflect, they begin to have a sense of themselves as part of a larger racial and racist historical context that precludes an easy exit. Indeed, as Barbara Applebaum writes, "White complicity pedagogy encourages white students to learn to be constantly vigilant as there is no innocence to hide behind."[12] They begin to have a sense of their own role in the repetition of various forms of normative white bonding and how they now have begun to feel something of a shock, something of an emotional piercing. Yet "such trauma is required because white ignorance and denials of complicity mutually reinforce each other and support a refusal to engage in learning."[13] This is what loving wisdom is all about; it deploys a critical pedagogy "as a way of transforming individuals, providing opportunities for them to become more empowered and perceptive of the influences that shape their thinking and how and what they are encouraged to think and feel."[14]

What was previously axiomatic, a mere "given," has become dubious, fraudulent, and unstable. Once the admission has been made, there is no return to the chimera of white innocence, though there is always the seduction of bad faith, of eliding what one has now come to understand about one's social reality. For the moment, though, my students begin to feel the gravitas of their raced (white) existential predicament, the reality that their fleshy white bodies are agents and vehicles of white power. They begin to feel their whiteness as a weight, a burden to "dismantle." While not fully spoken, one can hear it on the tip of their tongues: "L—L—L—L— Look, a white!" When they see themselves as Cartesian subjectivities, self-transparent identities, and sociohistorically deracinated liberal subjects, there is suddenly a feeling of loss, a feeling of dispossession.

While I theorize the concept of dispossession in greater detail in Chapter 6, my contention here is that many of my white students, perhaps many unconsciously, have thought of themselves as being in total possession of their identities, of knowing who they are. Creating that pedagogical space of danger results in vertigo and self-doubt, but not the sort that René Descartes bemoans. My white students' sense of dispossession drives home the reality of the external world, the reality of white others, the reality of a world and a history of continued white violence, a world that has already claimed and constituted their identities. They begin to feel opaque. This feeling of opaqueness is a manifestation of awareness that whiteness (as the transcendental norm) is the condition of their formation, is the condition of dispossession, is the condition that links them to heteronomous white networks and matrices of power and privilege.

I have had white graduate students privately share with me their sense of feeling distraught over the ways in which the field of philosophy avoids the whiteness question. I have encouraged them to stay in the field and make an intellectual and political difference and not to confuse the act of loving wisdom with the uncritical love of themselves/whiteness; I have encouraged them to see through Western philosophy's obsessive gazing on itself—a form of white narcissism gone wild. My goal, at the end of the day, is to encourage all of my students to be gadflies, troublemakers, and fearless speakers (or *parrhesiastes*) when it comes to whiteness, especially as whiteness is so resilient and continues to be a "permanent" and deeply problematic and pervasive feature of North America's reality.

I want dreamers. However, not any dreamers will do. I encourage dreamers who are wide awake, eyes open; dreamers who are capable of envisioning a different world, a better world, a more just and humane world; dreamers who engage in the efforts of liberation. As Charles R. Lawrence writes, "Dreamers, be they prophets, politicians, or philosophers, challenge established understandings with the new and unfamiliar."[15] In my courses on race and whiteness, I fight hard to introduce the new and the unfamiliar. The objective is to unsettle students by introducing a form of loving wisdom that has the impact of a powerful *sting*.

I teach the *Apology*[16] as a way of encouraging my students to appreciate the daring of someone like Socrates, of someone who would dangerously risk speaking fearlessly in the Agora. I encourage my students to envision how it would be for them to confront white racism with such daring, to engage in a form of public elenchus that makes white racism its focus. Yet Socrates knew all too well that most of us prefer to "sleep," which is a powerful metaphor to describe what it means to live a life uninterrogated. He was thus aware of the constant need "to be stirred up by a kind of gadfly."[17] Some of my white students prefer to remain asleep when it comes to understanding the reality of white power and privilege. They often fidget, a few yawn, and some may even stare off into the distance as if transfixed by something light-years away when asked to examine their whiteness. Others openly resist change, strike out verbally, and stubbornly refuse to accept the implications of their whiteness for them *and* for people of color. There are times, though, when a white student will help nurture a space of danger and dare to risk, dare to dream, and thereby dare to awaken many in my courses from their soporific assumptions and illusions.

Socrates was aware that gadflies can very easily be hit by the tail of an annoyed horse. One of America's greatest fearless speakers/gadflies, Martin Luther King, Jr., refused to be silent in the face of white racism, poverty, war, and imperialism. Indeed, he valued Socrates for fostering the importance of creative analysis and tension in a time of complacency. In keeping with Socrates, King recognized the importance of "gadflies to create the kind of tension in society that will help men [and women] to rise from the dark depths of prejudice and racism to the majestic heights of understanding and brotherhood."[18] Along with countless others, he collectively forced white America to examine itself, to confront its demons. Socrates forced Athenians to examine themselves regarding issues of wealth, reputation, and a kind of epistemic arrogance bordering on the profane.

My effort, however, is not to encourage my white students to become lone figures, especially not white "saviors." We already have too many of those in the fictive world of Hollywood film. I want them to think *collectively*, to seize the moment *together*, though never independently of the powerful and courageous voices, epistemic standpoints, and political praxes of people of color. So, even as my aim is to "shake things up"[19] in the classroom, I encourage my white students to realize that the classroom is a microcosm of society and that it is also within the larger context of our collective and experimental democracy that things need to be shaken up, that *citizens* need to be shaken up; the *demos* needs to be awakened, *stung*. The objective is to become better citizens, better human beings, to instigate a conception of citizenry and what it means to be human that does not reinscribe whiteness as the benchmark of either. I agree with Omar Swartz, Katia Campbell, and Christina Pestana when they argue that to be a citizen is a collective process whereby one is cognizant of his or her connection "to others through a larger community, has opportunities to participate actively in shaping that community, and understands that communal engagement is a primary way of developing individual and collective human potential."[20]

As I engage students in a relatively small classroom space, my attention remains on the larger goal of helping to bring forth citizens who are dedicated to social transformation. Thus, just as we need students who are capable and willing to raise dangerous questions in classrooms, we need citizens who are not afraid to critique hegemonic forces that belie the open-ended direction of critical engagement. We need those who possess the courage to speak fearlessly in the effort "to continuously improve the quality and experience of life for all members of society."[21] Yet as I continue to create classroom spaces that foster risk and openness in critically engaging whiteness and race, I am reminded that there are other, larger extra-academic publics with which one must contend. In short, *looking at whiteness*, even in our so-called postracial moment, can be a dangerous affair. After all, *looking at whiteness* implicates the brutal history of black bodies that dared to return the gaze.

After the publication of my book *Black Bodies, White Gazes, The Continuing Significance of Race*,[22] I was invited to do a radio interview on the Chris Moore Show, KDKA Radio 1020, in Pittsburgh, which has a listener call-in component. I was eager to engage different publics through a form of edifying communication, one that stresses mutual intellectual transformation and moral examination.[23] I was eager to engage my work on racial embodiment, whiteness, white privilege, and power outside the classroom. I found the interview experience rewarding. Chris Moore was a delightful and engaging host.

While some callers responded positively to what I said in the interview, some did not. I recall that one white woman complained about my use of "all those big words." I thought to myself, "What, a black man can't be articulate?" Another white woman accused me of perpetuating racism through the simple act of talking about it. Somehow I was given this incredible magical power to speak into existence the reality of racism. This was not new. In retrospect, I should have asked her if women who are raped create the reality of rape by simply talking about it. Her statement was an insult to me and black people more generally, just as it would be an egregious claim to say that women literally speak into existence the reality of male sexual brutality against them.

As I recall, this same white woman refused to accept my characterization of whites vis-à-vis white privilege and shared with me and the larger listening audience that she suffered from a disability and was bedridden. She went on to explain how she made it on her own, that whiteness played no role in making her life just a bit easier. I think that it is very important to critically discuss the ways in which whiteness and disability intersect. However, her point was not to complicate how whiteness works but to reject the thesis that it makes any difference at all. Indeed, perhaps undergirding her point was an analogous argument to the effect that she was just like me. As Cris Mayo insightfully notes, "The gesture of analogy or complication seems an ill-timed attempt at connection with people of color in a discussion that is about racial division [and differential power and privilege based on 'raced' bodies]."[24] While I was empathetic to the ways in which disability inflects whiteness, this does not change the fact that she was a disabled *white* woman. Given the theme of this book, I'll say it now: "Look, A white!" I wonder what sort of discussion would have ensued had a disabled *black* woman called in and shared her quality-of-life experience of what it means to be black *and* disabled in white America.

It was also after giving the public radio interview that I began to receive e-mail messages that were unfavorable to say the least, although one or two were very positive.[25] I received one message with the subject heading: "You f#cking fool!" Because of the impact of the radio discussion, I reluctantly opened it. It read:

> My dear Yancy: Do you know what you remind me of? You remind me of somebody like that stupid Henry Gates who got a Ph.D. and ivy league tenure at Harvard by being an expert on himself. Maybe you ought to go to the White House and have a beer with yourself and wait for Obama at his door to show up like his dog, "Bo."

I leave it to the reader to make sense of this message, but I suspect that the writer was not edified by my talk. It became even clearer to me that loving wisdom can come at a price, that one can become the target of nasty epithets.

But is it not my aim to create "unsafe" spaces, spaces that refuse to be complacent and uncritical of dominant narratives that render our intellectual capacities and imaginations comatose? "You f#cking fool!" was not what I had in mind. I wanted to come lithe into a dialogue and construct knowledge together. As Paulo Freire writes, "Authentic education is not carried on by 'A' *for* 'B' or by 'A' *about* 'B,' but rather by 'A' *with* 'B,' mediated by the world—a world which impresses and challenges both parties, giving rise to views or opinions about it."[26] "You f#cking fool!" was clearly not an invitation by "A" to carry on a pedagogical dialogue *with* "B." Rather, it was an exclusionary act, one designed to put me "in my place," to mark me as that "fucking fool."

There was a much longer e-mail message from another listener that was not directly sent to me, though it was copied to me by the writer. It was, however, directly sent to the president of my university, to a number of philosophy graduate students in my department, and to the Catholic Diocese of Pittsburgh, specifically to its Department of Communications. The letter was designed to cost me my livelihood. The writer wanted me fired, pure and simple. He could not fathom how a Catholic university would hire and retain someone who would dare to discuss with white students the various ways in which they are implicated directly/indirectly in the reproduction of white racism or the ways in which they are complicit in it. Indeed, he was in no way receptive to the claim that there is a connection between the benefits and privileges of being white in America and the use of the term "racist" to describe those whites who reap them. I imagine that the writer was even more perturbed by the fact that I was African American.

In the context of a radio interview and allowing for time limitations, it was not possible for me to explain the full complexity of my analysis of whiteness. So, to be fair, there was room for misunderstanding. The writer, however, presumed that he did understand my position, its complexity, and its nuances and went on to find ways of *silencing* me. Sadly, he neglected to tarry longer with—and should have tarried longer with—what I said and perhaps gone out and purchased my book. This failure to tarry added to the weak content of his charges. Moreover, he had no knowledge that many white scholars not only publicly declare their white racism, something that I address more critically in Chapter 6, but also theorize white racism as a *system* that specifically implicates whites in its perpetuation.

Unfortunately, his campaign against me did not stop with one letter. The next one was sent not only to the president of my university and the Catholic Diocese of Pittsburgh but also to the secretary and administrative assistant to the university president and to the executive vice president for student life. His third letter was even bolder. Again complaining that my views on whiteness are, as he said, "inappropriate for a Christian University classroom," he sent this one to the Chris Moore Show, to the *Pittsburgh Post-Gazette*, and to the Archdiocese of Washington, D.C. Indeed, the letter was directly addressed to Archbishop Wuerl. Given his obsession with getting me fired, I thought that perhaps the writer's fourth letter would be sent to Rome.

One of the writer's charges reminded me of Meletus of Pithus from Plato's *Apology*, who charged Socrates with corrupting the youth of Athens. For example, in his first letter the writer said, "It does not seem to be appropriate philosophy to be teaching to young Catholic minds." Before that, he had said, "I am sorry that negative pondering on race seems to be such a big part of Professor's Yancy's life. This does not seem like a happy existence." Ah, yes, look, a white! See him? Note the arrogance of his white privilege, how race does *not* play such a big part in *his* life. To be white in America is precisely to live a life in which race is believed not to play a big part, if any part at all. And notice how my existence is presumably unhappy because I spend so much time "pondering on race." Let me repeat: "Look, a white!" If only black people would stop "pondering on race," their lives would be so much happier. Damn, how could black people have overlooked this? It is the fact that black people spend so much time confronting overt and covert antiblack racism that makes them so fucking angry—that's right, *fucking angry*, not simply unhappy. And notice how the writer also takes the time to feel "sorry" for me with such condescension.

This is the substance of whiteness. See it! Don't blink! Whiteness presumes to reside above the fray of race matters, free of such superficial concerns, free of those poor souls who are burdened by such a trivial matter as race. "Look at those whites!" There they are: living a happy existence, thoughtless and serene, concealing their conscience through their collective pity for so many unhappy black souls who have only themselves to blame for their plight. This thing called whiteness is like innocent children, frightened and dependent. They live "on the surface of their days."[27] Is it better to leave white people striving for the "trivial material prizes of American life"? Or is it better to expose them to themselves? "Look, a white!" I choose the latter.

I have always been struck by the power of Socrates's critique of Meletus, for not pulling him aside and instructing him in the ways he ought to avoid corrupting the youth of Athens, especially as Socrates has shown that he does not corrupt the youth and, if he does, it is only unwillingly.[28] One might argue that Meletus contradicts his own name, which means "to care." The letter writer, who henceforward I refer to as "my Meletus," did not once write to me directly. To copy me on these e-mails clearly functioned to intimidate. I became the "object" spoken about, not the *subject* addressed. I remained voiceless as he reported on my pedagogical "incompetence" and "anti-Catholic" sensibilities.

My Meletus obviously did not want to instruct me on how best to educate white Catholic students at my university. He did not desire to enter into a mutually beneficial critical dialogue about the meaning of whiteness, white privilege, race, and racism. Knowing absolutely nothing about my pedagogical practices, and not revealing any desire to ask *me* about them, he wrote, "Professor Yancy's views simply shut down discussion on a very important topic for our country—race." It was actually my Meletus's attempt to shut me down. He wrote, "It's disturbing to me that your university employs a professor who teaches such racial negativity to your students. It's also sad that a Catholic institution employs a professor who is teaching a philosophy that does not seem to me to be in line with Jesus's teachings of love and forgiveness," and he went on to say, "I question whether labeling an entire race in our nation as racist is in line with there being 'no difference between the Jew and the Greek.'"

First, to engage critically in a discussion about the systemic nature of whiteness is not about *arbitrarily assigning* labels but about engaging students to think through various social and philosophical theories on the nature of whiteness and allowing them the space to disagree, to agree, and to support their positions either way. I am, however, familiar with the willful and hateful labeling of an entire race in our nation as "niggers" and how that labeling was and is used to mark a fundamental difference between blacks and whites. The fact of the matter is that blacks and whites have undergone racialized experiences in North America that are significantly different and that speak to differently configured identities, identities that are *real* within the context of *lived* social reality, identities that make a difference in the world—a world that affects those identities. Such identities, while not fixed metaphysically, "are," according to Linda Alcoff, "fundamental to our selves as knowing, feeling, and acting subjects."[29] There are crucial differences between blacks and whites, for example, in terms of how the world "shows up." Hence, "Raced . . . identities operate as epistemological perspectives or horizons from which certain aspects or layers of reality are made visible."[30]

Second, while I understand my Meletus's appeal to the belief that speaks to the outpouring of Jesus's love and grace, this does not negate the fact that black embodied identities, for example, are racially profiled and marginalized against the backdrop of historically white racist negative stereotypes and assumptions in ways that white embodied identities are not. In white North America, then, there is a difference that indeed makes a difference between blacks and whites in terms of how race continues to play itself out differentially and problematically in the context of their everyday lives. By invoking the words of St. Paul, my Meletus problematically conflates important issues that are simply different. We must not avoid critically discussing whiteness, for example, in the name of a "color-blind" (or color-evasive) cosmopolitanism that only sustains the power of whiteness. As bell hooks writes,

"Repudiating us-and-them dichotomies does not mean that we should never speak of the ways observing the world from the standpoint of 'whiteness' may indeed distort perception, impede understanding of the way racism works both in the larger world as well as in the world of our intimate interactions."[31]

Third, since when did confronting white racism, identifying the ways in which it implicates whites in America, including my Meletus, become incompatible with discussions about love and forgiveness? To live a life of sanity and one that did not yield to a collective self-destructive vengeance against whites in an antiblack racist society like ours, black people certainly knew, and know, about the power of love and forgiveness. Moreover, love and forgiveness should never blind us to the continuing existence of white racism or any other forms of social evil. Neither King's deployment of active nonviolent resistance to white racism nor the importance of agape—that "willingness to forgive, not seven times, but seventy times seven to restore community"[32]— in his fight against white racism blinded him to the horrors of white racism during the civil rights movement. My Meletus incorrectly equates the importance of identifying the *lived* complexity of white racism with a lack of love and forgiveness—a blatant non sequitur.

In his second letter, my Meletus wrote, "In my mind, Professor Yancy's beliefs are not tolerant and only serve to divide us." I agree with him, with all due respect, that it is indeed in his mind. And while I would grant that my practice of parrhesia can be challenging and sometimes off-putting, it is not my beliefs as such that are intolerant and divisive. My claim that whites are racists does not require that they specifically hate black people. Why, some of my best friends are racist whites. To say that my views are intolerant and divisive because I hold that white racism is systemic and that white people undergo processes of racial interpellation that structure the ways in which they benefit from racism and become blind to those benefits, it would follow that many white scholars who write about the problems of white racism in a similar philosophical vein must also be intolerant and divisive.

What would my Meletus make of Charles E. Curran, a white Catholic theologian, who writes, "White privilege is a structural sin that has to be made visible and removed."[33] This is precisely what I do. I strive to make whiteness visible and to teach my white students about its *structural* dimensions. If Curran is correct, my Meletus needs to address how he and other whites are able to stand outside, as it were, the *structural* dimensions of white privilege, how they are able to avoid being interpellated by this sin. After all, my Meletus is white, and as such he is implicated in the perpetuation of white racism and racial injustice. Curran also writes, "I have to see myself as the oppressor and as the problem."[34] Curran's self-recognition as the oppressor and as the problem involves the sort of critical consciousness about whiteness that *all* whites in North America need to adopt. Unfortunately, my Meletus would see my suggestion here as a form of generalization and intolerance, not as an important and crucial move that would facilitate a more honest and less cowardly dialogue about white racism. Required, though, is also a form of critical consciousness that grasps the serious existential implications of white privilege for people of color. Curran writes, "Making matters worse, this privilege comes at the expense of others. I have to become much more aware of the role of white privilege in my daily life brought about by the systemic injustice of racism."[35]

In my courses on whiteness and race, I encourage my white students to think about the ways in which they are oppressors, even if unintentionally. In fact, I openly express the anger that they must feel when this consideration is put before them. Of course, I, too, am prepared to reveal ways in which male patriarchy and sexism interpellate and position me as an oppressor, even as I constantly attempt (and many times fail) to refuse the hail and counter the positioning. Curran also writes, "Acknowledging my failure as a Catholic theologian to recognize and deal with the problem of racism in society and the church is only the first step toward a recognition of white privilege."[36] I often have my white students think critically about the interconnections between their religious beliefs and the structural and intrapsychic dynamics of white racism. That is, I encourage them to think about how their religious beliefs (and their overall sense of religiosity) speak to or fail to speak to the reality of white privilege and power. This is not simply to reveal contradictions but to instigate deeper levels of religious and political consciousness; it is to encourage them to develop a more robust understanding of themselves and the complex ways in which all of us are fragile and broken and always in need of moral repair.

In a chapter boldly titled "Confessions of a White Catholic Racist Theologian," Jon Nilson writes, "So, I have to confess that I am a racist. I am a racist insofar as I rarely read and never cited any black theologians in my own publications. I never suspected that the black churches might teach me something that would make me a better Roman Catholic ecclesiologist. Occasionally, I have assigned a short article by a black theologian to my students but never a complete book."[37] Furthermore, Alex Mikulich, who describes himself as an antiracist Roman Catholic, writes about the toxicity of white racism: "I benefit psychologically, materially, and socially from hierarchies of gender and race that result in lethal racism."[38] He asks, "When and how will we collectively acknowledge, celebrate, and learn from the wisdom, insight, and experience of our black, Latina, and First American brothers and sisters?"[39] Curran, Nilson, and Mikulich demonstrate courage and risk. This is the stuff of loving wisdom. It is a mode of being that unflinchingly seeks to tackle the problem of white privilege and power, to be disruptive and dangerous. It says, "Look, *I'm* the white!" It says, "Look no further, *I'm* the problem!"

Critically discussing the complexity of whiteness is not the problem; it is partly the solution. My Meletus did not want to engage me directly about my views on white racism, their complexity or philosophical ramifications. He wanted to render my voice mute. Indeed, in my view, it was he who acted with intolerance and divisiveness. Furthermore, my Meletus acted with arrogant presumptuousness. In his third letter, to Archbishop Wuerl, he wrote, "As someone who donates what I can to the Catholic Church . . . I strongly prefer [my] donations do not go towards supporting a Catholic University that teaches racial intolerance—which [this] University seems to be doing for those students in professor Yancy's classes." My Meletus concludes his letter on a very revealing note: "I am White, while my wife is [Black]. We both found Professor Yancy's beliefs on race to be inappropriate for a Christian university classroom." Notice how he demeans the integrity of "Catholicism" or, at least in this case, the integrity of one *Catholic* university. He firmly believes that his threat to discontinue his donations will result in my being removed. This not only is disrespectful to the significance and integrity of my scholarship, teaching, and service to my university, but it also cheapens, at least in its presumptuousness, my university's moral and academic institutional integrity to stand on principles and refuse to be bought.

The entire threat was vicious and reeked of white power and privilege. At no point did my Meletus stop and think about how his letter-writing campaign was a reflection of white power as it is often wielded in this country. Indeed, I wonder if he thought that he would actually succeed in having me fired. I wonder to what extent, even if unconsciously, my Meletus bought into his own whiteness as a site of power and privilege. It is also important to note how he references his wife. What is the point of mentioning his wife's "racial" identity at all? Partly, it is designed to give credibility to his claim about my racial intolerance. After all, if a black person agrees with him, then surely it must be true that what I teach is a case of racism (or perhaps so-called reverse racism), and hence I must be silenced with all deliberate speed. Moreover, the reference to his wife is designed to deflect any suspicion that he is motivated by racism. My Meletus is perhaps under the illusion that to be white and to be married to a person of color automatically frees one from racism. Not true!

I do agree with my Meletus that "racial intolerance, from wherever it comes, including from African Americans . . . does not seem compatible with our Christian faith." Indeed, racial intolerance ought to be incompatible with the Christian faith. Frederick Douglass wrote, "The feeling of the nation must be quickened; the conscience of the nation must be roused; the propriety of the nation must be startled; the hypocrisy of the nation must be exposed; and its crimes against God and man must be proclaimed and denounced."[40] Douglass was all too familiar with many white racists who deemed themselves Christians. In fact, members of the Klan deemed themselves good Christian folk, "singing hymns at meetings and burning crosses as warnings to black people."[41] Lillian Smith, who has detailed many subtle contradictions in the South, notes, "I learned that God so loved the world that He gave His only begotten Son so that we might have segregated churches in which it was my duty to worship each Sunday and on Wednesday at evening prayers."[42]

My objective has never been to teach racial intolerance but to create a productive dialogical space within which students begin to rethink the ways in which they have been taught to think about race, racism, and whiteness. The objective is to encourage them to develop critical perceptual practices (seeing, listening) through which they are more effectively able to comprehend with greater complexity the workings of whiteness in their everyday lives. Many of my white students have become prisoners to a white epistemological framing that actually resists challenge. Recently, I was putting my soon to be three-year-old son to sleep. He asked me why the night sky was square. Initially, I did not understand his question, so I positioned myself to see the night sky from his angle. I could tell that he was seeing it as framed through the square window. Trying to explain to a two-year-old that the night sky is not square but only appears to be so because of the squared window through which he is viewing it was no easy task. Similarly, my white students comprehend social reality through the white gaze, a white frame according to which the world "shows itself" in particular ways. My objective is to encourage them to see beyond what they take to be real, to reframe reality, even as they equate their way of seeing the world with *the way* the world is *simpliciter*.

Many of my students are shocked by the implications of whiteness vis-à-vis their own lives and how white racism continues to be such a problem for people of color. I am unapologetically blunt when discussing white racism's past and present manifestations. It is a discursive move that is necessary, not so much for its shock value but for its lack of ambiguity. Initially, my bluntness elicits surprised looks and shocked faces with opened mouths. There is often a noticeably thick, awkward silence throughout the classroom. By the second week of class, I have effectively communicated that in our class we should not be "polite" if politeness means circumventing the racial messiness of our lives. My hope is that the dividends will be students who are not seduced by a form of discourse that sidesteps the funkiness of life. When it comes to matters of race and racism, my responsibility is not to let my white students off the proverbial hook. This is a form of critical pedagogy that strives to avoid irresponsibility, which means that I do not take the lives of my students for granted.

My Meletus accused me of using "racist" in a way that "only serves to exacerbate the problem of racism." Encouraging my white students to think critically through the complexity of the meaning of the word is, I must admit, a pedagogically arduous task but not one that exacerbates the problem of racism. While I might incur a great deal of defensiveness from my students—perhaps some even show expected signs of anger, the majority are thankful that I put questions to them that are often deemed taboo. It is as if racism is like the sinister character Voldemort from the movie *Harry Potter*—he who must not be named. Yet racism must be *named*. Its existence must be marked and unmasked. Not naming it, failing, or pretending to fail, to notice it, only helps to obfuscate its existence and thereby deceive us regarding its reality.

In one of my courses, I assigned my students the task of keeping a journal of their everyday encounters with racism. The idea for this assignment came from the significant and insightful sociological work done by Joe R. Feagin and his colleagues. As Feagin writes, "I have found that much blatantly racist thought, commentary, and performance has become concentrated in the social 'backstage,' that is, social settings where only whites are present."[43] I instructed my students, over the course of twelve to fifteen weeks, to record anything that they witnessed in the "backstage" that had racist implications. This was an unusual assignment for an undergraduate philosophy course, perhaps too empirical. Many of my white students seemed skeptical and initially thought that their diaries would be short and sparse. However, the assignment pushed them to new levels of attentive acuity and dispelled any illusions of racism as not being an intimate part of the fabric of their everyday existence. It is important to note that the following observations are from the same students to whom my Meletus insisted that I represent a danger. *Au contraire*, the enemy is white racist America that is permeated with micro-racist acts that shape the sensibilities, beliefs, and perceptual practices of my students, practices that they come into contact with on campus, in their homes, and in other social settings.

Typically in any given semester, white students will attempt to convince me that they constitute a new generation that has fundamentally changed when it comes to treating black people in racist ways. They assure me that they are different from their parents and grandparents. I have yet to be convinced. While optimistic, these white students have not really understood the social and existential dynamics of what it means to be black in America; they have not come to terms with white America's embedded and recalcitrant racist historical past and present. I agree with Richard Wright when he says, "I feel that for white America to understand the significance of the problem of [the vast majority of black people] will take a bigger and tougher America than any we have yet known. I feel that America's past is too shallow, her national character too superficially optimistic, her very morality too suffused with color hate for her to accomplish so vast and complex a task."[44] In the journal entries given here, the reader will note the overwhelming and pervasive themes of antiblack racism, racist imagery, racist jokes, hatred and fear of miscegenation, use of the term "nigger," and racist stereotypes. The journal entries speak to America's distorted optimism and its bad-faith discourse about our so-called postrace moment in American history. Consider the following:

> I was with my family and we were discussing my Super Bowl plans. My dad mentioned how he didn't want me to go downtown after the game because it could get crazy. Someone else agreed and said I shouldn't go off campus because it will be dark and there are black people.

> Walking with my friend, he said about black people, "They all look the same to me."

> I was sitting in my guy friends' room while they watched a movie. One friend poured half his Monster energy drink into a cup for another friend. I told him I was taking a sip, grabbed the glass, and did so. When I sat the glass back down he looked mortified. I asked what was wrong and he pointed to saliva left on the side of the glass and replied, "You nigger-lipped it!"

> I was on the phone with my boyfriend and he asked, "What's the difference between a large pizza and a black man?" I told him that I didn't know, and then he answered that "A large pizza can feed a family of four, but a black man can't."

I was out to dinner with my friend and my text message notification went off on my cell phone. My ringtone is a P. Diddy song, and my friend, joking around, said, ". . . I didn't know you liked nigger music."

Yesterday alone I can count many instances where I heard the word nigger, or a variation (niglet, nig-nog, nig). I was playing video games with my friend, not of African-American background, and he would say the word nigger after throwing an interception or when I would score. Another instance was when I received a text message from my friend, also a Caucasian, and after I answered his question, he said, "Alright, thanks nig nog."

I went to get my nails done with one of my friends, and while we were picking out our nail polish colors I asked her what she thought of a dark purple. Jokingly, she said that that dark of a nail polish would make my nails look like nigger nails.

A couple of friends and I were talking about guys we liked. One girl had a black guy who asked for her number. She said she was afraid because he was so intimidating, so she gave it to him. Later on in the conversation, she said she could never marry him because "if we had kids, I wouldn't know how to take care of their hair."

My friend and I were discussing ways to become rich. She suggested that she should adopt an African baby so he will be a sports star and share his millions with her once he grows up.

Last night, a group of friends were drinking in [M] and [G]'s room. I picked up a stuffed raccoon off of [G]'s bed. One of the boys in the room said, "Oh [M], that's something you and [G] have in common: you both sleep with koons."

One white girl was talking about why she could not date a black guy and she mentioned the black hands. "When they turn over their hand, that is really gross—they look like gorilla's hands."

I was listening to a speech from a white professor. The speech had nothing to do with racism in general, but there was one part he mentioned: "I am not a racist at all—I hang out with African Americans all the time!"

One white guy told me his secret [thoughts] while he was boxing . . . he always imagined his girlfriend being banged by some really big black guy and this [makes him] so pissed that he could go all out in boxing.

My friend's grandmother, while driving through a bad part of town, spotted some black people. "The neighborhood is going downhill," she sighed.

Some of my friends at [University] were talking about Wiz Khalifa before our class started and the one girl made the comment that "black people have two goals in life—sell drugs or try to be a rapper."

My mom and I [were] watching "Teen Mom" on MTV and one of the girls on the show started dating a black man. My mom made derogatory comments about a white girl dating a black guy, and said that he looked like he was "no good."

My dad and I were watching the Grammies and throughout the show there were a few different Black rap and hip hop artists that performed. When one of the artists was performing . . . my mom said she thought that he had already performed a song and my dad said that he was pretty sure this was [a] different guy but you can't be sure because they all look the same. I just gave my dad a look and he said he was just kidding but for some reason it bothers me more when my family make[s] jokes than when my friends make jokes.

I was talking to [a] Chinese girl while I was working. After she was gone, one white customer came up and said: "Hey who were you talking to just now, your twin sister?" "No, we are just friends, and we look so different." I could feel the annoyance coming. "Oh no way, you guys look like you are sisters for real!"

Sometimes you have to stop when you lie down at night and think about what has happened the day before. We have one friend that is Indian. That speaks for about all the diversity in our everyday group of friends at [University]. I do have more diversity than this in my friends but not that I see every day. Comments are made daily towards this friend, about looking Middle Eastern, about bombings, he is called Kumar, and basically he is the butt of many jokes.

I was at a house party for St. Patrick's Day and a guy walked in and greeted his friend by saying "Sup nigga" [and] then stops, looks around and says, "O good there aren't any black people here, I can say that."

At the end of her journal, one white student entered an unsolicited personal reflection that summarized her feelings about the assignment, one that was both insightful and validating.

When I was given this assignment, I thought that I would have a really hard time getting journal entries, but I really have not, which was very surprising to me. Until you really listen to what people are saying and are making jokes about, you don't always realize how racist or negative the outcomes really are. This assignment really opened my eyes up to how many people I surround myself with are racist. I don't think that this means that they are horrible people, but I do think that it shows how ignorant they can be. I think that being white in America can really make someone racist without them even knowing. This is something that needs to be changed, but it will take time and effort to do that. Keeping this journal has also made me think twice sometimes about ideas in my head that I had about other people. This assignment was very interesting to do, and was very eye-opening to things that I never realized were occurring around me every day.

To return to Attorney General Eric Holder, and in conclusion, in many ways we indeed are cowards, but what we need is a nation of brave souls who are willing to confront the reality of white racism, who are willing to pose dangerous questions about the continuing existence of white racism, and who are willing to unsettle the rigidity of white racism through the dangerous act of loving wisdom. As Frederick Douglass said in 1852, "We need the storm, the whirlwind and the earthquake."[45]

6

Looking at Whiteness

Tarrying with the Embedded and Opaque White Racist Self

At the most intimate levels, we are social; we are comported
toward a "you"; we are outside ourselves, constituted in
cultural norms that preceded and exceed us, given over to a
set of cultural norms and a field of power that condition us
fundamentally. —Judith Butler, *Precarious Life*

The white complicity claim maintains that all whites, by virtue
of systemic white privilege that is inseparable from white ways
of being, are implicated in the production and reproduction
of systemic racial injustice. —Barbara Applebaum, *Being White,
Being Good*

I argue that I cannot escape whiteness, nor can I discount the
ways I am reproducing whiteness. I argue that I cannot claim to
be nonracist, to rest in the ideal of a positive racial identity.
—John Warren, "Performing Whiteness Differently"

Avoiding White Racist Exposure

"I see an angry black professor!" That was the response of a white male
professor after listening to a talk I had been invited to give on the
theme of racial embodiment and the phenomenological dimensions
of what it felt/feels like to be an "essence" vis-à-vis the white gaze. I engaged
in a critical discussion of the ways in which black bodies are profiled, stereotyped, and dehumanized within the context of antiblack racism. I theorized
the ways in which the white gaze functions to foreclose the black body from
the realm of personhood, how the white gaze renders the black body ontologically truncated, fixed like an essence. My aim was to bring attention to
the racial and racist dynamics of quotidian social encounters, to defamiliar-
ize everyday social encounters in order to expose the *lived* reality of white
racism and its impact on the everyday experiences of, in this case, black

people. I wanted to create a receptive space within which whites in attendance would be willing to make an effort to suspend (to the extent this is possible) their own assumptions about the operations of white racism and allow themselves to be touched by, affected by, black *Erlebnis*, to glimpse, from the perspective of a site of critical black subjectivity, what it means to encounter white gazes. My aim was to create a space of trust, vulnerability, and risk. The white male professor's response, though, was not one of empathetic identification or trust; rather, it functioned as a form of dismissal. For him, I was simply angry, my judgment was clouded, and therefore my philosophical observations were nugatory. It was about *my* anger, *my* inability to discard cumbersome and misplaced (perhaps even fabricated) charged emotions that for him were clearly the real problem.

While I certainly spoke with passion, which is something that I hope we all do on matters that are dear to us, there was no physical display of anger. All that he could see, though, was my "anger," my "hostility." His response quickly triggered what seemed to be miniature side discussions among others in the audience. I recall seeing another white male in the audience shake his head in disagreement about the imputation of anger. I heard him say, "Righteous indignation, sure." Unfortunately, no one else heard him. On further reflection, I asked myself: What if I had been angry? When did anger and the simultaneous truthful disclosure of pain and suffering become incompatible? After the white professor's dismissal, I raised the ethical problem of pornography and its objectification of women's bodies, asking the women in the audience if they were angry about the ways in which pornography can function as an act of violence and violation, as a form of bodily fragmentation, "visual mutilation," and reduction. Most of them openly agreed, though in barely audible voices. My use of this example was to communicate the point that anger can function as a place of passion, as a place of urgency. I even quoted Toni Morrison: "Anger is better. There is a sense of being in anger. A reality and presence. An awareness of worth."[1]

My sense is that my "anger" functioned as the fulcrum around which the professor's entire narrative of my talk revolved. He could see *only* my "anger." In "seeing" only my "anger," he not only failed to hear me but also, in the process, managed to shore up his whiteness. In other words, "I see an angry black professor!" can be theorized as an instance of distancing whiteness from examination and critique, of safeguarding whiteness. Hence, "I see an angry black professor!" can be described as the deployment (whether consciously or unconsciously) of a white "distancing strategy" to "avoid being positioned as racist or implicated in systemic oppression."[2]

During the talk, part of my objective, as on many other occasions when the theme has to do with racism and racial embodiment, was to put whiteness on display, to mark it, to counter-gaze from the perspective of critical black male subjectivity. Marking whiteness in the presence of whites can be a profoundly disquieting experience for them, especially when the agent doing the marking is a person of color—in this case, a *black male*. As raced and engendered, I am a black male professor, and yet I am also the "hypersexual beast," the "raper of white women," the "shadow lurking in the dark." The context can become downright volatile. "I see an angry black professor!" functioned to erase my critical subjectivity. I felt the shock and sting of gross misrecognition. I became the quintessential angry black man, a powerful racist trope that signified that I was out of control and possibly in need of discipline. Perhaps for this professor and for other whites too timid to voice their views, I was the epitome of the raging black male on the precipice of violence, the academic Willie Horton.

Toward the end of my talk, another white male professor, this time an older gentleman, felt that I had failed members of the audience. He said, and one could sense the irritation in his voice, "You leave us with *no* hope." In fact, he inferred from this that I must be angry because I did not talk about ways to deal effectively with white racism, ways of overcoming it. The faulty inference aside, I responded, "Why do you want hope? My objective here is not to bring white people hope, to make them walk away feeling good about themselves." He reiterated, "Then you must be angry!"

Hope has always played an essential existential role in the lives of black people living in white America. Black people have long rebelled against the absurdity of white racism through a blues sensibility that continues to emphasize the power of transcendence through hope. Thus, it was not that I was unfamiliar or unconcerned with the power of hope, that incredible capacity to look absurdity in the face and yet affirm life. Rather, I was curious about the function of this older professor's desire that I should have left my audience with hope. Indeed, for me, "I see an angry black professor!" and "You leave us with *no* hope" functioned as two sites of white obfuscation. In the former case, as already argued, I was reduced to the mythical angry black male, a one-dimensional caricature, rendering all that I had to say about whiteness and white racism of little or no value. The latter case functioned to elide the gravitas of the immediacy of black pain and suffering and the virulent ways in which white racism continues to function with such frequency in our contemporary moment. In my analysis, both men failed to *tarry* with the reality of racism and the profound ways in which people of color must endure it.

This refusal to tarry with the reality of racism and black pain and suffering is not new. In many invited talks, including the one just discussed, I explore what I have come to call the "elevator effect." I describe how, in the context of an elevator, white racism is performed through the activity of a white woman pulling on her purse and what this means in terms of the interpellation of the black body as always already criminal. I have noticed that many whites, after I present the elevator effect, immediately ask questions that challenge my epistemic status as a black person (and by extension other black people) and my capacity *to know* when an act is racist. For example, I have been asked the following:

- What if the purse strap broke and instead of holding it for fear of being robbed, the white woman is attempting to fix it?
- What if the white woman on the elevator is physically blind and so does not even notice the "race" of the man?
- What if the white woman is claustrophobic and therefore she is simply anxious about being in an enclosed space as opposed to being in an enclosed space with a black man?
- What if there is a *virtual* white woman engaging in racist gestures (pulling on her purse, looking at the black body suspiciously)?
- What if the white woman on the elevator is really a cardboard image of a white woman, one that the black man only assumes to be real?
- What if the white woman is exhibiting behavior that resembles racist behavior, but such behavior is really the result of obsessing about not wanting to appear racist? In short, what if the white woman ends up emulating racist behavior for fear of appearing racist?

Two points follow. First, I reject the epistemic metaphor that is implied in the questions. I am reduced to something of a Cartesian subject cut off from the reality of the racialized social world. Also, by implication, upon entering the elevator, it is as if for the very first time I am faced with something called white racism. Hence, my epistemic task appears to be one in which I must now figure out if what I see before me is an act of white racism. It is as if I find myself in an epistemic predicament, enclosed within my own epistemic bubble, such that I have to ascertain some way of being sure that what I see is true. This sounds like a familiar Cartesian predicament of dubitability, not one infused with and informed by frequent racist and racialized experiences, experiences that are ready-to-hand. When it comes to race and racism, I am already "out there," so to speak. In fact, I am always already ensconced within a social matrix where white racism and the black body (my black body) are continuous and, more specifically, *contiguous*—the meeting ground has already taken place. Black bodies have already been exposed to a daily enactment of white racialized drama; it's not about establishing epistemic certainty but about securing existential and psychological safety in a white racist world already known. There is something artificial and questionable about the fundamental structure of the epistemic picture that is invoked in the above scenarios. It is not as if I am trying to get beyond my skin to know, with indubitable certainty, a world that continuously eludes my epistemic grasp and of which I must therefore remain skeptical. Before long, I will find myself in a solipsistic dilemma that simply has no room for insidious and blatant white racist dynamics. Indeed, skepticism within such contexts may cost me and perhaps even my life. American philosopher Wilfrid Sellars once suggested that I remain critically aware of my choice of philosophical metaphors and the work that they do. Within this context, I like the metaphor of "epistemic contiguity," a form of familiar and embodied entanglement or an intimately shared social integument through which our racial identities are shaped, as opposed to a form of "epistemic distanciation," which invokes the entire problem of representation.

Second, it is the sheer *alacrity* with which these questions are posed that makes me skeptical. Rare are the times when whites actually attempt to understand what the experience is like for the black male on the elevator. Take the last example. The failure or refusal to tarry might very well indicate the power of white narcissism. This question may result from feelings of guilt, of having been in precisely the same circumstances/physical spaces where the racist fear of black bodies erupted. It is as if the white woman, who in this case posed the question, has glimpsed her own guilt and begins to obsess about (lie about) her "innocence" in the form of declaring herself not racist but only mistaken as such. In short, the hypothetical objection is the vehicle through which she relives, at the level of fantasy, her experience of having been in the presence of a black body, only this time she can live that moment as racially innocent. In other words, the "innocent" white self is able to distance itself from any sense of racism through relocating the locus of the problem in the black person's distorted perception of what the white person on the elevator is actually doing. The declaration "I am not being racist, but exhibiting behaviors that mimic racism because I am really anxious about appearing to be racist to you" functions as a performance of a false moment of transcendence beyond racism. As Sara Ahmed writes, "The white subject might even be anxious about its own tendency to worry about the proximity of others,"[3] but in doing so there is a gesture toward white purity.

The listed questions are taken very seriously by whites who raise them. I do not deny this. Yet they are often communicated in a tone that says, "See! I got you. You were so wrong about me." Indeed, the "what if" structure of these questions has the effect of calling into question black people as epistemic subjects and installing whites as all-knowing epistemic subjects, especially regarding their own lack of racism. So many whites I have encountered are so quick to deploy the hypothetical scenario that they not only fail to tarry with the pain and suffering of black people but also fail *to hear* the complexity and reality of the racist situation that has been described. "You leave us with *no* hope" functions in precisely this way. The actual desire for hope, which is the subtext of the accusation, looks toward the future and can function to point beyond the racist mess that whites *currently* continue to perpetuate. Indeed, the presentation of the white self as hopeful can itself function as a way of disavowing one's own racism or mitigating the sheer weight of contemporary racism.

Hoping for the end of white racism or hoping for a panacea for it can function as a way of distinguishing oneself from those "really racist whites who are without hope." After all, the white who hopes for the end of white racism is no doubt a "good white." As a "good white," he or she is already positioned beyond the muck and mire of contemporary forms of white racism, has already come to terms with his or her racist *past*. Then again, I have encountered many whites who give the impression that they were born from the head of a god, as Athena was born from the head of Zeus, fully mature and unscathed by the reality of white racism. I firmly believe that whites ought to possess hope, "for without hope, the future would be decided, and there would be nothing left to do."[4] But I am critical of forms of hope that "rush to 'inhabit' a 'beyond' to the work of exposing racism, as that which structures the present."[5]

I encourage whites to dwell in spaces that make them deeply uncomfortable, to stay with the multiple forms of agony that black people endure from them, especially those whites who deny the ways in which they are complicit in the operations of white racism. I want them to *delay* the hypothetical questions, to *postpone* their reach beyond the present. Reaching too quickly for hope can elide the importance of exposure. As in the tale of Odysseus and the Sirens, whites often fail to run the risk of being truly touched by the Other, exposed to the Other's voice, narrative, and experiences. Odysseus wanted to hear the Sirens and yet play it safe. He wanted to be affected by them without risking fundamental transformation through a radical act of exposure. Indeed, he undermined the very possibility of genuine exposure by stipulating the conditions of the encounter, conditions that allowed some semblance of exposure without the important feature of letting go, both literally and figuratively. That is why he tied himself to a mast and made sure that his shipmates stuffed wax in their ears so that neither he nor they would succumb to death. Yet there are forms of "death" that should be welcomed. There is the death of obstinacy, the death of narcissism, and the death of fear of change for the better.

Ahmed writes:

> To hear the work of exposure requires that white subjects inhabit the critique, *with its lengthy duration,* and to recognize the world that is re-described by the critique as one in which they live. The desire to act in a non-racist or anti-racist way when one hears about racism, in my view, can function as a defense against hearing how that racism implicates white subjects, in the sense that it shapes the spaces inhabited by white subjects in the unfinished present.[6]

The unfinished present is where I want whites to tarry (though not permanently remain), to listen, to recognize the complexity and weight of the current existence of white racism, to attempt to understand the ways in which they perpetuate racism, and to begin to think about the incredible difficulty involved in undoing it. Ahmed *locates* this tendency to flee the unfinished business of white racism vis-à-vis whites who ask, "But what can we do?" She argues, "But the question . . . can work to *block* hearing; in moving on from the present towards the future, it can also move away from the object of critique, or place the white subject 'outside' that critique in the present of hearing. In other words, the desire to act, to move, or even to move on, can stop the message 'getting through.'"[7] I would not argue that *all* hypothetical scenarios or critiques of instances that black people point to as racist are actually modes of obfuscation or flight by whites who deny (consciously or not) their own racism. However, like Ahmed, I want to interrogate how various white responses move "too quickly past the exposure of racism and hence ['risk'] such concealment"[8] of their own white racism—indeed, conceal it. In short, then, my sense is that "I see an angry black professor!" and "You leave us with *no* hope" both functioned to relocate the two white males "outside" the framework of my analysis of the pervasive, complex, and insidious nature of white racism. As such, they were able to retreat from exposure and find shelter from acknowledging its unfinished present.

The metaphor of "seeking shelter" or "finding shelter" in the face of white racism's reality is powerful in terms of identifying the ways in which white people obfuscate the reality of their whiteness and insidiously reinscribe and reinforce white power and privilege. In a course that I regularly teach entitled "Race Matters," my students and I were discussing bell hooks's understanding of whiteness as a site of terror. I asked the class, which was predominantly white, in what ways they thought whiteness, in our contemporary moment, constitutes a site of terror. In retrospect, I see that I wanted to get a sense of how white students related to hooks's understanding of whiteness as a site of "traumatic pain and anguish that remains a consequence of white racist domination, a psychic state that informs and shapes the way black folks 'see' whiteness."[9] My hope was that they might get a sense of whiteness from the perspective of black people. I also wanted them to begin to interrogate whiteness as a site and signifier of "goodness," "purity," as something benign.[10] Indeed, I wanted them to begin to rethink ways in which they felt comfortable in their own white skin.

One white student said that she did not understand how her whiteness could possibly be a site of terror as she did not own any black people as slaves and was not violent toward black people. She was able to rush past the aim of the question by disassociating *herself* from a certain period in American history and thus relegate white terror to the remote past. In fact, I had the impression that she saw herself as just a *person*, pure and simple, free from any entanglements having to do with the socially chaotic and archaic history of slavery, black codes, and Jim Crow. It was then that a black student shared that she had attended an all-white school and was referred to as "the black girl." She specifically explained how she felt denuded of her subjectivity, her complexity. She made sure to specify how psychologically damaging it felt *to be treated* as "the black girl," not simply to be nominated as such. Another white student interjected, "I know exactly what she means! I lived in a black neighborhood and they referred to me as 'the white girl.'"

Without belittling my white student's experience, I must say that this was an important pedagogical and philosophical moment to point out how the failure of exposure operates insidiously. There was the need to mark whiteness *publicly*, to call it out: "Look, a white!" I was not looking for a public confession of guilt or an admittance of shame. Within the context of whiteness, it is easy to move from a "badge of shame or guilt" to a "badge of honor or goodness." After all, such public displays can easily function to reinstall the "moral purity" of the white self. Through an act of white prestidigitation, as it were, public confessions of shame and guilt become instantiations of white ethical pride. "The presumption that saying is doing—that being sorry means that we have overcome the very thing we are sorry about—hence works to support [the continuing existence of] racism in the present."[11]

It is not enough, though, to point to the fact *that* whiteness is insidious; one must show *how*. Again, in the classroom situation I am speaking about, there was the alacrity, the rush. More specifically, there was the rush to identify with the black student's experience. However, this form of "identification" forced a conflation that both undermined the uniqueness of the black student's experience of what she saw as an instance of white terror, and it obfuscated the specific power and privilege of the historical uniqueness of white racism. The white student placed under erasure the reality and gravitas of the black student's experience of whiteness as terror by shifting the discussion away from the black student's experiences to *her own* (white) situation of being an object of insult in a black neighborhood. "I am just like you" also suggested that there is nothing special about being white (or black for that matter) in America, despite the fact that America is a country predicated on white privilege and white power.

The fact is that there is a morally atrocious and enduring history of black people as the objects of white insults, which is not to deny that whites have experienced the sting of black insults. Black people, however, have been the targets not only of white vitriolic speech and a long history of racial stereotyping but also of state-sanctioned racial violence inextricably linked to such speech and stereotyping. In short, whites have had the historical collective ideological and material power to enforce such hate speech and degrading racist stereotypes. Through conflating or flattening important differential experiences, the white student sought shelter; she avoided the exposure of how she, *as white*, undergoes processes of racial interpellation that are different from the ways in which black people undergo processes of specific *white racist* interpellation.[12] She was not attentive to the unfinished present of whiteness and how it positions her differently. She did not tarry with or allow herself to be addressed by the experiences of the black student.

In this way, my white student did not hear what was being communicated. In fact, she became the hub of the discussion. Her feelings of white fragility became valorized at the expense of the black student's feelings. Moreover, the discussion of whiteness as terror was replaced by one of whiteness as innocence through both white students' responses. In fact, in both cases each white student was able to disarticulate herself (or certainly imagine herself to have done so) from the history of whiteness and the ways in which whiteness continues to assert its power, privilege, and hegemony. In both cases, especially the latter, the white students reasserted their whiteness qua privilege precisely through the presumption of themselves as simply individuals, autonomous and nondescript—that is, interchangeable with anyone else.

Exploring whiteness either in an invited talk or in a classroom, I have witnessed many whites attempt to position themselves beyond the fray of white privilege and power. Indeed, I would argue that they imagine themselves as *completely* autonomous agents, free from the power of white racist effective history. Yet whiteness is precisely the *historical* meta-narrative that affects their sense of themselves as atomic individuals and as sites of exclusive transcendence.[13] Whites see themselves, even if unconsciously, as raceless, as abstract minds, spectral beings, as constituting the transcendental norm. And because this conception of the white self has complex historical links with European modernity and imperialism, it presupposes a problematic philosophical anthropology that comes with a misanthropic dialectic—that is, that black people vis-à-vis whites are ontologically collapsed into pure facticity, constituting the very quintessence of racial assignment and racial degeneracy/inferiority. This view of the white subject, though, obscures its status as *raced* and elevates it to the status of human qua human. As a result, white subjects come to see the problem of race as an issue for people of color. After all, as white, they "transcend" the particularity and messiness of race. They inhabit the sphere of universality. They are "free" to move through the stream of history unmarked by race, for the problem of race pertains to "those Others."

The ease with which many whites presume to distance themselves from white privilege and power can be shown in the following example. I was asked by a white colleague, who teaches at a relatively small private college, to give a talk in one of his philosophy classes about my work on racial embodiment and whiteness. I have had the pleasure of giving many such invited talks at various universities and colleges since the publication of my book *Black Bodies, White Gazes: The Continuing Significance of Race.*[14] There was one white male student in the class who, after my talk, was very insistent about how he conceptualized his relationship to white privilege, race, and racism. He announced to the entire class that he could, and so would, live his life without concern for such issues. He said this with no hint of irony, humor, or doubt. He publicly narrated a sense of himself as completely detached and detachable from such issues and did so in a cavalier fashion.

Seconds afterward, one of the two female students in the room launched into an astute critique that also functioned as a passionate plea. With tears flowing down her face, she pointed out to him how her life is constantly inundated with issues of social responsibility and how she experiences pain and dread directly related to race, racism, and sexism. Explaining that she was white and Arab, she said that she was constantly on edge about doing the "right thing," doing well on exams, and so forth, lest whites generalize from her to all Muslims. Within our post-9/11 context, she had all the more reason to be concerned about prejudices against persons of the Islamic faith. She talked about how she was perceived when in Muslim garb and how she felt as a woman living in a sexist society. It was one of the most passionate responses that I had heard from an undergraduate in discussions of whiteness, white privilege, and sexism. I turned to look into the eyes of the only African American female student who was sitting next to her, and she too was crying, wiping her eyes. This was no longer about abstract philosophical responses but about suffering bodies that navigate social spaces that are oppressive, complex, and ambiguous.

I felt myself growing impatient with what seemed familiar: white privilege, white hubris, and white solipsism. I encouraged the white male student to think about the ways in which his understanding of his identity vis-à-vis white privilege, race, and racism was itself an expression of white privilege. Barbara Applebaum argues that "the mere fact that they [whites] can question the existence of systemic oppression is a function of their privilege to choose to ignore discussions of systemic oppression or not."[15] I also raised the question of whether it was even possible for him, as white, to live his life without already being complicit in the systemic operational power of white privilege. I questioned his conception of the atomic, liberal self that he assumed. I argued that he had already been constituted as white and that it was therefore already too late to make claims about a social identity that undergirded aspirations and assumptions that presupposed an *asocial* self. I also suggested that his view of himself might very well border on moral apathy in the face of white racism.

Toward the end of the class, I sensed what may have been a slight nod of agreement from this student. What was unclear to me was whether or not he really understood the deeper social justice issues that were at stake given his social ontological constitution as white and the complex ways in which his identity was always already ensconced in a matrix of racial and racist relations. I left him to think seriously about the ways in which his white self-declaration of "autonomy" from race constituted a slap in the face of those bodies of color who continue to be the victims of whiteness and racism. After all, they do not have the luxury to exist in the guise of Cartesian subjects and *to play* philosophically at wondering whether or not they exist.

After class, the professor who had invited me said that this sort of thing had never happened before in this class. My visit reinforced my dedication to create fearless spaces within classrooms, spaces that take transformation seriously, spaces that must be made "unsafe." There was a moment when I wasn't even sure whether we were still doing philosophy. Something else permeated that classroom. There was the sense that doing philosophy was not simply about clarifying abstract ideas but about individuals who struggle in the flesh to make sense of their lives at an existentially deep and passionate level.

The Embedded White Racist Self

When introducing undergraduate and graduate students to questions of white privilege, I deploy Peggy McIntosh's seminal article (1988) that explores white and male privilege. This article has become staple reading in critical whiteness studies. In it, McIntosh gives forty-six examples of white privilege, the majority powerfully identifying ways in which white privilege continues to exist. For example, in the first person singular, she writes, "I can go shopping alone most of the time, pretty well assured that I will not be followed or harassed."[16] A significant part of what makes McIntosh's article so powerful is the way in which she conceptualizes the white self as complicit in the systemic operational power of white privilege. I have had white students object to the example just given, only later to recant, realizing, for example, that they were probably stopped by security as they entered a store because of their age or attire or because of their multiple tattoos and piercings. I have never had a white student say that she has been stopped *because she is white*.

My objective in using McIntosh's work is to have white students think about the deeper ways in which their whiteness functions to sustain and contribute to white racism, even as they are, understandably, resistant to the appellation "racist." It is important to note that McIntosh actually clears a conceptual space for understanding her own white identity as racist. She writes, "In my class and place, I did not see myself as racist because I was taught to recognize racism only in individual acts of meanness by members of my own group, never in invisible systems conferring unsought racial dominance on my group from birth."[17] In other words, seeing herself as *not* racist is the result of a narrow understanding of racism—as a site of individual acts of meanness—an understanding that is typically held and expressed by my white students. Thinking about racism in terms of what is systemically conferred or bestowed, it is logically uncontroversial to say that, for McIntosh, the extension of the term "racist" includes herself *and* those from her group (other whites) who are recipients of the conferral or bestowal of racial dominance from birth.

One of my white students argued that, if he and a black man walk into a store together and the black man is followed by a white security guard, this in no way makes him (my white student) the racist. Rather, it is the white security guard, the one who carries out the "individual act of meanness," the one who initiates the actual following, the one who has the racist stereotype, who is the racist. However, this student was overlooking the way in which *he* is still the recipient and perpetrator of racial dominance. Indeed, the fact that he is not racially profiled and followed (because he is white) is inextricably linked to the fact that the black man is racially profiled and followed. As white, my student can walk into stores without anyone doubting the integrity of his character and intentions. As Zeus Leonardo notes, "[White] privilege is granted even without a subject's cognition that life is made a bit easier for her."[18] And while he may not suspect that the black man will commit a crime in this situation, my student, nevertheless, can walk into the store on the basis of presumptive innocence that is dialectically linked to the blacks man's presumptive guilt. As Applebaum notes, "Privilege also consists in the presumption of white moral integrity that is, in the larger picture, contingent upon the co-construction of the Black as morally suspect."[19]

There is, in short, a parasitic relationship, one governed by a racial Manichean divide where whites position themselves as its positive term. Indeed, within the context of white racist domination, this hierarchical binary assumes the form of a "metaphysical" structure. As stated earlier, whiteness functions as the transcendental norm, as that which defines nonwhites as "different" or "deviant" while it, whiteness, remains the same. Referring to whiteness as a master signifier, Kalpana Seshadri-Crooks argues, "The system of race as differences among black, brown, red, yellow, and white makes sense only in its unconscious reference to Whiteness, which subtends the binary opposition between 'people of color' and 'white.'"[20] Steve Martinot emphasizes the relationship of dependence in this racial binary: "If whites were to cease to dominate, or cease to exercise a determining white power over any situation, they would lose their identity because they would lose control over the source of that identity in others."[21]

The difficult part is to have white students understand the profound ways in which they are implicated in a complex network of racist power relationships, the ways in which racism constitutes a heteronomous web of white practices to which they, as whites, are linked both as its beneficiaries and as co-contributors to its continual function. White racial oppression, power, and privilege can be conceptualized, though not exclusively, as uneventful acts of being white, such as walking into a store and not being followed. In this way, white racial oppression, power, and privilege are "connected to one's very being constituted as white."[22] As Stephanie M. Wildman and Adrienne D. Davis argue:

Because part of racism is systemic, I benefit from the privilege that I am struggling to see. . . . All whites are racist in this sense of the term, because we benefit from systemic white privilege. Generally whites think of racism as voluntary, intentional conduct, done by horrible others. Whites spend a lot of time trying to convince ourselves and each other that we are not racist. A big step would be for whites to admit that we are racist."[23]

Robert Jensen has a similar line of argument:

I have struggled to resist that racist training and the racism of my culture. I like to think I have changed, even though I routinely trip over the lingering effects of that internalized racism and the institutional racism around me. But no matter how much I 'fix' myself, one thing never changes—I walk through the world with white privilege. . . . White privilege is not something I get to decide whether I want to keep. Every time I walk into a store at the same time as a black man and the security guard follows him and leaves me alone to shop, I am benefiting from white privilege.[24]

Many of my white students have difficulty accepting what I call the "conception of the embedded white racist." In my view, however, this conception helps them to appreciate the ways in which they have missed the socio-ontologically robust ways in which they are *not* self-identical substances moving through space and time, fully self-present and fully autonomous, etymologically a "law" unto themselves. Theorized as embedded in a preexisting social matrix of white power,[25] one that is fundamentally constitutive, though not deterministic, my students are encouraged to think critically about ways in which they are *not* sites of complete self-possession but, rather, sites of dispossession.[26] Part of the meaning of the process of dispossession is that one is not *the* ego-logical sovereign that governs its own meaning, definition, and constitution. The white embodied self, on this score, is "transitive" (etymologically, "passing over"); its being presupposes others, signifying a relational constitution that takes place within material history and situational facticity. The white embodied self is always already constituted through its connectivity to discursive and material practices that are fundamentally racist and in terms of which the white self is already consigned a meaning; it is an embodied white self that has already been given over, as it were, to embedded and embodied white others. My white students, then, have already undergone processes of racist interpellation by the time white racism even becomes an issue for them, something to be critically and seriously reckoned with. Some of them have even gestured toward the desire to "abandon" their whiteness.

Tamara K. Nopper elaborates on a variation of this theme of desiring to "abandon" whiteness. She argues that whites remain "structurally white" (her term) despite the fact that they "go around saying dumb things such as, 'I am not white! I am a human being!' or, 'I left whiteness and joined the human race," or my favorite, 'I hate white people! They're stupid.'"[27] Another way of stating this is that "privilege is also granted despite a subject's attempt to dis-identify with the white race."[28] The embedded and embodied white self is already the product of an anterior multitude of white epistemic assumptions, privileges or immunities, perceptual practices, and forms of white bonding that are experienced as unextraordinary. The white self is already cared for by other whites, who are themselves invested in whiteness in different ways. Judith Butler writes, "The body has its invariably public dimension. Constituted as a social phenomenon in the public sphere, my body is and is not mine. Given over from the start to the world of others, it bears their imprint, is formed within the crucible of social life."[29] While Butler is not theorizing whiteness in that quote, what she says is relevant to my understanding of white constitution.

I try to have my white students understand the ways in which they are materially linked to the public and private worlds of white others, and how the simple act of walking into a store with (white) racial impunity/immunity constitutes the site of a body that "bears the imprint" of white silent assumptions, moral integrity, and greater freedom of bodily mobility/comportment. My white students often rush to think of themselves as purely autonomous selves, especially when the issue of white racism is raised. Here, too, they fail to tarry with the reality of their embeddedness. Again, inflecting the work of Butler, they attempt to elide their racist constitution and, by extension, their vulnerability. Constitution-cum-vulnerability is the process by which their emergence in the world as white is put into play *ab initio*. However, there is no preexisting, stable, vulnerable *white self* that is exposed to white racism. Moreover, there is no ahistorical material "white" vulnerable body that is the starting point of the white self. Referring to the "whiteness" of certain bodies, John Warren argues, "The color of one's skin cannot be separated from the practices that have historically constructed it—pigment is a product of a stylized repetition of acts."[30] I would argue that vulnerability and racial constitution/ subjection are coextensive.

My white students attempt to "build a notion of 'autonomy'"[31] on the rejection of this deeper sense of their white historical constitution and precariousness. In doing so, they reject their existential fragility and white racist sociohistorical conditionedness in the name of an untenable conception of autonomy.[32] Thus, no matter how much my white students attempt to "fix" themselves or attempt to make themselves invulnerable, they are "already given over,"[33] beyond themselves. They are already dispossessed by social forces that fundamentally belie the assumption that the white self is a site of auto-genesis or self-creation beyond social structures that have always already positioned them in particular ways. In short, the white self is heteronomous, though not exclusively so. To rephrase this, I encourage my white students to think about their white embedded and embodied selves as products of *the "law" of the other*—that is, ways of having undergone interpellation, citation, and socio-structural positioning beyond their intentions, especially their "good intentions," beyond their sense of themselves as "self-lawed" or as the site of exclusive transcendence. My aim, of course, is also to get them *not* to rush past the question of accountability or responsibility. Conceptualizing themselves as autonomous subjects, they understand themselves as disconnected from the systemic nature of white racism. Indeed, they often imply that, if they are not directly causally linked to oppressing someone or directly causing racist harm, then they are free from any responsibility.

Part of the problem, as Applebaum brilliantly argues,[34] is that whites presume a causal nexus within which racist responsibility can be directly and causally traced back to their actions. While it is not my aim in this chapter or in this book to examine the philosophically fruitful issue of *responsibility* vis-à-vis systemic white power and racism, it is important to note that my white students fail to understand the ways in which a conception of the embedded white racist self, a self that is also linked to perpetuating structural injustice, highlights their being part of a larger white racist social network of "belonging together with [white] others in a system of interdependent processes of cooperation and competition through which [whites] seek benefits and aim to realize projects."[35]

Then again, some of my white students think that the mere act of acknowledging their complicity is sufficient or that their newfound resolve to fight against white racism—especially now that after taking my course they have a broader comprehension of white racism's socio-structural dimensions—places them squarely outside the social matrix of whiteness. As Applebaum notes, however, "No white person can stand outside the system"[36] of white power. And although it is true, within the context of white power and privilege, that not all whites are impacted by whiteness in the same way, "all whites," according to Barbara Trepagnier, "are infected"[37] by whiteness. It is at this juncture that my students begin to discover that the rabbit hole of whiteness is deeper than they had initially imagined. I explore with them what it means to say that they (and other whites) do not "stand outside" the system of whiteness. I also explain to them that they (along with other whites) are also *infected* in profound ways at the site of their white psyches. This is a point that they are often either reluctant or simply refuse to acknowledge.

The Opaque White Racist Self

Just as my white students have difficulty accepting the "conception of the embedded white racist," they resist what I refer to as the "conception of the opaque white racist." Most of them rely on the assumption that they can ascertain their own racism through a sincere act of introspection, if they "look" deep enough, shine the light of consciousness bright and long enough. Indeed, they assume that the process of ascertaining the limits of one's white racism is guaranteed by an "all-knowing" consciousness that is capable of peeling back, as it were, various levels of internalized racism and at once discovering a nonracist, innocent white core. My white students presume that when it comes to the complexity and depth of their own racism, they possess the capacity for absolute epistemic clarity and that the self is transparent, fully open to inspection.

Given contemporary whites' moral investment in the rhetoric of a color-blind United States, despite their embeddedness within systemic white racist practices, and the social stigma of being called a racist, I would argue, with Ann Berlak, that "introspection as ordinarily understood is more often an imaginative *construction* than a retrieval process"[38] or an effective method for ascertaining the "truth" about the internal depth of one's white racism. In short, the act of introspection is itself interest-laden and protective. Yet I find problematic the very conception of the white racist self as fully capable of such levels of epistemic depth.

When one begins to give an account of one's "racist limits," the white racist self has already "gotten done" by white racism in fundamentally and profoundly constitutive ways, ways that are densely complex. The white self that attempts to "ascertain such limits" has already arrived too late[39] to determine the complex and insidious ways in which white racism has become embedded within her white embodied self. It is not that there is no transparency at all, that one is incapable of identifying various aspects of one's racist/nonracist white self. Rather, the reality of the sheer depth of white racialization is far too opaque.

In *Black Bodies, White Gazes*, I argue that whiteness is a profound site of concealment, that whiteness is embedded in responses, reactions, good intentions, postural gestures, and denials. Deploying the root meaning of the term "insidious" (*insidiae*), which means to *ambush*, I posit that whiteness is a form of ambushing. I argue that the moment a white person claims to have "arrived"—that is, to have achieved "complete" antiracist mastery—he or she often undergoes a surprise attack, a form of attack that belies any sense of arrival. Indeed, the surprise attack points to how whiteness ensnares even as one strives to fight against white racism. In *Black Bodies, White Gazes*, however, I do not connect the process of ambush to what I now see as indicative of a deeper opaque white self, one that is alien to itself, one that is a site of dispossession. Indeed, it seems to me that the condition for ambush is linked to, presupposes, a *relational* white self, one that has undergone processes of *arrival*. In short, arrival signifies that one has undergone anterior processes of white subject formation that profoundly limit direct introspective access to aspects of the white racist self.

Antiracist activist Tim Wise shares a story that demonstrates the insidious nature of whiteness and the opacity of the white racist self, though he does not theorize the complexity of what that insidious nature entails for the white self that his story presupposes. In 2003, he boarded a 737 headed to St. Louis. He notes, "I glanced into the cockpit . . . and there I saw something I had never seen before in all the years I had been flying: not one but two black pilots at the controls of the plane."[40] Despite all of his antiracist work and the antiracist training that he provided, and continues to provide, for other whites, Wise admits that he thought: "Oh my God, can these guys fly this plane?"[41]

What is powerful about this disclosure is that Wise also points out that what *he knew to be true* was of little help. The domain of justified true beliefs was of little help. So, despite what he knew—that is, that black pilots are more than capable of flying planes—his racism triumphed, perhaps accompanied by deep *feelings* of trepidation, anxiety, and images of so-called perpetually incompetent black bodies.[42] It was not about what he knew to be true through self-reflection; rather, it was about formative racist dynamics that exceed the site of an epistemic subject possessed of so-called full self-knowledge. Wise's experience demonstrates how white racism is embedded within one's embodied perceptual engagement with the social world and how it is woven into, etched into, the white psyche, forming an opaque white racist self that influences (and often overshadows) everyday mundane transactions. Wise is always already linked to the domain of otherness in the form of prior social relationships involving formative, in this case, racist influences. "Oh my God, can these guys fly this plane?" is not a disinterested, individualistic epistemic inquiry; rather, Wise was challenged by "the otherness that marks the boundaries of the self 'within'"[43]—that is, the opaque self.

So, just as the white subject undergoes white racist interpellation in white racist systemic structures and institutional practices, the white self undergoes processes of interpellation vis-à-vis the psychic opacity of the white racist self. One responds, as it were, to the hail of one's "immanent other"—the opaque white racist self. If Wise had been asked before he got on the plane to share his thoughts about black pilots, he probably would have said how important it is to see more "racial" diversity and how this challenges the white monochromatic field of commercial piloting. Yet Wise was *not* asked to provide such an account, an account that would have involved a narrative of racially blinkered introspection, even if sincere. His response, in short, would not have revealed anything racist. Yet he was besieged by what he would otherwise have disavowed had he been asked. The besieging or the ambush is intelligible against the background of a white racist prehistory that "has never stopped happening."[44]

I would argue that these moments of ambush, moments of unknowing, are profound moments of dispossession, which implicate forms of white racist relationality that install white racist sensibilities and iterative white racist norms. As Wise entered the plane, whiteness as the transcendental norm never stopped happening; it had already installed an opaque white racist self. And while Butler theorizes dispossession/foreignness as an important basis of ethical connection with others, I theorize dispossession/foreignness as a source of insight for understanding the phenomenon of ambush. Thus, Wise's dispossession/foreignness to himself within the context of white racism takes the form "I *don't* know myself as I thought I had" or "I am other to myself despite my assumptions to the contrary."

Given my theorization of white self-formation as involving one's "immanent other"—that is, the opaque white racist self—one that presupposes the reality of various destructive processes of white iterative racist practices, some overt, many covert, my sense is that this opacity places a limit on self-knowledge regarding one's own white racism. The experience of ambush interrupts and undermines a form of white epistemic arrogance to give a full account (a belief held by so many of my white students) of the complex dimensions of one's white racist self. My white students gain solace from such a belief. That they believe they possess the capacity to give a transparent and full account of their "nonexistent" racism has the impact of securing the illusion of self-control and a conception of themselves as postrace or as postracist. Given the sheer density of internalized white racism, however, their accounts of themselves *will* fail. They will undergo the upsurge of an ambush experience, its sting, and perhaps experience the feeling of vertigo that discloses profound uncertainty regarding the white racist self—that is, an experience of aspects of the white self as outside their control.

This upsurge was demonstrated when comedian Michael Richards (best known as Kramer on *Seinfeld*) launched into an explosive racist tirade at the Laugh Factory. Pointing to a group of blacks in the audience who allegedly had been talking or heckling him during his performance, he shouted:

Shut up. Fifty years ago we'd have you upside down with a fucking fork up your ass. You can talk, you can talk, you can talk. You brave now motherfucka. Throw his ass out, he's a nigger! He's a nigger! He's a nigger! A nigger! Look, it's a nigger![45]

Later, Richards appeared via satellite on the Dave Letterman show (with Jerry Seinfeld as a guest) and offered an apology. He said, "I'm not a racist. That's what's so insane about this."[46] How does one reconcile his understanding of himself as not a racist in light of his blatant racism? Indeed, in his tirade Richards used the N-word six times, seven if you include "nigga."

How many times does it take a white man to use the N-word before he acknowledges himself as a racist? What is very insightful, though he does not provide any additional explanation of what this means, is Richards's remark "And yet, it's said. It comes through. It fires out of me."[47] Part of what is insane is that Richards thinks that he is not a racist. Perhaps he sees himself as a "good white" who had an otherwise very bad evening. Perhaps he sees himself as the "less bad" white as opposed to the "bad" white. That is, he sees himself as innocent and untouched by the really bad forms of racism.[48] Or perhaps he understands "genuine racism" only in the form of Klan rallies or contemporary formations of the Nationalist Socialist movement. Yet he says that racism "comes through" and that it "fires out" of him.

This is a powerful example of ambush. His claim, "I am not a racist," is falsified and postponed by the weight of what comes through and fires out. His alleged "nonracism" is deferred in relationship to his opaque racist white self. What fires out is the white racist surplus, the white residue, as it were, that exceeds Richards's disavowal. What fires out points to profound and pivotal forms of relational constitution that have taken place over time, forms of exposure to white racist practices that have undergone processes of calcification and sedimentation.[49] Keep in mind that he makes a clear reference to the spectacle of lynching and sodomy. To scream out the N-word seven times with such hatred in his voice for the black body is clear evidence that Richards underwent a powerful intrusion, one that signifies "a prior exposure"[50] to the racist myths of the black body as something deeply problematic, perhaps even ontologically detestable. As Butler says, "Moments of [white racist] unknowingness about oneself tend to emerge in the context of relations to others, suggesting that these relations call upon primary forms of relationality that are not always available to explicit and reflective thematization."[51]

Richards's declaration, "I am not a racist," as I have argued thus far, suggests the limits of reflective consciousness in penetrating white racist opacity. Butler writes that "conscious experience is only one dimension of psychic life, and that we cannot achieve by consciousness or language a full mastery over those primary relations of dependency and impressionability that form and constitute us in persistent and obscure ways."[52]

Lillian Smith provides a profound example of the dynamics of the opaque white racist self in a white woman who, along with other white church women determined to break segregation laws, ate with black people. Smith demonstrates just how relations of dependency and impressionability are fundamentally constitutive, in this case, of aspects of the white racist self. Smith writes that she and other southern whites in their childhood were taught that it was a sin to touch their bodies, for example in masturbation. Along with this lesson, she was simultaneously taught that it was sinful to eat with or play with Negroes.[53] To touch one's body or to violate segregation laws was believed to be abominable and to result in God's punishment. These lessons were subtle, uneventful, and formed everyday white ways of being-in-the-world. Not to play with a Negro was *not* something that needed to be self-consciously reflected on; rather, such modes of comportment functioned as ready-to-hand against the backdrop of a "totality" (not totalization) of other racist practices.

Smith explains one white woman's first experience eating with black people: "Though her conscience was serene, and her enjoyment of this association was real, yet she was seized by an acute nausea which disappeared only when the meal was finished. She was too honest to attribute it to anything other than anxiety welling up from the 'bottom of her personality,' as she expressed it, creeping back from her childhood training."[54] Despite the fact that the white woman in this case was morally at peace while fighting against racial segregation, she was on the verge of vomiting as a result of eating with black people. It was from the "bottom of her personality" that a deep and disturbing anxiety emerged. One can imagine the influx of images: smelly Negroes; hypersexed Negroes; ugly Negroes; savage-like

Negroes. It wasn't the case that the white woman had failed to bracket epistemologically false beliefs. It was not as though she was morally torn regarding the ethics of desegregation. The fact that her "conscience was serene" was of little help in terms of staving off the disruptions of the "immanent other," the opaque white racist self. This is an incredible example because it demonstrates that having a serene conscience or having an epistemologically correct belief does not ipso facto militate against the impact of one's white racism. In the white woman's case, it was clear that her conscience had a strong sense of integrity, but the opacity of the white racist self also seemed to have had a strong degree of "realness" that inevitably manifested itself in acute nausea.

Wise, Richards, and the white woman in Smith's example constitute, as Butler might say, sites of inscrutability in relationship to the opacity of their white racism. They come face to face with themselves as enigmas, astounded by just how deep is the rabbit hole of whiteness. Faced with important facets of themselves that belie the metaphysics of self-grounding and the metaphysics of presence, whites, more generally, find themselves as already having undergone insidious racist forces that delimit the specious claims to absolute self-knowledge or self-transparency. More compelling, perhaps this psychic configuration of white racist opacity has a structural "permanence" that has no exit. It would seem that the attempt to "stand outside" white racist configurations of embedded, systemic power and privilege is also "pointless," also providing no exit. To use Otto Neurath's analogy of "sailors who must rebuild their ship on the open sea, never able to dismantle it in dry-dock and to reconstruct it there out of the best material,"[55] there is no "dry-dock" where white people can go to rehabilitate their whiteness. The white self is already on the open sea of white power, privilege, and narcissism. To invoke the discourse of repair or rehabilitation, there is *no exit* where the problematic white self, the fractured and broken white vessel, can be repaired or rehabilitated in toto and from the bottom up. One must begin with the *racist* white self.

In René Descartes's metaphor, one *cannot* "raze everything to the ground and begin again from the original foundations."[56] And there is no innocent, fictive tabula rasa to which one can return. The white self that *desires* to flee white power and privilege is precisely the problematic white self of power and privilege, a white self whose desire may constitute a function of that very white power, privilege, and narcissism *ab initio*. Indeed, the white self that desires and attempts to "rebuild" or "rehabilitate" itself does so precisely within the context of complex and formative white racist social and institutional material *and* intrapsychic forces.

Conclusion

It is important that whites tarry under the weight of this analysis. The process of tarrying, in this case, is not meant to encourage them in an abstract flirtation with some species of philosophical nihilism, to play Sisyphus, perhaps eventually throwing their hands up in theatrical gestures of ultimate failure, or to engage in some form of disinterested cynicism or to treat the analysis that I have provided as a philosophical puzzle, a kind of Rubik's Cube of white racism. Part of my objective is to have whites to tarry with the question *How does it feel to be a problem?* The goal, though, is not to guilt white people or, more specifically, my white students. After sharing with his father that we would discuss whiteness in my class, one white student said that his father warned him that I—no doubt the marked *black* professor, the one filled with unfounded anger—would attempt to instill guilt in him. Such a warning could have effectively jeopardized exposure, framing in advance what this student listened to and what he silenced.

Tarrying or lingering with the analysis in this chapter is not meant to paralyze action and critique but to instigate action and critique, though always with the understanding that white antiracist action and critique take place within a systemic white racist context of white power and privilege, where white psychic life is formed through sociality—a site of relational constitutionality—resulting in an opaque (and dispossessed) white self that is always already prior to a conscious and deliberate act of taking up the issue of one's own white racism. Tracing the complexity of whiteness does not mean that one does not believe in the *possibility* of something different. The tracing process is not an analytical cul-de-sac. As with cancer, we do not simply examine it because we are enthralled by its cellular morphology.

Fanon writes, "Today I believe in the possibility of love; that is why I endeavor to trace its imperfections, its perversions."[57] Similarly, I have traced deficiencies and distortions. I see myself as adding to the "semantic availability to understand whiteness."[58] But I am by no means a Pollyanna when it comes to the persistence and complexity of white racism and the colossal difficulties involved in whites effectively confronting their whiteness. In the process of confronting her own white complicity and finding different ways to combat white racism, Alice McIntyre writes with honesty and risk: "I've made mistakes in that process. . . . I've learned from them—which is not to say that I still don't make them, or that I won't again. I do and I will."[59] While I'm certainly excited by this sort of realism, I am not seduced into a state of ecstatic optimism.

The reality of "*having been given over from the start*"[60] signifies the reality of a profound white racist social embeddedness and a racist psychic opacity that operates insidiously. As whites resist or take a stand against white racism, it is within this complex social and psychic arena, as traced and explored in this chapter, that the battle takes place. Unlike Tamara K. Nopper, I do not think that being a white antiracist as such is an oxymoron,[61] though I do hold that white antiracists are indeed *racists*. There is nothing contradictory in that statement. Being a white antiracist and yet being racist are not mutually exclusive. Rather, being a white antiracist racist signifies tremendous tension and paradox but not logical or existential futility. In fact, it is from this site of paradox, tension, frustration, and descriptive complexity, and the weight thereof, that white antiracist racists must begin to attempt to give an account of themselves, critique themselves, and continue to reimagine themselves even as these processes will inevitably encounter limitations and failures; indeed, even as these processes will be burdened by the possibility of no *clear* exit.

Notes

FOREWORD

1. Yancy's words implied that, in having no nonracist *core*, the students were exactly like onions.

INTRODUCTION

1. Frantz Fanon, *Black Skin, White Masks*, trans. Charles Lam Markmann (New York: Grove Press, 1967), 112.

2. Ibid., 114.

3. Robert Gooding-Williams, "Look, a Negro!" in *Reading Rodney King, Reading Urban Uprising*, ed. Robert Gooding-Williams (New York: Routledge, 1993), 165.

4. Judith Butler, "Endangered/Endangering: Schematic Racism and White Paranoia," in *Reading Rodney King, Reading Urban Uprising*, ed. Robert Gooding-Williams (New York: Routledge, 1993), 18.

5. Fanon, *Black Skin, White Masks*, 113.

6. Ibid., 191.

7. For more on this subject, see Chapter 1.

8. Mike Hill, *After Whiteness: Unmaking an American Majority* (New York: New York University Press, 2004), 215.

9. Fanon, *Black Skin, White Masks*, 109.

10. Ibid., 116.

11. Ibid.

12. Whites hear names, bear marks, have histories, but such burdens characteristically are not *racialized*.

13. Fanon, *Black Skin, White Masks*, 177.

14. Ibid., 116.

15. Butler, "Endangered/Endangering," 18.

16. See Drew Griffin and Scott Bronstein, "Video Shows White Teens Driving over, Killing Black Man, Says DA," CNN, August 8, 2011, available at http://www.cnn.com/2011/CRIME/08/06/mississippi.hate.crime/index.html?hpt=hp_p1&iref=NS1.

17. Butler, "Endangered/Endangering," 20.

18. James Baldwin, clip from *Take This Hammer*, available at http://www.youtube.com/watch?v=L0L5fciA6AU. Baldwin made these remarks in 1963 while reflecting on racial inequality in the United States.

19. Geneva Smitherman, *Black Talk: Woods and Phrases from the Hood to the Amen Corner* (Boston: Houghton Mifflin, 1994), 133.

20. Butler, "Endangered/Endangering," 17.

21. In personal correspondence, Floyd Hayes wonders whether whites, caught in the clutches of whiteness, are amenable to the "gift" that I seek to offer them. My sense is that part of the logic of gift giving is that the recipient is under no obligation to accept the gift. This, it seems to me, raises larger questions regarding public policy and legislation that protect people of color from the hegemony of whiteness.

22. Bell hooks, *Killing Rage, Ending Racism* (New York: Henry Holt, 1995), 194.

23. W.E.B. Du Bois, "The Souls of White Folk," in *W.E.B. Du Bois: A Reader*, ed. David Levering Lewis (New York: Henry Holt, 1995), 465.

24. Steve Martinot, *The Machinery of Whiteness: Studies in the Structure of Racialization* (Philadelphia: Temple University Press, 2010), 62.

25. Sara Ahmed, "Declarations of Whiteness: The Non-performativity of Antiracism," *borderlands* e-journal 3, no. 2 (2004), available at http://www.borderlands.net.au/vol3no2_2004/ahmed_declarations.htm.

26. George Lipsitz, *The Possessive Investment in Whiteness: How White People Profit from Identity Politics* (Philadelphia: Temple University Press, 1998), 1.

27. Ibid.

28. Richard Dyer, *White* (New York: Routledge, 1997), 3.

29. Terrance MacMullan, *Habits of Whiteness: A Pragmatist Reconstruction* (Bloomington: Indiana University Press, 2009), 142.

30. Ahmed, "Declarations of Whiteness."

31. Ibid.

32. Ibid.

33. Lipsitz, *The Possessive Investment in Whiteness*, vii.

34. Bell hooks, *Black Looks: Race and Representation* (Boston: South End Press, 1992), 167–168.

35. Crispin Sartwell, *Act Like You Know: African-American Autobiography and White Identity* (Chicago: University of Chicago Press, 1998), 9.

36. Supreme Court Justice Sonia Sotomayor, then an appeals court judge, delivered a speech in 2001 arguing that legal judgments are influenced by one's ethnicity and gender. She stated, "I would hope that a wise Latina woman with the richness of her experiences would more often than not reach a better conclusion than a white male who hasn't lived that life." Charlie Savage, "A Judge's View of Judging Is on the Record," *New York Times*, May 14, 2009, available at http://www.nytimes.com/2009/05/15/us/15judge.html.

37. Du Bois, "The Souls of White Folk," 453.

38. Ibid.

39. See Chapter 5 regarding a project that I assigned my students that involved keeping a journal of their daily experiences of race/racism.

40. Ahmed, "Declarations of Whiteness."

41. Zeus Leonardo and Ronald K. Porter, "Pedagogy of Fear: Toward a Fanonian Theory of 'Safety' in Race Dialogue," *Race Ethnicity and Education* 13, no. 2 (July 2010): 150.

42. Ibid.

43. Richard Wright, "The Man Who Went to Chicago," in *Eight Men*, introduction by Paul Gilroy (New York: Harper Perennial, 1996), 214.

44. Dyer, *White*, 14.

45. Fanon, *Black Skin, White Masks*, 109.

46. Ibid.

47. See Christine E. Sleeter's foreword in Alice McIntyre, *Making Meaning of Whiteness: Exploring Racial Identity with White Teachers* (Albany: State University of New York Press, 1997), xi.

48. John T. Warren, "Performing Whiteness Differently: Rethinking the Abolitionist Project," *Educational Theory* 51, no. 4 (2001): 459.

49. Alecia Youngblood Jackson, "Performativity Identified," *Qualitative Inquiry* 10, no. 5 (2004): 677.

50. Martinot, *The Machinery of Whiteness*, 43.

51. Charles W. Mills, "White Supremacy," in *A Companion to African-American Philosophy*, ed. Tommy L. Lott and John P. Pittman (Malden, MA: Blackwell, 2003), 272.

52. Du Bois, "The Souls of White Folk," 454.

53. In 2009, South Carolina Representative Joe Wilson shouted, "You lie" at President Obama during a televised address to a joint session of Congress. The accusation came as President Obama commented on his health care reform bill vis-à-vis "illegal immigrants."

54. This is a quote by Democratic Senate Majority Leader Harry Reid regarding the electability of Barack Obama to the presidency of the United States in 2008. Reid was quoted in John Heilemann and Mark Halperin, *Game Change: Obama and the Clintons, McCain and Palin, and the Race of a Lifetime* (New York: Harper, 2010), 36.

55. Cheryl Harris, "Whiteness as Property," in *Black on White: Black Writers on What It Means to Be White*, ed. David R. Roediger (New York: Schocken Books, 1998), 110.

CHAPTER 1

1. By "conceptually thin," I mean failing to deal with the messiness of race as lived, not conceptually superficial.

2. Clevis Headley, "The Existential Turn in African American Philosophy: Disclosing the Existential Phenomenological Foundations of *Black Bodies, White Gazes: The Continuing Significance of Race*," in *CLR James Journal: A Review of Caribbean Ideas* 16, no. 1 (Spring 2010): 252.

3. Maurice Natanson, *The Journeying Self: A Study in Philosophy and Social Role* (Reading, MA: Addison-Wesley, 1970), 47.

4. Frantz Fanon, *Black Skin, White Masks*, trans. Charles Lam Markmann (New York: Grove Press, 1967), 11.

5. Cynthia Willett, "A Phenomenology of Racialized Space and the Limits of Liberalism," in *Racism in Mind*, ed. Michael P. Levine and Tamas Pataki (Ithaca, NY: Cornell University Press, 2004), 249.

6. Ruth Frankenberg, "The Mirage of an Unmarked Whiteness," in *The Making and Unmaking of Whiteness*, ed. Birgit Brander Rasmussen, Eric Klinenberg, Irene J. Nexica, and Matt Wray (Durham, NC: Duke University Press, 2001), 75.

7. Steve Martinot, *The Machinery of Whiteness: Studies in the Structure of Racialization* (Philadelphia: Temple University Press, 2010), 63.

8. John Warren, "Performing Whiteness Differently: Rethinking the Abolitionist Project," *Educational Theory* 51, no. 4 (2001): 463.

9. Barbara Applebaum, *Being White, Being Good: White Complicity, White Moral Responsibility, and Social Justice Pedagogy* (Lanham, MD: Lexington Books, 2010), 166.

10. Sara Ahmed, "A Phenomenology of Whiteness," *Feminist Theory* 8, no. 2 (2007): 161.

11. Debra Van Ausdale and Joe R. Feagin, *The First R: How Children Learn Race and Racism* (Lanham, MD: Rowman and Littlefield, 2001), 1.

12. Ibid.

13. Ahmed, "A Phenomenology of Whiteness," 152.

14. David J. Kahane, "Male Feminism as Oxymoron," in *Men Doing Feminism*, ed. Tom Digby (New York: Routledge, 1998), 221.

15. Ahmed, "A Phenomenology of Whiteness," 155.

16. Ibid., 154.

17. Judith Butler, *Giving an Account of Oneself* (New York: Fordham University Press), 22.

18. Applebaum, *Being White, Being Good*, 68.

19. Ibid., 59.

20. Ahmed, "A Phenomenology of Whiteness," 152.

21. Ibid., 161.

22. Ibid.

23. Linda Martín Alcoff, *Visible Identities: Race, Gender, and the Self* (New York: Oxford University Press, 2006), 5.

24. Mike Hill, *After Whiteness: Unmaking an American Majority* (New York: New York University Press, 2004), 177.

25. I thank Charles Mills for inspiring this concern.

26. Zeus Leonardo and Ronald K. Porter, "Pedagogy of Fear: Toward a Fanonian Theory of 'Safety' in Race Dialogue," *Race Ethnicity and Education* 13, no. 2 (July 2010): 150.

27. George Lipsitz, *The Possessive Investment in Whiteness: How White People Profit from Identity Politics* (Philadelphia: Temple University Press, 1998), vii.

28. Kahane, "Male Feminism as Oxymoron," 227.

29. Sara Ahmed, "Declarations of Whiteness: The Non-performativity of Anti-racism," *borderlands* e-journal 3, no. 2 (2004), available at http://www.borderlands .net.au/vol3no2_2004/ahmed_declarations.htm.

30. Aimee Sands, *What Makes Me White?* (Aimee Sands Productions, 2009), 1:00.

31. Ibid., 1:34.

32. For a more robust conceptualization of habits vis-à-vis whiteness, I appreciate Shannon Sullivan's *Revealing Whiteness: The Unconscious Habits of Racial Privilege* (Bloomington: Indiana University Press, 2006). I would also recommend Terrance MacMullan's *Habits of Whiteness: A Pragmatist Reconstruction* (Bloomington: Indiana University Press, 2009). While I admire MacMullan's courage, I am somewhat skeptical of his optimism for reconstructing new habits vis-à-vis whiteness.

33. Sands, *What Makes Me White?* 2:30 (my emphasis).

34. Ibid., 3:22.

35. Ibid., 4:46.

36. See Steve Martinot's excellent review of *Black Bodies, White Gazes: The Continuing Significance of Race* in *Socialism and Democracy* 23, no.3 (2009): 199–203.

37. Then again, the act is one that is incredibly *eventful*, particularly in terms of its racially interpellative consequences.

38. See Sara Salih, *Judith Butler* (London: Routledge, 2002), 62.

39. Sara Ahmed, "A Phenomenology of Whiteness," 155.

40. Robert Bernasconi, "The Invisibility of Racial Minorities in the Public Realm of Appearances," in *Race*, ed. Robert Bernasconi (Malden, MA: Blackwell, 2001), 288.

41. Leonardo and Porter, "Pedagogy of Fear," 148.

42. Ibid.

43. John J. Ansbro, *Martin Luther King, Jr.: Nonviolent Strategies and Tactics for Social Change* (New York: Madison Books, 2000), 109.

44. Sands, *What Makes Me White?* 4:38.

45. Ahmed, "A Phenomenology of Whiteness, 155.

46. Thomas F. Slaughter, Jr., "Epidermalizing the World: A Basic Mode of Being Black," in *Philosophy Born of Struggle: Afro-American Philosophy from 1917*, ed. Leonard Harris (Dubuque, IA: Kendall/Hunt, 1983), 284.

47. James Baldwin, *The Cross of Redemption: Uncollected Writings*, ed. Randall Kenan (New York: Pantheon, 2010), p. 79

48. Ibid., 79.

49. Judith Butler, "Endangered/Endangering: Schematic Racism and White Paranoia," in *Reading Rodney King, Reading Urban Uprising*, ed. Robert Gooding-Williams (New York: Routledge, 1993), 18.

50. Charles Johnson, "A Phenomenology of the Black Body," in *America and the Black Body: Identity Politics in Print and Visual Culture*, ed. Carol E. Henderson (Madison, NJ: Fairleigh Dickinson University Press, 2009), 258.

51. Fanon, *Black Skin, White Masks*, 134. Although this quote is retrieved from a section of *Black Skin, White Masks* where Fanon critiques Jean-Paul Sartre's "Black Orpheus," the quote is nevertheless apropos.

52. Brent Staples, *Parallel Time: Growing up Black and White* (New York: Harper Collins, 1995), 202 (my emphasis).

53. Robert Gooding-Williams, "Look, a Negro!" in *Reading Rodney King, Reading Urban Uprising*, ed. Robert Gooding-Williams (New York: Routledge, 1993), 164.

54. Charles Johnson, "A Phenomenology of the Black Body," 258.

55. Marcia Y. Riggs, "A Clarion Call to Awake! Arise! Act!' The Response of the Black Women's Club Movement to Institutionalized Moral Evil," in *A Troubling in My Soul*, ed. Emilie M. Townes (New York: Orbis Books, 1997), 68.

56. Fanon, *Black Skin, White Masks*, 111.

57. Bell hooks, *Ain't I a Woman: Black Women and Feminism* (Boston: South End Press, 1981), 39–40.

58. Ibid., 18.

59. Ibid., 36.

60. Ibid., 38.

61. Patricia Hill Collins, *Black Feminist Thought* (New York: Routledge, 1991), 69.

62. Ibid., 77.

63. Taunya Lovell Banks, "Two Life Stories: Reflections of One Black Woman Law Professor," in *Critical Race Theory: The Key Writings That Formed the Movement*, ed. Kimberle Crenshaw, Neil Gotanda, Gary Peller, and Kendall Thomas (New York: New Press, 1995), 331.

64. Ibid.

65. Ibid.

66. For example, in chapter 4, "The Agential Black Body: Resisting the Black Imago in the White Imaginary," of *Black Bodies, White Gazes: The Continuing Significance of Race*, I theorize black agency and identity vis-à-vis whiteness.

67. *The Heartbreak Kid*, directed by Peter Farrelly and Bobby Farrelly (Universal City, CA: Dreamworks Pictures, 2007), 44:30.

68. Ralph Ellison, *Shadow and Act* (New York: Vintage Books, 1995), 304.

69. Malcolm X with Alex Haley, *The Autobiography of Malcolm X* (New York: Ballantine Books, 1965), 32.

70. Patricia Hill Collins, *Black Feminist Thought: Knowledge, Consciousness, and the Politics of Empowerment* (New York: Routledge, 1991), 70.

71. *Deuce Bigalow: Male Gigolo*, directed by Mike Mitchell (Culver City, CA: Happy Madison Productions, 1999), 1:21:25.

72. Fanon, *Black Skin, White Masks*, 158.

73. *Big Stan*, directed by Rob Schneider (Warner Home Video, 2007), 2:05.

74. Ibid., 2:29.

75. Ibid., 2:39.

76. Lillian Smith, *Killers of the Dream*, with a new introduction by Margaret Rose Gladney (New York: W. W. Norton, 1949), 121.

77. Bell hooks, *Black Looks: Race and Representation* (Boston, MA: South End Press, 1992), 175.

78. See "Video of California Police Shooting Spurs Investigation," CNN, January 6, 2009, available at http://articles.cnn.com/2009-01-06/justice/BART .shooting_1_fruitvale-station-oscar-grant-video?_s=PM:CRIME.

79. See Beverly Ford and Rich Schapiro, "Sgt. James Crowley, Cop Who Arrested Harvard Professor Henry Louis Gates Jr., Denies He's Racist," *NY Daily News*, July 23,

2009, available at http://articles.nydailynews.com/2009-07-23/news/17928870_1_gates-cambridge-police-department-james-crowley.

80. Fanon, *Black Skin, White Masks*, 112–113.

81. Ibid., 114.

82. W.E.B. Du Bois, "China and Africa," in *W.E.B. Du Bois: A Reader*, ed. David Levering Lewis (New York: Henry Holt, 1995), 93.

83. Richard Wright, "Big Black Good Man," in *Eight Men*, with an introduction by Paul Gilroy, (New York: Harper Perennial, 1996), 93. I thank my student Molly Emmett for reminding me about the sheer force of Olaf's racist prejudices.

84. See "Amadou Diallo," Times Topics, *New York Times*, available at http://topics.nytimes.com/topics/reference/timestopics/people/d/amadou_diallo/index.html.

85. See "Racial Manipulation in Boston," *New York Times*, January 6, 1990, available at http://www.nytimes.com/1990/01/06/opinion/racial-manipulation-in-boston.html?src=pm.

86. Cornel West, *Race Matters* (Boston: Beacon Press, 1993), x–xi.

87. Ibid., x.

88. Ahmed, "A Phenomenology of Whiteness," 161.

89. Ibid., 161.

90. Joe R. Feagin, *The White Racial Frame: Centuries of Racial Framing and Counter-Framing* (New York: Routledge, 2010), 137.

91. Peggy McIntosh, "White Privilege and Male Privilege: A Personal Account of Coming to See Correspondences through Work in Women's Studies," in *Critical Whiteness Studies: Looking behind the Mirror*, ed. Richard Delgardo and Jean Stefancic. (Philadelphia: Temple University Press, 1997), 294.

92. Tim Wise, *White Like Me: Reflections on Race from a Privileged Son* (Brooklyn, NY: Soft Skull Press, 2005), 39.

93. Ibid., 39.

94. West, *Race Matters*, x. I have examined this incident in a broader theorized black/white dialectic in the context of Carol E. Henderson's important edited book. See my afterword, "The Black Body: Under the Weight of White America's Microtomes," in Carol E. Henderson, ed., *America and the Black Body: Identity Politics in print and Visual Culture* (Madison, NJ: Fairleigh Dickinson University Press, 2009). I thank Carol for her enthusiasm about my work on racial embodiment and for the inclusion of parts of the afterword in the current text.

95. Ralph Ellison, *Invisible Man* (New York: Vintage Books, 1995), 3.

96. Fanon, *Black Skin, White Masks*, 117.

97. West, *Race Matters*, 86.

98. Ibid., 85.

99. John T. Warren, *Performing Purity: Whiteness, Pedagogy, and the Reconstruction of Power* (New York: Peter Lang, 2003), 29.

100. Bernasconi, "The Invisibility of Racial Minorities, 288.

101. West, *Race Matters*, 85.

102. Feagin, *The White Racial Frame*, 13.

103. Robert J. C. Young, *White Mythologies: Writing History and the West*, 2nd ed. (New York: Routledge, 2004), 48.

104. See "Take This Hammer," KungPowVoodo blog, February 25, 2011, available at http://kungpowvoodo.blogspot.com/2011/02/take-this-hammer.html.

105. Fanon, *Black Skin, White Masks*, 109.

106. West, *Race Matters*, 85.

107. Ahmed, "A Phenomenology of Whiteness," 161.

108. Fanon, *Black Skin, White Masks*, 166.

109. Feagin, *The White Racial Frame*, 102.

110. Ann Berlak, "Challenging the Hegemony of Whiteness by Addressing the Adaptive Unconscious," in *Undoing Whiteness in the Classroom: Critical Educultural Teaching Approaches for Social Justice Activism*, ed. Virginia Lea and Erma Jean Sims (New York: Peter Lang, 2008), 60.

111. Joy James, *Shadowboxing: Representations of Black Feminist Politics* (New York: St. Martins Press, 1999), 127.

112. Robyn Wiegman, *American Anatomies: Theorizing Race and Gender* (Durham, NC: Duke University Press, 1995), 81.

113. *Higher Learning*, written and directed by John Singleton (Culver City, CA: Columbia Tristar, 1995), 43:06.

114. I do not deny that poor whites have occasionally felt that America has failed in its promise of economic prosperity. It is not clear to me, though, that this situation has created in poor whites a profound sense of homelessness, of being an outsider. Moreover, my suspicion is that poor whites ought to feel a sense of injustice at their economic situation. Yet, or so I would argue, their indignation comes from a place of racial (white) entitlement. And I can imagine many whites who would rather be white and poor than black and poor. Indeed, there are probably many whites who would rather be white and poor than black and wealthy.

CHAPTER 2

1. Ann DuCille, *Skin Trade* (Cambridge, MA: Harvard University Press, 1996), 144.

2. Dorothy Roberts, *Killing the Black Body: Race, Reproduction, and the Meaning of Liberty* (New York: Vintage, 1997), 12.

3. Ibid., 8.

4. Ibid.

5. George Yancy, "Situated Vices: Black Women in/on the Profession of Philosophy," *Hypatia: A Journal of Feminist Philosophy* 23, no. 2 (April-June 2008), 172.

6. Ibid., 171.

7. George Yancy, *African-American Philosophers, 17 Conversations* (New York: Routledge, 1998), 59.

8. Quoted in Brian Leiter, "Is There Any Hope for the Racial Diversity of the Philosophy Profession?" Leiter Reports: A Philosophy Blog, June 6, 2011, available at http://leiterreports.typepad.com/blog/2011/06/is-there-any-hope-for-the-racial-diversity-of-the-philosophy-profession.html.

9. Ronald L. Jackson, *Scripting the Black Masculine Body: Identity, Discourse, and Racial Politics in Popular Media* (New York: State University of New York Press, 2006), 9.

10. Roberts, *Killing the Black Body*, 16.

11. I thank Alasdair MacIntyre for invoking the link between states of unhappiness vis-à-vis genuine critical self-reflection that can happen (and ought to) within a classroom that takes seriously the education of students. He made this insightful connection in a public lecture given at Duquesne University in 2010.

12. Bell hooks, *Teaching to Transgress: Education as the Practice of Freedom* (New York: Routledge, 1994), 207.

13. Margaret A. Simons, *Beauvoir and the Second Sex: Feminism, Race, and the Origins of Existentialism* (Lanham, MD: Rowman and Littlefield, 1999), 224.

14. Hooks, *Teaching to Transgress*, 192.

15. Ibid., 191.

16. Ibid., 16.

17. Ibid.

18. Ibid., 15.

19. Bell hooks, *Yearning: Race, Gender, and Cultural Politics* (Boston: South End Press, 1990), 219 (my emphasis).

20. Ibid., 15–16.

21. Ibid., 16–17.

22. Ibid., 145.

23. Personal correspondence.

24. Zeus Leonardo and Ronald K. Porter, "Pedagogy of Fear: Toward a Fanonian Theory of 'Safety' in Race Dialogue," *Race Ethnicity and Education* 13, no. 2 (July 2010): 149.

25. Ibid., 149.

26. Personal correspondence.

27. Christine E. Sleeter, foreword in *Making Meaning of Whiteness: Exploring Racial Identity with White Teachers*, by Alice McIntyre (New York: State University of New York Press, 1997), x.

28. Alice McIntyre, *Making Meaning of Whiteness: Exploring Racial Identity with White Teachers* (New York: State University of New York Press, 1997), 31.

29. Hooks, *Teaching to Transgress*, 194.

30. Ibid., 195.

31. Ibid.

32. Ibid., 14.

33. Ibid., 16.

34. Ibid., 17.

35. Ibid.

36. Ibid., 13.

37. Ibid., 92.

38. Bell hooks, *Talking Back: Thinking Feminist, Thinking Black* (Boston: South End Press, 1989), 5.

39. Hooks, *Teaching to Transgress*, 186.

40. Ibid., 149.

41. Ibid.

42. Ibid.

43. Ibid.

44. Ibid., 153.

45. Ibid.

46. Ibid., 187.

47. Ibid., 19.

48. Ibid., 198.

49. Ibid., 199.

50. Ibid., 198.

51. Patricia Williams, *Seeing a Color-Blind Future: The Paradox of Race* (New York: Farrar, Straus and Giroux, 1997), 6.

52. Ibid.

53. Hooks, *Teaching to Transgress*, 5.

54. Ibid., 202.

55. Ann Berlak, "Challenging the Hegemony of Whiteness by Addressing the Adaptive Unconscious," in *Undoing Whiteness in the Classroom: Critical Educultural Teaching Approaches for Social Justice Activism*, ed. Virginia Lea and Erma Jean Sims (New York: Peter Lang, 2008), 54.

56. Paulo Freire, *Pedagogy of the Oppressed, 30th Anniversary Edition* (New York: Continuum International Publishing Group, 2000), 51.

57. Hooks, *Teaching to Transgress*, 203 (my emphasis).

58. Ibid. (my emphasis).

59. Freire, *Pedagogy of the Oppressed*, 81.

60. Ibid.

61. Hooks, *Teaching to Transgress*, 18.

62. Ibid., 14.

63. Ibid., 46.

64. Ibid., 73.

65. Ibid., 72.

66. My point here is to suggest ways in which the sensibilities embedded in the banking system of education actually function to render whites passive with respect to rendering problematic their whiteness.

67. Freire, *Pedagogy of the Oppressed*, 79.

68. Ibid., 83.

69. Ibid., 84.

70. Ibid.

71. Ibid., 83.

72. Ibid.

73. Ibid.

74. Berlak, "Challenging the Hegemony of Whiteness," 59.

75. Ibid.

76. Freire, *Pedagogy of the Oppressed*, 92.

77. Ibid., 81.

78. Ibid., 88.

79. Leonardo and Porter, "Pedagogy of Fear," 153.

80. Ibid.

81. Hooks, *Teaching to Transgress*, 39.

82. Freire, *Pedagogy of the Oppressed*, 90.

83. Leonardo and Porter, "Pedagogy of Fear," 149.

84. Hooks, *Teaching to Transgress*, 202.

85. Ibid., 67.

86. Ibid., 59.

87. Freire, *Pedagogy of the Oppressed*, 84.

88. Ibid., 84.

89. Søren Kierkegaard, *Concluding Unscientific Postscript to Philosophical Fragments*, ed. and trans. (with notes) Howard V. Hong and Edna H. Hong (Princeton: Princeton University Press, 1992), 167.

90. Ibid., 167.

91. Peggy McIntosh, "White Privilege and Male Privilege: A Personal Account of Coming to See Correspondences through Work in Women's Studies," in *Critical Whiteness Studies: Looking Behind the Mirror*, ed. Richard Delgardo and Jean Stefancic (Philadelphia: Temple University Press, 1997), 291.

92. Ibid.

93. Ibid., 292.

94. Nelson M. Rodriguez, "Emptying the Content of Whiteness: Toward an Understanding of the Relation between Whiteness and Pedagogy," in *White Reign: Deploying Whiteness in America* ed. Joe L. Kincheloe, Shirley R. Steinberg, Nelson, M. Rodriguez, and Ronald E. Chennault (New York: St. Martin's Press, 1998), 45.

95. Frances E. Kendall, *Understanding White Privilege: Creating Pathways to Authentic Relationships across Race* (New York: Routledge, 2006), 41.

96. Of course, being black does not mean ipso facto that one has not internalized ways of thinking and being that reflect white-approved ways of thinking and being.

97. Bell hooks, *Black Looks: Race and Representation* (Boston: South End Press, 1992), 167.

98. Ibid.

99. Ibid., 167–168.

100. Ibid., 165.

101. Freire, *Pedagogy of the Oppressed*, 91.

102. Ibid., 88.

103. Hooks, *Teaching to Transgress*, 21.

104. Ibid.

105. Freire, *Pedagogy of the Oppressed*, 84.

106. Ibid., 90.

107. Ibid., 84.

108. Michael Apple, Foreword to *White Reign: Deploying Whiteness in America*, ed. Joe L. Kincheloe, Shirley R. Steinberg, Nelson M. Rodriguez, and Ronald E. Chennault (New York: St. Martin's Press, 1998), xii.

109. Hooks, *Teaching to Transgress*, 144.

110. Ibid.

111. Helen Tworkov, "No Right, No Wrong: An Interview with Pema Chodron," *Tricycle*, June 1993, available at http://www.mandala.hr/5/pema.html.

112. Ibid., 207.

113. In Chapter 6, I give greater attention to the concept of the opaque white racist self.

CHAPTER 3

1. Charles W. Mills, *The Racial Contract* (Ithaca, NY: Cornell University Press, 1997), 18.

2. Ibid., 18–19.

3. Abdul R. JanMohamed, "The Economy of Manichean Allegory: The Function of Racial Difference in Colonialist Literature," in *"Race," Writing, and Difference*, ed. Henry Louis Gates, Jr. (Chicago: University of Chicago Press, 1986), 86.

4. Kamau Brathwaite, nationally and internationally known literary figure, is the winner of the Neustadt International Prize for Literature and the Casa de las Americas Prize for poetry and literary criticism.

5. Paget Henry, "Whiteness and Africana Phenomenology," in *What White Looks Like: African-American Philosophers on the Whiteness Question*, ed. George Yancy (New York: Routledge, 2004), 208.

6. Kamau Brathwaite, *Magical Realism* (New York: Savacou North, 2002), 2:666.

7. Ibid.

8. Maryse Condé, *I, Tituba, Black Witch of Salem* (New York: Ballantine Books, 1992), 175.

9. Lola Young, *Fear of the Dark: "Race," Gender and Sexuality in the Cinema* (New York: Routledge, 1996), 64.

10. Emmanuel C. Eze, ed., Introduction to *Postcolonial African Philosophy: A Critical Reader* (Cambridge, MA: Blackwell, 1997), 9–10.

11. Aimé Césaire, *A Tempest*, trans. Richard Miller (New York: Theatre Communications Group, 2002), 18.

12. Ibid.

13. Kamau Brathwaite, "Metaphors of Underdevelopment: A Proem for Hernan Cortez," in *The Art of Kamau Brathwaite*, ed. Stewart Brown (Bridgend, UK: Seren, 1995), 242.

14. See photographs in Adam Hochschild's *King Leopold's Ghost: A Story of Greed, Terror, and Heroism in Colonial Africa* (New York: Mariner Books, 1999), 116–117.

15. Kamau Brathwaite *Magical Realism* (New York: Savacou North, 2002), 1:193.

16. Brathwaite, "Metaphors of Underdevelopment," 246.

17. Brathwaite, *Magical Realism*, 1:196.

18. Ibid., 180.

19. Ibid., 169.

20. Austin Clarke, *The Polished Hoe* (New York: Armistad, 2003), 11.

21. Ibid.

22. Kamau Brathwaite, *Missile and Capsule* (New York: Savacou North, 2004), 27.

23. Brathwaite, *Magical Realism*, 1:171–172.

24. Ibid., 173.

25. Brathwaite, "Metaphors of Underdevelopment," 251.

26. Christopher Small, *Music of the Common Tongue: Survival and Celebration in African American Music* (Hanover, NH: First University Press of New England/Wesleyan University Press, 1998), 168.

27. Aimé Césaire, *Discourse on Colonialism* (New York: Monthly Review Press, 1972), 34.

28. Robert J. C. Young, *White Mythologies* (New York: Routledge, 2004), 160.

29. Frantz Fanon, *The Wretched of the Earth* (New York: Grove Press, 1963), 24–25.

30. On Kant's view of the inherent "inferiority" of blacks, see Cornel West, *The Cornel West Reader* (New York: Basic Civitas Books, 1999), 83–84.

31. Henry Louis Gates, Jr., "Talkin' That Talk," in *"Race," Writing, and Difference,* ed. Henry Louis Gates, Jr. (Chicago: University of Chicago Press, 1986), 408.

32. Brathwaite, *Missile and Capsule*, 23.

33. Brathwaite, *Magical Realism*, 2:654–655; also see Brathwaite, *Missile and Capsule*, 42.

34. Brathwaite, *Magical Realism*, 1:37.

35. W.E.B. Du Bois, "The Souls of White Folk," in *W.E.B. Du Bois: A Reader,* ed. David Levering Lewis (New York: Henry Holt, 1995), 456.

36. Brathwaite, *Missile and Capsule*, 18.

37. Brathwaite, *Magical Realism*, 1:36.

38. Brathwaite, "Metaphors of Underdevelopment," 250.

39. Brathwaite, *Magical Realism*, 1:65.

40. Jacob Burckhardt, *The Civilization of the Renaissance in Italy* (New York: Harper and Row, 1958), 2:280–281.

41. Brathwaite, *Magical Realism*, 2:653.

42. Fanon, *The Wretched of the Earth*, 16.

43. Simone de Beauvoir, *The Ethics of Ambiguity* (New York: Citadel Press, 1976), 47.

44. Césaire, *Discourse on Colonialism*, 21.

45. Brathwaite, *Missile and Capsule*, 18.

46. Ibid., 20.

47. Ibid., 14.

48. William Shakespeare, *The Tempest*, ed. Robert Langbaum (New York: Signet Classic, 1998), 5.1.275. References throughout are to act, scene, and line.

49. Ibid., 1.2.280.

50. Ibid., 1.2.285.

51. Ibid., 1.2. 315.

52. Ibid., 1.2.305.

53. Ibid., 1.2.355.

54. Ibid., 1.2.305.

55. Joane Nagel, *Race, Ethnicity, and Sexuality: Intimate Intersections, Forbidden Frontiers* (New York: Oxford University Press, 2003), 93.

56. Frantz Fanon, *Black Skin, White Masks*, trans. Charles Lam Markmann (New York: Grove Press, 1967), 107.

57. Toni Morrison, *Playing in the Dark: Whiteness and the Literary Imagination* (New York: Vintage Books, 1993), 6–7.

58. Ibid., 44.

59. Brathwaite, *Missile and Capsule*, 18.

60. Graham Richards, *"Race," Racism and Psychology: Towards a Reflexive History* (New York: Routledge, 1997), 16.

61. Jan Nederveen Pieterse, *White on Black: Images of Africa and Blacks in Western Popular Culture.* (New Haven, CT: Yale University Press, 1992), 221.

62. Brathwaite, *Missile and Capsule*, 51.

63. Ibid., 36.

64. Brathwaite, *Magical Realism*, 1:36.

65. Brathwaite, *Missile and Capsule*, 35.

66. Ibid.

67. Ibid.

68. It is here that Caliban has undergone a critical moment of de-Calibanization, exercising his capacity as agent to reject Prospero's ideology.

69. Césaire, *A Tempest*, 61–62. I think it is important to note that when Caliban refers to crushing the world of Prospero, he is not simply referring to the crushing and crumbling of the destructive imago. Rather, his resistance suggests the crushing and crumbling of white hegemony and systemic structural forms of white power, as well as white racist epistemic ways of constructing the black body.

70. Ibid.

71. Ibid.

72. See Melton A. McLaurin, *Celia, A Slave: A True Story* (New York: Avon Books, 1993), in which, in a pivotal moment, Celia, who had been purchased by Robert Newsom, raped by him at the age of fourteen, and eventually bore him at least two children, kills him as he forces himself on her yet again. The book raises significant issues regarding the concept of black women as property, as by nature promiscuous, and regarding their ability to resist sexual oppression.

73. Brathwaite, "Metaphors of Underdevelopment," 249.

74. Brathwaite, *Missile and Capsule*, 33

75. See Brathwaite's historical discussion, in *Missile and Capsule* (21–22) of Caribbean culture and its multiple and interrelated levels of fragmentation: geopsychic, politico-local, demographic, communication-related, social, racial, perceptual/expectation-related, ideational, ethnic, phenotypic, and cultural.

76. Brathwaite, *Missile and Capsule*, 53.

77. James W. Loewen, *Lies My Teacher Told Me: Everything Your American History Textbook Got Wrong* (New York: Touchstone/Simon and Schuster, 1995), 60.

78. Ibid., 61.

79. Brathwaite, "Metaphors of Underdevelopment," 234.

80. Brathwaite, *Missile and Capsule*, 34.

81. Ibid.

82. See Brathwaite's diagram of a missile/rocket on page 200 of *Magical Realism*, vol. 1, in which, on the bottom of the missile/rocket, is the word "colony." It is as if at the foundation or base of the missile/rocket is the power to create a colony.

83. Brathwaite, *Magical Realism*, 2:606.

84. Loewen, *Lies My Teacher Told Me*, 61.

85. Ibid.

86. Ibid., 62.

87. Ibid., 64–65.

88. Ibid., 65.

89. Brathwaite, *Missile and Capsule*, 18.

90. Ibid.

91. Hortense J. Spillers, "Mama's Baby, Papa's Maybe: An American Grammar Book," *Diacritics* (Summer 1987): 29.

92. Brathwaite, "Metaphors of Underdevelopment," 234–235.

93. Fred D'Aguiar, *Feeding the Ghosts* (Hopewell, NJ: Ecco Press, 1997), 11.

94. Ibid., 38–39.

95. Ibid., 39–40.

96. Ibid., 21–29.

97. Brathwaite, *Missile and Capsule*, 53.

98. Henry, "Whiteness and Africana Phenomenology," 207.

99. Bonnie Angelo and Toni Morrison, "The Pain of Being Black," *Time*, May 22, 1989, available at http://www.time.com/time/magazine/article/0,9171,957724,00.html.

CHAPTER 4

1. Jean-Paul Sartre, "Black Orpheus," in *Race*, ed. Robert Bernasconi (Malden, MA: Blackwell, 2001), 115.

2. Hernan Vera and Andrew M. Gordon, *Screen Savior: Hollywood Fictions of Whiteness* (Lanham, MD: Rowman and Littlefield, 2003), 3.

3. Winthrop Jordan, *The White Man's Burden: Historical Origins of Racism in the United States* (New York: Oxford University Press, 1974), 101.

4. V. Y. Mudimbe, *The Invention of Africa: Gnosis, Philosophy, and the Order of Knowledge* (Bloomington: Indiana University Press, 1988), 17.

5. Fatimah Tobing Rony, *The Third Eye: Race, Cinema, and Ethnographic Spectacle* (Durham: Duke University Press, 1996), 12–13.

6. Vera and Gordon, *Screen Savior*, 1.

7. Rony, *The Third Eye*, 11.

8. Vera and Gordon, *Screen Savior*, 17.

9. Ibid.

10. *White Chicks*, directed by Keenan Ivory Wayans, written by Keenan Ivory Wayans, Shawn Wayans, and Marlon Wayans (Culver City, CA: Columbia Pictures, 2004).

11. Sartre, "Black Orpheus," 116.

12. Ibid., 115.

13. Bell hooks, *Black Looks: Race and Representation* (Boston: South End Press, 1992), 168.

14. Linda Martín Alcoff, "Toward a Phenomenology of Racial Embodiment," in *Race*, ed. Robert Bernasconi (Malden: Blackwell, 2001), 268–269.

15. William Mahar, *Behind the Burnt Cork Mask: Early Blackface Minstrelsy and Antebellum American Popular Culture* (Chicago: University of Illinois Press, 1999), 330.

16. Robert Toll, *Blacking Up: The Minstrel Show in Nineteenth-Century America* (New York: Oxford University Press, 1974), 38.

17. Patricia Williams, *Seeing a Color-Blind Future: The Paradox of Race* (New York: Farrar, Straus and Giroux, 1997), 18.

18. Ibid., 22.

19. Rony, *The Third Eye*, 10.

20. Joe R. Feagin, *The White Racial Frame: Centuries of Racial Framing and Counter-Framing* (New York: Routledge, 2010), 76.

21. Ibid., 75.

22. James Snead, *White Screens, Black Images: Hollywood from the Dark Side*, posthumously ed. Colin MacCabe and Cornel West (New York: Routledge, 1994), 3.

23. Ibid.

24. Williams, *Seeing a Color-Blind Future*, 6.

25. Ibid., 7.

26. Ibid., 8.

27. Ibid., 9.

28. Peggy McIntosh, "White Privilege and Male Privilege: A Personal Account through Work in Women's Studies," in *Critical Whiteness Studies: Looking behind the Mirror*, ed. Richard Delgardo and Jean Stefancic (Philadelphia: Temple University Press, 1997), 291.

29. Ibid., 296.

30. Ibid., 292–293.

31. Ibid., 298.

32. Judith Butler, "Endangered/Endangering: Schematic Racism and White Paranoia," in *Reading Rodney King, Reading Urban Uprising*, ed. Robert Gooding-Williams (New York: Routledge, 1993), 18.

33. Ibid.

34. *White Chicks*, 12:25–28.

35. Ibid., 12:50–53.

36. Ibid., 15:22-35.

37. McIntosh, "White Privilege and Male Privilege," 294.

38. Alison Bailey, "Locating Traitorous Identities: Toward a View of Privilege-Cognizant White Character," in *Border Crossings: Multicultural and Postcolonial Feminist Challenges to Philosophy, Part II*, ed. Sandra Harding and Uma Narayan, special issue, *Hypatia: A Journal of Feminist Philosophy* 13, no. 3 (Summer 1998) 27–42, 34–35.

39. *White Chicks*, 20:44–52.

40. Ibid., 21:26–30.

41. Ibid., 21:33–46.

42. Shannon Sullivan, *Revealing Whiteness: The Unconscious Habits of Racial Privilege* (Bloomington: Indiana University Press, 2006), 10.

43. *White Chicks*, 19:56–58.

44. Ibid., 20:04–09.

45. Ibid., 34:26–47.

46. Tim Wise, *White Like Me: Reflections on Race from a Privileged Son* (Brooklyn, NY: Soft Skull Press, 2005), 91.

47. G.W.F. Hegel, "Geographical Basis of World History," in *Race and the Enlightenment: A Reader*, ed. Emmanuel Chukwudi Eze (Malden, MA: Blackwell, 1997), 134.

48. George M. Fredrickson, *The Black Image in the White Mind: The Debate on Afro-American Character and Destiny, 1817–1914* (Hanover, NH: Wesleyan University Press, 1971), 279.

49. Gail Bederman, *Manliness and Civilization: A Cultural History of Gender and Race in the United States, 1880–1917* (Chicago: University of Chicago Press, 1995), 8–9.

50. In fact, the reader should note that *White Chicks* does not simply mark whiteness but also plays with the theme of drag. The movie also implicitly critiques the site of heteronormativity. Exploring the film from the perspective of counternormative sexual identities might prove fruitful; however, this is not the aim of this chapter.

51. *White Chicks*, 31:20–30.

52. Franz Fanon, *Black Skin, White Masks* (New York: Grove Press, 1967), 158.

53. Ibid., 159.

54. *White Chicks*, 31:08–16.

55. Ibid., 31:31–44.

56. Ibid., 31:44–59.

57. Ibid., 32:09–17.

58. Ibid., 32:17.

59. Ibid., 1:42:07–11.

60. Fanon, *Black Skin, White Masks*, 159.

61. Ralph Ellison, *Invisible Man* (New York: Vintage Books, 1995), 16.

62. Fanon, *Black Skin, White Masks*, 165.

63. *White Chicks*, 57:18–33.

64. Ibid., 32:19–27.

65. Ibid., 32:37–42.

66. Ibid., 46:10–21.

67. Ibid., 1:01:34–50.

68. Ibid., 1:38:18–25.

69. Ibid., 1:38:25–30.

70. Ibid., 1:38:40–45.

71. Ibid., 1:38:45–48.

72. Ibid., 1:38:54–1:39:00.

73. Donald Bogle, *Toms, Coons, Mulattoes, Mammies, and Bucks: An Interpretive History of Blacks in American Films* (New York: Continuum, 1973), 10.

74. *White Chicks*, 52:30.

75. Ibid., 52:35.

76. Crispin Sartwell, *Act Like You Know: African-American Autobiography and White Identity* (Chicago: University of Chicago Press, 1998), 11.

77. *White Chicks*, 1:02:47–1:03:04.

78. Williams, *Seeing a Color-Blind Future*, 62.

79. For more on black minstrelsy, see Mel Watkins, *On the Real Side: Laughing, Lying, and Signifying—The Underground Tradition of African-American Humor That Transformed American Culture, from Slavery to Richard Prior* (New York: Simon and Schuster, 1994), especially chap. 3.

80. *White Chicks*, 23:17.

81. Ibid., 23:28.

82. Ibid., 23:31.

83. Ibid., 23:34–43.

84. Ibid., 49:15–18.

85. Ibid., 49:18–21.

86. Ibid., 1:14:38–1:15:50.

CHAPTER 5

1. U.S. Department of Justice, "Full Text: U.S. Attorney General Eric Holder Remarks on Black History Month, 'Nation of Cowards,'" *C²: Clips and Comment*, February 18, 2009, available at http://www.clipsandcomment.com/2009/02/18/full-text-us-attorney-general-eric-holder-remarks-on-black-history-month-nation-of-cowards/.

2. Charles Mills, *From Class to Race: Essays in White Marxism and Black Radicalism* (Lanham, MD: Rowman and Littlefield, 2003), 167.

3. Richard Wright, *Eight Men* (New York: HarperPerennial, 1996), 213.

4. "Acted stupidly" was President's Obama's response describing the Cambridge, Massachusetts, policemen who arrested Gates.

5. Sara Ahmed, "A Phenomenology of Whiteness," *Feminist Theory* 8, no. 2 (2007): 158.

6. Lewis R. Gordon, *Disciplinary Decadence: Living Thought in Trying Times* (Boulder, CO: Paradigm, 2006), 127.

7. Ibid.

8. Omar Swartz, Katia Campbell, and Christina Pestana, *Neo-Pragmatism, Communication, and the Culture of Creative Democracy* (New York: Peter Lang, 2009), 53.

9. I have made an initial effort to explore some of the phenomenological dynamics of attending predominantly white philosophy conferences in the inaugural issue of *Epistemologies Humanities Journal* (2011). There was also an attempt to address the theme of engaging philosophy in ways that require going against the grain or "doing philosophy my way." See http://www.epistemologies.org/thematizing-diy/.

10. Cynthia Willett, "A Phenomenology of Racialized Space and the Limits of Liberalism," in *Racism in Mind*, ed. Michael P. Levine and Tamas Pataki (Ithaca, NY: Cornell University Press, 2004), 255.

11. Joel Olson, *The Abolition of White Democracy* (Minneapolis: University of Minnesota Press, 2004), 104.

12. Barbara Applebaum, *Being White, Being Good: White Complicity, White Moral Responsibility, and Social Justice Pedagogy* (Lanham, MD: Lexington Books, 2010), 183.

13. Ibid., 45.

14. Swartz, Campbell, and Pestana, *Neo-Pragmatism*, 127.

15. Charles R. Lawrence, "The Word and the River: Pedagogy as Scholarship as Struggle," in *Critical Race Theory: The Key Writings That Formed the Movement*, ed. Kimberle Crenshaw, Neil Gotanda, Gary Peller, and Kendall Thomas (New York: The New Press, 1995), 350.

16. By the way, I do not deny the importance of teaching Western philosophy. The trick is to be sure to *mark* its particularity within the larger context of world philosophies.

17. Plato, *Five Dialogues: Euthyphro, Apology, Crito, Meno, Phaedo*, trans. G.M.A. Grube (Indianapolis: Hackett Publishing, 2002), 35.

18. Martin Luther King, Jr., "Letter from Birmingham City Jail," in *A Testament of Hope: The Essential Writings and Speeches of Martin Luther King, Jr.*, ed. James M. Washington (New York: HarperSanFrancisco, 1986), 291.

19. Swartz, Campbell, and Pestana, *Neo-Pragmatism*, 36.

20. Ibid., 43.

21. Ibid., 101.

22. See George Yancy, *Black Bodies, White Gazes: The Continuing Significance of Race* (Lanham, MD: Rowman and Littlefield, 2008).

23. Swartz, Campbell, and Pestana, *Neo-Pragmatism*, 40.

24. Cris Mayo, "The Whiteness of Anti-racist White Philosophical Address," in *The Center Must Not Hold: White Women Philosophers on the Whiteness of Philosophy*, ed. George Yancy (Lanham, MD: Lexington Books, 2010), 215.

25. One woman wrote, "Please continue the good fight and continue to express your viewpoints concerning the black experience. Many Jewish members of our society continue to speak out against anti-Semitism, although it is rare that they receive the backlash that black members of our society must endure during these dialogues. Our voices must be heard, not silenced; we must surely 'Never Forget.'"

26. Paulo Freire, *Pedagogy of the Oppressed* (New York: Continuum, 1997), 93.

27. Richard Wright, "Big Black Good Man," in *Eight Men* (New York: Harper Perennial, 1940), 212.

28. Plato, *Five Dialogues: Euthyphro, Apology, Crito, Meno, Phaedo*, 30.

29. Linda Martín Alcoff, *Visible Identities: Race, Gender, and the Self* (New York: Oxford University Press, 2006), 126.

30. Ibid.

31. Bell hooks, *Black Looks: Race and Representation* (Boston: South End Press, 1992), 177.

32. Martin Luther King, Jr., "An Experiment in Love," in *A Testament of Hope: The Essential Writings and Speeches of Martin Luther King, Jr.*, ed. James M. Washington (New York: HarperSanFrancisco, 1986), 20.

33. Charles E. Curran, "White Privilege: My Theological Journey," in *Interrupting White Privilege: Catholic Theologians Break the Silence*, ed. Laurie M. Cassidy and Alex Mikulich (Maryknoll, NY: Orbis Books, 2007), 81.

34. Ibid.

35. Ibid.

36. Ibid., 80.

37. Jon Nilson, "Confessions of a White Catholic Racist Theologian," in *Interrupting White Privilege: Catholic Theologians Break the Silence*, ed. Laurie M. Cassidy and Alex Mikulich (Maryknoll, NY: Orbis Books, 2007), 18.

38. Alex Mikulich, "(Un)Learning White Male Ignorance," in *Interrupting White Privilege: Catholic Theologians Break the Silence*, ed. Laurie M. Cassidy and Alex Mikulich (Maryknoll, NY: Orbis Books, 2007), 161.

39. Ibid.

40. Frederick Douglass, *Narrative of the Life of Frederick Douglass, an American Slave, Written by Himself*, ed. David W. Blight (New York: Bedford/St. Martin's, 1993), 145.

41. Karen Teel, *Racism and the Image of God* (New York: Palgrave Macmillan, 2010), 30.

42. Lillian Smith, *Killers of the Dream* (New York: W. W. Norton, 1949), 28.

43. Joe R. Feagin, *The White Racial Frame: Centuries of Racial Framing and Counter-Framing* (New York: Routledge, 2010), 124.

44. Wright, *Eight Men*, 213.

45. Douglass, *Narrative of the Life of Frederick Douglass*, 144.

CHAPTER 6

1. Toni Morrison, *The Bluest Eye* (1970; repr., New York: Alfred A. Knopf, 1998), 50.

2. Barbara Applebaum, *Being White, Being Good: White Complicity, White Moral Responsibility, and Social Justice Pedagogy* (Lanham, MD: Lexington Books, 2010), 42.

3. Sara Ahmed, "Declarations of Whiteness: The Non-performativity of Anti-racism," *borderlands* e-journal 3, no. 2 (2004), available at http://www.borderlands .net.au/vol3no2_2004/ahmed_declarations.htm.

4. Ibid.

5. Ibid.

6. Ibid.

7. Ibid.

8. Ibid.

9. Bell hooks, *Black Looks: Race and Representation* (Boston: South End Press, 1992), 169.

10. Ibid.

11. Ahmed, "Declarations of Whiteness."

12. This does not mean that the ways in which black people undergo white racist interpellation are exactly the same or are experienced exactly the same.

13. See Robert Birt, "The Bad Faith of Whiteness," in *What White Looks Like: African-American Philosophers on the Whiteness Question*, ed. George Yancy (New York: Routledge, 2004).

14. See George Yancy, *Black Bodies, White Gazes: The Continuing Significance of Race* (Lanham, MD: Rowman and Littlefield, 2008).

15. Applebaum, *Being White, Being Good*, 43.

16. Peggy McIntosh, "White Privilege and Male Privilege: A Personal Account of Coming to See Correspondences through Work in Women's Studies," in *Critical Whiteness Studies: Looking Behind the Mirror*, ed. Richard Delgado and Jean Stefancic (Philadelphia: Temple University Press, 1997), 293–294.

17. Ibid., 298.

18. Zeus Leonardo, *Race, Whiteness, and Education* (New York: Routledge, 2009), 75.

19. Applebaum, *Being White, Being Good*, 29.

20. Kalpana Seshadri-Crooks, *Desiring Whiteness: A Lacanian Analysis of Race* (New York: Routledge, 2000), 20.

21. Steve Martinot, *The Machinery of Whiteness: Studies in the Structure of Racialization* (Philadelphia: Temple University Press, 2010), 24.

22. Applebaum, *Being White, Being Good*, 30.

23. Stephanie M. Wildman and Adrienne D. Davis, "Making Systems of Privilege Visible," in *White Privilege: Essential Readings on the Other Side of Racism*, ed. Paula S. Rothenberg (New York: Worth, 2008), 114–115.

24. Robert Jensen, "White Privilege Shapes the U.S.," in *White Privilege: Essential Readings on the Other Side of Racism*, ed. Paula S. Rothenberg (New York: Worth, 2008), 130–132.

25. Of course, people of color are also embedded within this matrix, but the results of their embedded reality are differently experienced. I must also caution against conflating the ways in which people of color experience their embedded reality within this matrix. This also applies to the ways in which people of color are differentially positioned along multiple axes vis-à-vis whites.

26. I use this term in the philosophical spirit of Judith Butler, particularly in terms of its poststructural implications, though I restrict its use here to speak to white subject formation.

27. Tamara K, Nopper, "The White Anti-racist Is an Oxymoron: An Open Letter to 'White Anti-racists,'" *Race Traitor* (Fall 2003), available at http://racetraitor .org/nopper.html.

28. Leonardo, *Race, Whiteness, and Education*, 75.

29. Judith Butler, *Precarious Life: The Powers of Mourning and Violence* (New York: Verso, 2004), 26.

30. John T. Warren, "Performing Whiteness Differently: Rethinking the Abolitionist Project," *Educational Theory*, 51, no. 4 (2001): 462.

31. Butler, *Precarious Life*, 26.

32. Ibid., 26.

33. Ibid., 28.

34. Applebaum, *Being White, Being Good*, 158. Applebaum, in my view, is the leading scholar of what she calls white complicity pedagogy. Deploying the work of Iris Marion Young and Judith Butler, she provides us with a rich and conceptually sophisticated picture of responsibility that does not rely on an inadequate liability model that fails to understand the social connectedness of whites in the context of systemic white racist injustice.

35. Iris Marion Young, *Global Challenges: War, Self-Determination and Responsibility for Justice* (Malden, MA: Polity Press, 2008), 175.

36. Applebaum, *Being White, Being Good*, 46.

37. Barbara Trepagnier, *Silent Racism: How Well-Meaning White People Perpetuate the Racial Divide* (Boulder, CO: Paradigm, 2006), 15.

38. Ann Berlak, "Challenging the Hegemony of Whiteness by Addressing the Adaptive Unconscious," in *Undoing Whiteness in the Classroom: Critical Educultural Teaching Approaches for Social Justice Activism*, ed. Virginia Lea and Erma Jean Sims (New York: Peter Lang, 2008), 55.

39. Judith Butler, *Giving an Account of Oneself* (New York: Fordham University Press, 2005), 79.

40. Tim Wise, *White Like Me: Reflections on Race from a Privileged Son* (New York: Soft Skull Press, 2005), 133.

41. Ibid., 133.

42. As Bettina Bergo notes, "One can change or alter one's concepts and one's use of language; but it is a harder matter to eradicate images that have become massively unconscious and attached to affects." This was a personal communication in June 2011.

43. Drucilla Cornell, *Transformations: Recollective Imagination and Sexual Difference* (New York: Routledge, 1993), 41.

44. Butler, *Giving an Account of Oneself*, 78.

45. See "'Kramer's' Racist Tirade—Caught on Tape," TMZ, November 20, 2006, available at http://www.tmz.com/2006/11/20/kramers-racist-tirade-caught-on -tape/.

46. See "Kramer's Apology," available at http://www.youtube.com/watch?v=EC 26RI-Ria8.

47. Ibid.

48. Applebaum, *Being White, Being Good*, 145.

49. For those interested in how two fictional characters function as fascinating examples of the opaque white racist self, I suggest looking at Spike Lee's *Do the Right Thing* (1998) and Paul Haggis's *Crash* (2004). In the former, the character Sal (played by Danny Aiello), who owns a pizzeria in a predominantly black and Latino neighborhood in Brooklyn, functions throughout the movie as a voice of reason, as someone who is "concerned" with people of color. Yet toward the end, in an unforgettable confrontation with three black characters, Radio Raheem (Bill Nunn), Buggin' Out (Giancarlo Esposito), and Smiley (Roger Guenveur Smith), Sal's white racism fires out with violent aggression, negative references to Africa, the word "nigger," and a few other dehumanizing expletives. In *Crash*, the character Tom Hansen (Ryan Phillippe) is a police officer who is clearly against and uncomfortable with white racism, especially as demonstrated by his LAPD partner John Ryan (Matt Dillon). As in *Do the Right Thing*, it is toward the end of the movie that Hansen's white racism fires out of him, which results in the tragic death of the black character Peter Waters (Larenz Tate), who innocently reaches into his pocket for a small religious statue. Hansen shoots Peter as he does so, a scene reminiscent of the 1999 real-life shooting of Amadou Diallo, who was shot at 41 times and hit with 19 bullets as he reached for his wallet. It would prove very fruitful to examine in greater detail the ways in which the fictional characters Sal and Hansen exemplify the opaque white racist self that I theorize here.

50. Judith Butler, *Giving an Account of Oneself*, 72.

51. Ibid., 20.

52. Ibid., 58.

53. Lillian Smith, *Killers of the Dream* (New York: W. W. Norton, 1949), 84.

54. Ibid., 148.

55. Otto Neurath, "Protocol Sentences," in *Logical Positivism*, ed. A. J. Ayer, trans. George Schlick (Chicago: Free Press, 1959), 201.

56. René Descartes, *Meditations on First Philosophy*, trans. Donald A. Cress (Indianapolis: Hackett Publishing, 1993), 13.

57. Frantz Fanon, *Black Skin, White Masks*, trans. Charles Lam Markmann (New York: Grove Press, 1967), 42.

58. Peter McLaren, "Whiteness Is . . . the Struggle for Postcolonial Hybridity," in *White Reign: Deploying Whiteness in America*, ed. Joe L. Kincheloe, Shirley R. Steinberg, Nelson M. Rodriguez, and Ronald E. Chennault (New York: St. Martin's Press, 1998), 68.

59. Alice McIntyre, *Making Meaning of Whiteness: Exploring Racial Identity with White Teachers* (New York: State University of New York Press, 1997), 7.

60. Butler, *Giving an Account of Oneself*, 77.

61. Nopper, "The White Anti-racist Is an Oxymoron."

Index

George Yancy is Associate Professor of Philosophy at Duquesne University and Coordinator of the Critical Race Theory Speaker Series. He is the author of *Black Bodies, White Gazes: The Continuing Significance of Race*, which received an Honorable Mention from the Gustavus Myers Center for the Study of Bigotry and Human Rights. He has edited twelve influential books, three of which have received *Choice* awards, and was recently nominated for the Duquesne University Presidential Award for Excellence in Scholarship.